STATUS QUAESTIO

STATUS QUAESTIONIS

Questionnaire on the Provision of Legal Interpreting and Translation in the EU

AGIS project JLS/2006/AGIS/052

Erik HERTOG

Jan VAN GUCHT (eds.)

AGIS 2006
With financial support from the AGIS programme
European Commission
Directorate General Justice,
Freedom and Security

Antwerp – Oxford – Portland

Distribution for the UK:
Hart Publishing Ltd.
16C Worcester Place
Oxford OX1 2JW
UK
Tel.: +44 1865 51 75 30
Fax: +44 1865 51 07 10

Distribution for Switzerland and Germany:
Schulthess Verlag
Zwingliplatz 2
CH-8022 Zürich
Switzerland
Tel.: +41 1 251 93 36
Fax: +41 1 261 63 94

Distribution for the USA and Canada:
International Specialized Book Services
920 NE 58th Ave Suite 300
Portland, OR 97213
USA
Tel.: +1 800 944 6190 (toll free)
Tel.: +1 503 287 3093
Fax: +1 503 280 8832
Email: info@isbs.com

Distribution for other countries:
Intersentia Publishers
Groenstraat 31
BE-2640 Mortsel
Belgium
Tel.: +32 3 680 15 50
Fax: +32 3 658 71 21

Status Quaestionis. Questionnaire on the Provision of Legal Interpreting and Translation in the EU. AGIS project JLS/2006/AGIS/052
Erik Hertog and Jan van Gucht (eds.)

© 2008 Intersentia
Antwerp – Oxford – Portland
http://www.intersentia.com

ISBN 978-90-5095-804-2
D/2008/7849/47
NUR 820

PREFACE AND ACKNOWLEDGEMENTS

This book is the result of a research project carried out under the auspices and with the support of the AGIS Programme of the Directorate-General Justice, Freedom and Security of the European Commission.

It must be seen as part of a concerted effort to establish guarantees and mechanisms for compliance with the procedural safeguards in criminal proceedings as set out in the European Convention for the Protection of Human Rights and Fundamental Freedoms ('ECHR'), as developed in the case law of the European Court of Human Rights (ECtHR) and in line with the objectives and ambition of the European Union and many Member States to shape the EU into an area of freedom, security and justice.

More particularly, this project is a follow-up project to a number of previous Grotius and later Agis projects, launched after the 1998 Tampere summit. It examines the state of affairs concerning one such fundamental procedural right, i.e. the right to access to justice across languages and culture or in other words, the right to a free interpreter and the translation of all relevant documents in criminal proceedings.

In 2002 the EU Commission launched a processus to try and make five fundamental procedural rights practical and effective throughout the EU. This momentum, which culminated in a proposal for a Framework Decision, ultimately and unfortunately enough, collapsed in 2007. However, the need, or indeed the challenge to provide all citizens of the EU with the right to a fair trial, including the provision of quality legal interpreting or translation, has not gone away.

This project therefore sets out to provide more detailed and objective information about the existing provisions – the *status quaestionis* – on legal interpreting and translation throughout the European Union. We have chosen to carry out this task by means of an EU-wide questionnaire, so that best practices as well as differences in policy and thus a different implementation of this procedural right may be ascertained.

The parties participating in this project were:

> Lessius Hogeschool, Antwerp, Belgium
> The Chartered Institute of Linguists, London, United Kingdom
> The University of Alicante, Alicante, Spain
> The Raad voor Rechtsbijstand and the Ministry of Justice, the Netherlands

and with the cooperation of

> The European Criminal Bar Association (ECBA)
> The Council of Bars and Law Societies of Europe (CCBE).

As editor and project coordinator it is a privilege, first of all, to thank all the governmental and professional respondents who have taken the time to answer the questionnaire. It is a platitude, but without their interest and support the project would never have gleaned the invaluable information we now dispose of and which is a treasure trove indeed for further research, reflection and action both on EU and Member State level.

I would also like to thank Ann Matthyssen for her dedicated assistance in the process of collating the database of the respondents, Francis Note for his diligent compilation of all the information that could be collected on individual Member States level and Peter van de Vijver and Nancy Vink of Intomart GfK for providing professional expertise in the design and processing of the online questionnaire.

When it comes to thanks, my sincere gratitude goes out to the project participants for all the work they have done and for the commitment they have brought to this undertaking. This book is truly the collaborative effort of all and everyone who participated in this project. José Delgado, John Hammond, Jeroen Blomsma, Mirjam Schuurman, Sonsoles Plaza, Taru Spronken and Peter McNamee attended various meetings and made invaluable contributions to the discussion and the success of the project. Cynthia Giambruno hosted the important meeting at the University of Alicante and helped to shape both the format and the analysis of the data from the questionnaire. Evert-Jan van der Vlis, Hans Warendorf and Yolanda vanden Bosch provided information on the legal aspects and background of the project and they are the main authors of Chapter I. Ann Corsellis coordinated the writing of the Conclusions and Recommendations, with substantial input from Han von den Hoff who deserves special thanks not only for hosting a number of extra meetings at the Raad voor Rechtsbijstand in 's Hertogenbosch but also for generously providing extra funds to allow for an online questionnaire in addition to the print version. His important contribution to this project must be acknowledged and cannot be overestimated. A very special word of thanks must go to Jan van Gucht who developed the methodology to analyse and present the data resulting from the questionnaire. Without him the results would undoubtedly have been less illuminating and substantial. All of us in the project owe him thanks and admiration for his work.

The full text of this report is also available on the website of our projects (www. agisproject.com) including the full country profiles materials of each Member State. Thus colleagues throughout the EU can carry on this research project by disseminating the questionnaire to larger and other audiences as well as by analysing in depth the data relevant to their own Member State.

Finally, we want to express our gratitude to the European Commission for the financial support provided by the DG Justice, Freedom and Security under the AGIS programme. Their awareness of and interest in the issue of interpreting and translation in criminal proceedings have featured prominently on their agenda from the first Grotius projects on and this commitment has never waned. Without their support it would have been impossible to carry out this project.

April 2008

Erik Hertog, editor

TABLE OF CONTENTS

PREFACE AND ACKNOWLEDGEMENTS. v

EXECUTIVE SUMMARY 1

RÉSUMÉ. 5

KOMMENTIERTE ZUSAMMENFASSUNG 9

CHAPTER I
CO-OPERATION AND PROTECTION OF PROCEDURAL RIGHTS
IN THE AREA OF CRIMINAL JUSTICE THROUGHOUT THE
EUROPEAN UNION 13

Responsibility for a good and trustworthy interpreter or translator. 14
Green Paper on Procedural Safeguards 15
Framework Decision on Specific Procedural Rights in Criminal
    Proceedings 17
Minimum standards 19
Conclusion 21
References 22

CHAPTER II
METHODOLOGY 23

Introduction 23
Previous Questionnaires. 23
Drafting the Questionnaire 24
Response to the questionnaire. 30
Performance Indicators 31
    Indicator 1: Procedural safeguards. 33
    Indicator 2: Regulation of the profession. 37
    Indicator 3: Quality provisions 40
    Indicator 4: Quantitative provisions. 41

Analysis and Presentation Format 42
    T-scores 42
    Contrasting government and professionals' perspectives. 43
    Individual country profiles. 43
    Sample extended country profile. 44
    EU Topographical maps of linguistic assistance. 44
    EU Topographical maps of Green Paper indicators. 44

CHAPTER III
EU MEMBER STATES PROFILES

EU MEMBER STATES PROFILES 47

Introduction 47
1.   General Observations 48
    1.1. Sample Composition 48
    1.2. Indicator Composition 51
    1.3. General Observations 51
2.   Member State Indicator Profiles 52
    2.1. Austria. 52
    2.2. Belgium 54
    2.3. Bulgaria 56
    2.4. Cyprus 58
    2.5. Czech Republic. 60
    2.6. Denmark 62
    2.7. Estonia 64
    2.8. Finland. 66
    2.9. France 68
    2.10. Germany 70
    2.11. Greece 72
    2.12. Hungary. 74
    2.13. Ireland 76
    2.14. Italy. 78
    2.15. Latvia 80
    2.16. Lithuania 82
    2.17. Malta 84
    2.18. The Netherlands. 86
    2.19. Poland 88
    2.20. Portugal. 90
    2.21. Romania 92
    2.22. Slovakia 94
    2.23. Slovenia 96

2.24. Spain. 98
2.25. Sweden. 100
2.26. United Kingdom 102

CHAPTER IV
SAMPLE COUNTRY PROFILE: AUSTRIA 105

Introduction 105
1.   Legal Interpreting 107
      Indicator 1   Procedural Safeguards EU Contextual Information 107
      Basic Level Indicator 1 Procedural Safeguards. Underlying Question
            Profiles. 109
            I1.1 Procedural guarantees. 109
            I1.2 Number of phases in the procedure 112
            I1.3 Criteria for interpretation. 113
            I1.4 Vulnerable groups 114
      Indicator 2   Regulation of the Profession EU Contextual Information 116
      Basic Level Indicator 2 Regulation of the Profession. Underlying
            Question Profiles 118
            I2.1 Protection and regulation. 118
            I2.2 Accreditation body 119
            I2.3 Register 120
            I2.4 Code of conduct and procedure. 121
      Indicator 3   Quality Provisions EU Contextual Information. 123
      Basic Level Indicator 3 Quality Provisions. Underlying Question
            Profiles. 125
            I3.1 Quality provisions 125
            I3.2 Training level 127
            I3.3 Video taping 128
            I3.4 Directives for magistrates. 129
            I3.5 Recruitment programme 130
      Indicator 4   Quantitative Provisions EU Contextual Information 131
      Indicator 4   Quantitative Provisions. Underlying Question Profiles . . 133
      Apex Indicator EU Contextual Information. 134
      Apex Austria Indicator Profile. 135
2.   Legal Translation 136
      Indicator 1   Procedural Safeguards EU Contextual Information 136
      Basic Level Indicator 1 Procedural Safeguards. Underlying Question
            Profiles. 138
            I1.1 Procedural guarantees. 138

I1.2 Number of phases in the procedure 139
I1.3 Criteria for translation. 140
I1.4 Vulnerable groups 141
Indicator 2   Regulation of the Profession EU Contextual Information 142
Basic Level Indicator 2 Regulation of the Profession. Underlying
Question Profiles 144
I2.1 Protection and regulation. 144
I2.2 Accreditation body 146
I2.3 Register 147
I2.4 Code of conduct and procedure. 148
Indicator 3   Quality Provisions EU Contextual Information. 150
Basic Level Indicator 3 Quality Provisions. Underlying Question
Profiles 152
I3.1 Quality provisions 152
I3.2 Training level 154
I3.4 Directives for magistrates. 155
I3.5 Recruitment programme 156
Indicator 4   Quantitative Provisions EU Contextual Information 157
Indicator 4   Quantitative Provisions. Underlying Question Profiles . . 158
Apex Indicator EU Contextual Information. 159
Apex Austria Indicator Profile. 160
3.   Future Developments 161
Indicator 1: Procedural Safeguards. 161
Indicator 2: Regulation of the Profession. 161
Indicator 3: Quality Provisions: Standards and Training. 162
Indicator 3: Quality Provisions: Management Provisions 164
Working Conditions for Interpreters and Translators. 165
4.   Additional Country Information 166

CHAPTER V
EU LINGUISTIC ASSISTANCE INDICATOR PROFILES 167

Introduction 168
Indicator 1   Procedural Safeguards – Government Sources. 170
Indicator 1   Procedural Safeguards – Professionial Sources. 171
Indicator 2   Regulation of the Profession – Government Sources. 172
Indicator 2   Regulation of the Profession – Professional Sources 173
Indicator 3   Quality Provisions – Government Sources 174
Indicator 3   Quality Provisions – Professional Sources. 175
Indicator 4   Quantitative Provisions – Government Sources. 176

Indicator 4   Quantitative Provisions – Professional Sources 177
Apex Indicator – Government Sources 178
Apex Indicator – Professional Sources. 179

CHAPTER VI
EU GREEN PAPER INDICATOR PROFILES 181

Introduction 181
GP Indicator 1   Vulnerable Groups – Interdisciplinary Sources 182
GP Indicator 2   Accreditation Body – Interdisciplinary Sources. 183
GP Indicator 3   Register – Interdisciplinary Sources. 184
GP Indicator 4   Code of Conduct and Disciplinary Procedures –
                 Interdisciplinary Sources 185
GP Indicator 5   Training Level – Interdisciplinary Sources 186
Green Paper Overall Indicator – Interdisciplinary Sources 187

CONCLUSIONS AND RECOMMENDATIONS 189

Core conclusion 189
General points 189
Comments. 190
Recommendations. 191
Key indicators. 192
1.   Procedural Safeguards 193
Comments. 193
Recommendations. 194
2.   Regulation of the interpreting and translation professions 195
Comments. 195
Recommendations. 196
3.   Quality Assurance. 197
Comments. 198
Recommendations. 199
Final points. 200

APPENDIX I
QUESTIONNAIRE. 201

APPENDIX II
ADDITIONAL CEPEJ AND SPRONKEN-ATTINGER DATA ON
THE MEMBER STATES 233

APPENDIX III
PUBLIC SERVICE INTERPRETING & TRANSLATION:
COMPONENTS OF THE PROFESSION 249

APPENDIX IV
SUGGESTIONS ON DATA TO BE COLLECTED. 251

APPENDIX V
PROJECT PARTICIPANTS 253

EXECUTIVE SUMMARY

Facing new and multiple challenges such as immigration, cross border crime, terrorism, the movement of people and goods, etc., the European Union has come to realize the increased importance of the need for judicial cooperation and mutual recognition between Member States in order to guarantee security and justice in the EU.

However, at the same time there is a deep concern that, with regard to these challenges, the citizens' freedom and fundamental rights must be safeguarded.

This project (AGIS project JLS/2006/AGIS/052) must be seen as part of a concerted effort to establish guarantees and mechanisms for compliance with procedural safeguards in criminal proceedings in all Member States of the European Union.

Since the Tampere summit (1998), the EU has taken several initiatives in this area culminating eventually in a Green Paper (2003) and a proposal for a Framework Decision on Specific Procedural Rights in Criminal Proceedings (2004). Unfortunately enough, this proposal did not succeed in getting the unanimous support of all Member States and was abandoned in 2007.

This AGIS project focuses particularly on one such fundamental procedural safeguard, the right to access to justice across languages and culture or in other words, the right to a free interpreter and the translation of all relevant documents in criminal proceedings.

The need to provide all citizens of the EU with the right to a fair trial, including the provision of quality legal interpreting or translation, is both a major ambition and challenge for the EU, given the disparity and the patchy and uneven provision of legal interpreting and translation throughout the EU.

In order to remedy these discrepancies and to arrive at minimum guaranteed standards in all Member States, one needs, first of all, more detailed and objective information on the existing provisions, a *status quaestionis* on legal interpreting and translation in the EU. This will in turn allow for considered reflection and action both on EU and on Member State level.

We have chosen to carry out this task by means of a EU-wide questionnaire, so that both best practices but also differences in policy and the different implementation of this procedural right may be ascertained.

The core sections of this report provide an analysis of the responses from each Member State (Luxemburg excepted) on the basis of indicators that are relevant to assess the provision of legal interpreting and translation. These indicators allow us to draw up a composite country profile of each Member State for interpreting as well as translation. A more detailed, thorough analysis of one Member State has been included by way of example to show how the information has been gleaned and to stimulate colleagues to delve for themselves into the materials and exhaust the full potential of the responses.

These country profiles are then weighed and ranked, first of all, on a number of essential performance indicators (e.g. procedural safeguards, regulation of the interpreting and translation professions and quality assurance…) and subsequently on five Green Paper indicators (accreditation, register, code, training, vulnerable groups). This has allowed us to draw up overall apex indicators ranking all Member States on a EU scale and shows in composite maps how the Member States are performing with regard to this particular procedural safeguard.

The core conclusion of this survey on the provision of legal interpreting and translation in criminal proceedings in the EU is twofold. Firstly, the survey shows that sufficient legal interpreting and translation skills and structures are *not yet* in place to meet the goals that all individuals, irrespective of language and culture, have their procedural right respected in each Member State. Secondly, however, it also shows a process of development to do so *is* in progress across the EU, albeit still variable in coherence, quality and quantity.

The full text of this report is also available on the website of our projects (www. agisproject.com) including the full country profiles materials of each Member State.

Criminal justice systems form the essential framework for just and fair societies. The increase in movement of people between countries has found most Member States ill-prepared to deal with the inevitable resulting language barriers. As part of that, there is a paucity of relevant statistics on such basic facts as how many people will need the services of legal interpreters and translators, in which languages and where and how the quality of such provision can be guaranteed.

Nonetheless, through eliciting information from a variety of sources this questionnaire has managed to grasp a worthwhile map of what provisions exist. It is the view of the project group that the point has been reached where foundations have been laid. Worthwhile progress could be made if co-ordinated management strategies were put in place to reach long-term goals through incremental stages, within a sensible time-scale.

Finally, we want to express our gratitude to the European Commission for the financial support provided by the DG Justice, Freedom and Security under the AGIS programme.

RÉSUMÉ

Face à de nombreux nouveaux défis, tels que l'immigration, la criminalité transfrontalière, la libre circulation de gens et de biens, etc., l'Union Européenne s'est rendue compte de l'importance accrue de la coopération judiciaire et de la reconnaissance mutuelle entre États Membres afin de garantir la sécurité et la justice au sein de l'Union.

Cependant, dans le même temps, il subsiste un sentiment profond de préoccupation au sujet de ces défis, notamment que les libertés et les droits essentiels des citoyens doivent être préservés.

Il faut donc voir ce projet (AGIS projet JLS/2006/AGIS/052) comme un élément parmi les efforts concertés dans l'objectif de mettre en place des mécanismes et des assurances de respect des garanties procédurales en matière de droit pénal dans tous les Pays Membres de l'Union Européenne.

Depuis le sommet de Tampere (1998), l'UE a lancé plusieurs initiatives dans ce domaine, dont le point culminant a été la rédaction d'un Livre Vert (2003) et d'une proposition de décision-cadre du Conseil relative à certains droits procéduraux accordés dans le cadre des procédures pénales dans l'Union européenne (2004).

Ce projet AGIS vise spécifiquement l'une de ces garanties procédurales, notamment le droit d'accès à la justice, indépendamment des langues et des cultures, ou, en d'autres mots, le droit de pouvoir accéder gratuitement à un interprète ou de pouvoir obtenir une traduction de tous les document pertinents à la procédure pénale.

En vue de la disparité actuelle et des provisions incomplètes et hétérogènes en matière de traduction et d'interprétariat judiciaire, le besoin impératif de garantir à tous les citoyens de l'Union le droit à un procès juste, y compris la mise à disposition d'interprétariat et de traduction judiciaire de qualité, forme en même temps une ambition et un défi pour l'Union Européenne.

Si l'on veut remédier à cette disparité et mettre en place des normes minimales garanties par tous les États Membres, il faudra avant tout obtenir des informations plus détaillées et objectives par rapport aux dispositions existantes. Il faudra un *status quaestionis* concernant la traduction et l'interprétariat judiciaire au sein de l'UE, donnant lieu à un processus approfondi de réflexion et à une action concertée, aussi bien au niveau de l'Union Européenne, que celui des États Membres.

Dans le but d'identifier les meilleures pratiques, mais également les différentes politiques et pratiques existantes par rapport à ce droit procédural, nous avons opté pour une enquête, menée dans tous les États Membres.

Les sections-clef de ce rapport contiennent une analyse des réponses qui nous sont parvenues de tous les États Membres (à l'exception du Luxembourg), sur base d'indicateurs pertinents à l'accès aux dispositions en matière d'interprétariat et de traduction judiciaire. Ces indicateurs nous ont permis de rédiger des profils nationaux composites des États Membres concernant l'interprétariat ainsi que la traduction. Une analyse plus approfondie d'un État Membre a également été inclus afin de déconstruire le processus de transformation de données, mais également dans l'objectif de stimuler nos collèges à s'immerger dans le matériel disponible et à capitaliser pleinement le potentiel en réponses.

En premier lieu, les profils des États Membres ont été pondéré et comparé par rapport à un nombre d'indicateurs essentiels de prestation (par exemple: les garanties procédurales, la règlementation de la profession d'interprète ou de traducteur ou encore en matière de garanties de qualité …) et, en suite, par rapport à cinq indicateurs issus du Livre Vert (l'agrément, le registre, le code, la formation et les groupes vulnérables). Finalement, nous avons compilés des indicateurs principaux, permettant la classification des Pays Membres à l'échelle Européenne ainsi que la création de cartes topographiques comparatives, visualisant la performance relative des États Membres en relation à un indicateur spécifique.

Il y a deux conclusions principales à tirer de cette enquête concernant les dispositions en matière d'interprétariat et de traduction lors des procédures pénales. Premièrement, l'étude démontre que les structures et les capacités suffisantes en interprétariat et traduction judiciaire ne sont *pas encore* en place afin de pouvoir garantir dans chaque Pays Membre à tout individu, indépendamment de sa langue ou culture, le respect de ses droits procéduraux. Néanmoins, la seconde conclusion à tirer serait que l'on peut observer un processus de développement en cours dans toute l'Union, même s'il y a une variance en matière de cohérence, de qualité et de quantité.

Le rapport complet est également disponible sur le site web de nos projets (www. agisproject.com), y compris les profils complets des Pays Membres.

Les systèmes pénaux forment un cadre essentiel pour les sociétés justes et équitables. Suite à une mobilité accrue, la plupart des États Membres s'avère mal préparé à faire face aux inévitables barrières linguistiques résultantes. Cela implique, entre autres, un manque de statistiques pertinentes concernant les questions les plus fondamentales, comme, par exemple, le nombre de personnes ayant besoin d'interprétariat ou de traduction judiciaire, les langues requises ou la façon de se porter garant de la qualité des dispositions.

Cependant, en se basant sur différentes sources d'information, cette étude a su dresser un inventaire valable des dispositions en place. Le comité de pilotage du projet est d'avis que les premières fondations ont su être jetées. Des stratégies co-ordinées de gestion pourraient, par étapes successives et selon un échéancier raisonnable, réaliser d'importants progrès.

Finalement, nous tenons à exprimer notre gratitude à la Commission Européenne pour l'appui financier de la DG Justice, Liberté et Sécurité sous l'égide du programme AGIS.

KOMMENTIERTE ZUSAMMENFASSUNG

Die Europäische Union wird in zunehmenden Maße mit neuen und vielfachen Herausforderungen so wie Migration, Terrorismus, grenzüberschreitender Kriminalität und freiem Personen- und Dienstenverkehr konfrontiert und realisiert sich wie wichtig justizielle Zusammenarbeit und gegenseitige Anerkennung zwischen den Mitgliedstaaten ist, um Sicherheit und Justiz in der EU zu gewährleisten.

Im gleichen Moment gibt es aber auch eine große Besorgnis, dass im Rahmen dieser Herausforderungen die Freiheit und Grundrechte der Bürger geschützt werden müssen.

Dieses Projekt (AGIS JLS/2006/AGIS/052) ist Teil eines gemeinsamen Vorgehens, um Verfahrensrechte bei Stafverfahren in allen Mitgliedstaaten der Europäischen Union zu schützen.

Seit dem Tampere Gipfel (1998) hat die EU verschiedene Initiative in diesem Bereich, die kulminierten in einem Grünbuch (2003) und einem Vorschlag für einen Rahmenbeschluss des Rates über bestimmte Verfahrensrechte in Strafverfahren (2004), ergriffen. Dieser Vorschlag fand leider keine einstimmige Unterstützung der Mitgliedstaaten und er wurde 2007 auf verzichtet.

Dieses AGIS Projekt widmet sich im Besonderen einem dieser Verfahrensrechte, nämlich dem Recht auf Zugang zur Justiz in verschiedenen Sprachen und Kulturen, oder dem Recht auf einen Dolmetscher und auf die Übersetzung der wesentlichen Schriftstücke in Strafverfahren.

Durch die großen Unterschiede zwischen den Mitgliedstaaten im Bereich der Erbringung von Gerichtsdolmetsch- und Übersetzungsdienstleistungen ist das gewährleisten eines fairen Verfahrens für alle EU-Bürger, inklusive die Erbringung von qualitativen Gerichtsdolmetsch- und Übersetzungsdienstleistungen, zugleich eine große Ambition und Herausforderung für die Europäische Union.

Um eine Übersicht über diese Unterschiede zu verschaffen, wurde ein Fragebogen versand an Ansprechpartner in der ganzen Union, um so gute Methoden aber auch politische Unterschiede und die unterschiedliche Anwendung dieser Verfahrensrechte festzustellen.

Die Kernkapitel dieses Berichts bieten eine Analyse der Antworten von jedem Mitgliedstaat (außer Luxemburg) gegründet auf Indikatoren die für die Bewertung der Erbingung von Gerichtsdolmetsch- und Übersetzungsdienstleistungen relevant sind. Diese Indikatoren ermöglichen es ein Länderprofil für jede Mitgliedstaat zusammenzustellen für sowohl Dometschen als Übersetzen. Eine detailliertere, gründliche Analyse von einem Mitgliedstaat wurde als Beispiel aufgenommen, um zu zeichen wie die Auskünfte gesammelt wurden und um KollegInnen dazu anzutreiben das Maximum aus den Antworten herauszuholen.

Diese Länderprofile werden zunächst gewogen und geordnet auf Grund einer Zahl von wesentlichen Erfolgsindikatoren (zum Beispiel Verfahrensrechte, Vorschrifte des Dolmetsch- und Übersetzungsberufs und Qualitätssicherung,...) und danach auf Grund von fünf Grünbuchindikatoren (Akkreditierung, Register, Code, Bildung, schutzbedürftige Gruppen). Auf diese Weise konnten Apex Indikatoren aufgestellt werden und konnten alle Mitgliedstaaten auf einer europäischen Skala geordnet werden. Zusammengesetzte Karten zeigen wie die Mitgliedstaaten leisten im Bereich von diesem spezifischen Verfahrensrecht.

Die Kernschlussfolgerung dieses Fragebogens über die Erbringung von Gerichtsdolmetsch- und Übersetzungsdienstleistungen in Strafverfahren in der EU ist zweifach. Erstens zeigt der Fragebogen, dass die bestehenden Strukturen und Kompetenzen im Bereich des Gerichtsdolmetschens- und Übersetzens nicht ausreichend sind, um Verfahrensrechte für alle Bürger, ungeachtet ihrer Sprache und Kultur, zu gewährleisten. Zweitens zeigt er aber auch, dass dieser Prozess sich, zwar mit großen Unterschieden in Koherenz, Qualität und Quantität, in der ganzen EU entwickelt.

Der Volltext dieses Berichts ist zur Verfügung auf der Webseite unseres Projekts (www.agisproject.com), inklusive die Länderprofile der Mitgliedstaaten.

Strafrechtsysteme bilden den westenlichen Rahmen für eine gerechte und faire Gesellschaft. Der zunehmende freie Personenverkehr zwischen Länder bringt Sprachbarrieren mit sich, auf die die Mitgliedstaaten slecht vorbereitet sind. Das bedeutet, dass es keine relevante Statistiken über die Zahl der Personen die Gerichtsdolmetscher oder –Übersetzer brauchen, welche Sprachenkombinationen gefragt werden, und wie die Qualität der Dienstleistung gesichert werden kann, gibt.

Durch Auskünfte von verschiedenen Quellen einzuholen, hat dieser Fragebogen aber eine Übersicht über die bestehenden Erbringungen verschafft. Die

Projektgruppe glaubt, dass jetzt die Grundlagen gelegt worden sind. Koordinierte Managementstrategien, um langfristige Ziele innerhalb von einem realistischen Zeitraum zu erreichen, können dafür sorgen, dass wichtige Fortschritte erzielt werden können.

Wir möchten zum Schluß die Europäische Kommision danken für die finanzielle Unterstützung der GD Justiz, Freiheit und Sicherheit unter dem AGIS Programm.

CHAPTER I
CO-OPERATION AND PROTECTION OF PROCEDURAL RIGHTS IN THE AREA OF CRIMINAL JUSTICE THROUGHOUT THE EUROPEAN UNION

These past few years, co-operation in the area of criminal justice between the Member States of the European Union (EU) has gained momentum. The common desire of the Parties to the EEC Treaty of 1957 was to foster economic and social progress of their countries by eliminating the barriers that divided Europe. At that time criminal law was governed by the Conventions concluded within the Council of Europe. With the Treaty of Maastricht (1992) criminal law became part of the area for joint action of the European Union itself. In this so-called *third pillar,* elements of criminal law were prudently introduced. In that pillar, regulation can only take the form of a Framework Decision, not a Directive, and moreover requires the unanimous decisions of the Council, while the European Parliament may put forward recommendations. In 1997, the Treaty of Amsterdam stated in so many words that its target is the harmonisation of legislation in the field of organised crime, terrorism and drug trafficking. In the programme of the Tampere summit (1999), mutual recognition in criminal cases was stressed, so that decisions of judicial authorities in a Member State would be recognised and enforced in another Member State as if it were a national decision and this as expeditiously as possible with the least possible checks.

Co-operation in Europe in the area of criminal law is necessary to counter the security risks arising from the abolition of controls at internal frontiers in the second half of the eighties of the last century. It was based on the assumption that crime would increase at a cross-border level by the abolition of internal frontiers, while the countering of crime would take place within national frontiers. There is no European enforcement agency based on the EU Convention. National agencies are, in principle, not authorised to act in the territory of other Member States, so that co-operation and exchange are essential to ensure that a criminal may not move from one Member State to another without proper punishment. The expansion of the Union, the consequences of 11 September 2001 and 11 March 2004 and the urgent need to combat terror, reinforced the need for further co-operation in the area of criminal justice. But such co-operation can be effective only if there is mutual confidence between the authorities of the Member States. Confidence is two-sided: the Member States whose cooperation is sought must be confident that the proceedings in the executing state take place in accordance with the rules of law. Confidence is, moreover, not only of importance between the authorities (the police and the judicial authorities), but also for the citizens involved who must be able to trust that their rights will be duly respected.[1]

The European Arrest Warrant, which replaced the diverging extradition procedures within the European Union, is a clear example. This makes it simpler to extradite someone to the Member State concerned. A French national, for example, suspected of a criminal offence elsewhere within the EU may be surrendered to stand trial there. Furthermore, there are now Framework Decisions for obtaining evidence in criminal matters and for the harmonisation of the regulation for the punishment of offences like human trafficking, money laundering, child pornography, drug trafficking, terrorism and the protection of victims. In brief, more and more EU citizens are confronted with the consequences of co-operation in the area of European criminal justice.

From the perspective of the European citizen it is of importance, where the protection of his procedural rights are concerned, that he will be able to understand the language of the court in the country where he is an actor in criminal proceedings. In order to exercise his rights adequately, the citizen must in any case obtain knowledge and information on his legal (im-) possibilities in a language he can understand. Differences in language must be bridged correctly and reliably. Interpreters and translators therefore constitute a critical link in the communication between the citizen and the judicial authorities, which requires safeguards as to quality and integrity.

RESPONSIBILITY FOR A GOOD AND TRUSTWORTHY INTERPRETER OR TRANSLATOR

The right to have a good interpreter and translator is also based on international law. By virtue of Article 6 of the European Convention on Human Rights and Fundamental Freedoms (ECHR) a suspect is entitled, from the moment that there is question of a criminal charge, to be informed, in a language which he

---

[1]   Mutual confidence is also the essence of the case of Gözútuk and Brügge (ECtoJ 11 February 2003 C187/C and C-385/01). According to the Court it is necessary that the Member States have mutual confidence in their respective systems of criminal law and that each Member State accepts application of the criminal law in effect in the other Member States even if a different solution would result from the application of its own criminal law.

understands, of the nature and cause of the accusation against him. This is also one of the minimum safeguards for criminal prosecution mentioned in Article 14 par. 3 of the International Covenant on Civil and Political Rights (ICCPR).

Based on Article 5 par. 2 ECHR and Article 9 par. 2 ICCPR, everyone who is arrested is entitled to be informed immediately at his arrest of the reasons for his arrest and of any charge against him. The provision of the Convention pertains to the arrest of the suspect but, in addition, there is the situation that a suspect is stopped for questioning and the matter is dealt with on the spot. For instance, the suspect is briefly interviewed without any further constraint on his liberty. This occurs e.g. when specific checks on the possession of alcohol and drugs are made. The present questionnaire makes clear that the Member States implement the obligations arising from the ECHR and ICCPR each in their own way, as a result of which divergences arise which have far-reaching consequences for the suspects concerned.

GREEN PAPER ON PROCEDURAL SAFEGUARDS

Having regard a.o. to the differences in legal protection throughout the EU, the European Commission presented on 19 February 2003 a Green Paper on Procedural Rights in Criminal Proceedings for Suspects throughout the EU.[2] Chapter 5 of this Green Paper deals with the right to the assistance of a sufficiently qualified interpreter or translator as soon as the suspect is charged, so that the latter will be aware of the charge and can effectively take part in the proceedings. The Green Paper states that, in the interest of the right to an impartial trial, a formal mechanism must be introduced to ensure that suspects will properly understand the language in which the proceedings take place, so that they may be able to defend themselves. It is furthermore stressed that the assistance of an interpreter or translator must be free. With regard to the manner in which the provisions must be made, the Green Paper states that the Member States:

1. must have a system for training specialised interpreters and translators ending with a recognised certificate
2. must have a system for accreditation of such translators and interpreters
3. must introduce regulations for registration which must not be unlimited so as to encourage the persons involved to keep up their knowledge of the language and of legal procedure, if and when they wish to renew their registration

---

[2]   http://europa.eu.int/cgi-bin/eur-lex/udl.pl?GUILANGUAGE=nl&DOCID=503PC0075&LANGUAGE.

4. must set up a system of continuous professional development so that legal interpreters and translators will be able to maintain their skills at a proper level
5. must draw up a code of conduct and guidelines for proper working standards which must be equivalent throughout the EU or correspond as far as possible
6. must provide training for judges, public prosecutors and lawyers so that they will have a better insight into the role of the translator and the interpreter, resulting in a more efficient mutual collaboration.[3]

Most reactions of the Member States to the Green Paper were negative, although they were positive as regards the need for safeguards for suspects in criminal cases throughout the European Union. Many Member States, however, considered this mostly a domestic matter. Most Member States did not subscribe to the view that the European Union should play a role in the harmonisation of safeguards for the rights of suspects, next to that of the European Court of Human Rights (ECHR), while some Member States considered that the ECHR already provides sufficient safeguards. The financial consequences that an implementation of the Green Paper would entail, was also the subject of criticism.

The reaction of the European Parliament was considerably more positive.[4] In a Resolution on 6 November 2003, the European Parliament expressed the view, where the right of assistance of an interpreter or translator is concerned, that common basic standards must ensure that courts are reminded of their obligation to ensure, in conformity with international case law, that the various actors understand each other (Consideration 8). The Resolution further stated (Consideration 9) that common minimum standards must provide as from the first interview of the suspect (or when the person is accused of an offence), that there must be free interpretation at all hearings so that the suspect will be able to understand what is said and that, in the case of a conflict of interests, two different interpreters or translators are required, one for the defence and one for the public prosecution service (or the court, depending on the legal system); that all those documents must be translated which the suspect needs to understand in order to be assured of an impartial judgment as well as the documents required for consultation in respect of the defence of the suspect. The Resolution mentions in particular the translation of:

- the official police record
- the declarations of the person(s) who made the complaint and witnesses

---

[3]   These recommendations in the Green Paper were essentially based on Grotius Projects *Aequitas* (2001) and *Aequalitas* (2003).
[4]   http://europa.eu.int/abc/doc/off/bull/en/200311/p104025.htm.

- the statements of the suspect/the person made at the police station and before judicial authorities
- the indictment issued by the public prosecution service and the complaints reported by other parties
- the judicial decision whereby the indictment or the charge against the accused is confirmed.

With regard to the required level of quality, the Resolution states that each Member State needs to provide for a register of legal interpreters and translators. Each Member State must also institute a national body charged with the accreditation and periodical registration as well as the continuous professional development of specialised legal interpreters and translators. Within that framework, Member States must also draw up a code of conduct for the profession, the non-compliance with the code resulting in forfeiture of the accreditation or expulsion from the profession. When drawing up such a code of conduct, account must be taken of the views of organisations that train translators and interpreters, Ministries of Justice and professional organisations. The Resolution further stresses that by means of appropriate training courses Member States must ensure awareness among legal interpreters and translators of the legal procedures and terminology of the legal system in which they work (Considerations 9 and 10). It is notable that the European Parliament is of the opinion that all actors professionally involved in criminal proceedings, including the police, defence counsel, the persons who made a complaint and members of the judiciary, must be trained to work together with and via an interpreter (Consideration 10).

FRAMEWORK DECISION ON SPECIFIC PROCEDURAL RIGHTS IN CRIMINAL PROCEEDINGS

Subsequent to the Green Paper, the European Commission presented a proposal for a Framework Decision on Specific Procedural Rights in Criminal Proceedings throughout the EU.[5] It is clear in this text that, in response to the objections raised against the Green Paper, the Commission considerably adjusted and lowered the level of the ambitions outlined in the Green Paper.

In the proposed Framework Decision the term 'suspect' is limited to suspects who are aware that a criminal investigation is instituted against them, i.e. in most

---

[5]   COM (2004) 328 definitive.

cases when suspects are arrested. The proposal concentrated on the same five procedural rights that made up the core of the Green Paper:

1. the right to legal assistance and representation by defence counsel
2. the right to an interpreter and/or translator so that the suspect will be aware of what the charges are and will understand the procedure
3. an appropriate protection of suspects who cannot hear or follow the criminal procedure on account of a handicap or impairment
4. the right to consular assistance for foreign prisoners
5. the written notification given to the suspect in respect of his rights.

With regard to interpreters and translators, Articles, 6, 7, 8, 9 and 16 are of particular interest. Article 6 imposes on the Member State the obligation to safeguard that a suspect who does not understand the language of the court will be assisted free, during the entire proceedings, by an interpreter or translator. The proposed Framework Decision states that this is a conditio sine qua non for a fair trial. The proposal also underlines that it is not limited to situations where a foreign language is spoken but will also apply to suspects with hearing or speech impediments (Article 6, par. 3).

Article 7 imposes the obligation on Member States to make arrangements for safeguarding that suspects who speak a foreign language will be provided free of charge with a translation of all relevant documents in their case. The second paragraph of this article stresses that lawyers acting for suspects who speak a foreign language, may request a translation of such documents.

Article 8 relates to the required accuracy of the translation and interpretation. The first paragraph of this article states that Member States must safeguard that the interpreters and translators whose services are used will be 'sufficiently qualified' to provide a correct translation or interpretation. Furthermore, Member States must arrange safeguards that an interpreter or translator who does not perform his work accurately will be replaced. To further ensure the quality of interpreters, Member States should, as provided in Article 9, record the interpretation by means of audio or video tapes.

MINIMUM STANDARDS

As stated above, safeguards for suspects to ensure that they will have a fair trial were already laid down in several international instruments.[6] The proposed Framework Decision did not envisage the creation of new rights or the monitoring of compliance of rights which exist pursuant to the ECHR or other instruments. Its aim was, based on the existing rights, to promote the visibility and efficiency thereof so that these rights become practical and effective and are complied with in a consistent and uniform manner throughout the European Union. Having regard to this aim it is understandable, also in the light of the above-mentioned criticism of the Green Paper, that the Commission opted for the time being for regulation of minimum standards. These minimum standards are, moreover, exactly that, a minimum for effective protection of rights only because when it really becomes important, they will often in practice only be put into effect after litigation taking many years because, first of all, all national juridical procedures must have been completed before it is possible to appeal to the European Court of Human Rights. The case of the English and Dutch plane spotters in Greece once more made clear that the ECHR is not yet so effective that a suspect who speaks a different language may at all times be assured that his rights will be adequately protected.[7] The European Court of Human Rights, moreover, only reviews the conduct of authorities of a Member State and not the course of affairs on a European level, e.g. any acts of several EU-Member States jointly (e.g. *joint teams* of functionaries of Europol). This means that the level of legal protection provided by the ECHR on a European level is in the end only relative.

The obligations formulated in Articles 6 and 7 of the proposed Framework Decision in respect of the free assistance of an interpreter or translator are based on the right to a fair trial as laid down in Article 6 of the European Convention of Human Rights and also, more in particular, on the landmark decisions of the European Court of Human Rights in such cases as Luedicke Belkacem and Koç v. Germany[8] and Kamasinski v. Austria.[9] In these cases the European Court of Human Rights decided that Article 6 par. 3 sub b entails that assistance of an interpreter to a suspect is free of charge and, as a result, that a suspect may not be

---

[6]   Vandenberghe, Brecht, The European Convention of Human Rights: The Right to the Free Assistance of an Interpreter (p. 53–59) and Vanden Bosch, Yolanda, Adequate legislation to 'Equal Access to Justice across Language and Culture' (p. 61–73) in Hertog, E. (ed.) 2003. *Aequalitas: Equal Access to Justice across Language and Culture in the EU.* Antwerpen: Lessius Hogeschool.

[7]   http://www.f-t-a.freeserve.co.uk/press/releases/2001/eurowarrant301101.htm   and   http://www.f-t-a.freeserve.co.uk/press/releases/2001/greece101201.htm.

[8]   28 November 1978, Application no. 6210/73; 6877/75; 7132/75.

[9]   ECtHR 19 December 1989, Series A 168.

obliged after his sentence to pay the costs. 'For anyone who cannot speak or understand the language used in court has the right to receive the free assistance of an interpreter, without subsequently having claimed back from him payment of the cost thereby incurred.'

Where the accuracy of the interpretation or translation is concerned, the proposed Framework Decision in Article 8 follows the standard of care which the European Court of Human Rights formulated in the case of Artico v. Italy.[10] In that case the Court observed that the State did not only have the duty to guarantee that rights are not theoretical or illusory but that rights are practical and effective. This is particularly so of the rights of the defence in view of the prominent place held in a democratic society by the right to a fair trial, from which they derive. This of course also relates to assistance at law and encompasses that of an interpreter and translator: 'the State is not liable for every defect but the governmental authorities must maintain an effective system of assistance of interpreters'. In each criminal case the court must always consider whether assistance of an interpreter is required and when this is the case, it must be of adequate quality. The court may not hide behind the indifferent attitude of a counsellor as was clear from the Cuscani-case.[11] The European Court of Human Rights observed that while it is true that the conduct of the defence is essentially a matter between the defendant and his counsel, whether counsel be appointed under a legal aid scheme as in the applicant's case or be privately financed[12], the ultimate guardian of the fairness of the proceedings, however, was the trial judge who had been clearly apprised of the real difficulties which the absence of interpretation might create for the applicant. It further observed that the domestic courts have already taken the view that in circumstances such as those in the instant case, judges are required to treat the interests of an accused with 'scrupulous care'.

In an other case, the case of Hermi v. Italy,[13] the Court observed that 'in the context of application of paragraph 3 (e), the issue of the defendant's linguistic knowledge is vital and that it must also examine the nature of the offence with which the defendant is charged and any communications addressed to him by the domestic authorities, in order to assess whether they are sufficiently complex to require a detailed knowledge of the language used in court'.

---

[10]   ECtHR 13 May 1980, Application No. 6694/74.
[11]   ECtHR 25 September 2002, Application No. 32771/96 (Cuscani v. United Kingdom). .
[12]   See also the Kamasinski v. Austria judgment of 19 December 1989, Series A no. 168, pp. 32–33, §65; the Stanford v. United Kingdom judgment of 23 February 1994, Series A. 282-A, p. 11, §28.
[13]   18 October 2006, Application No. 18114/02.

CONCLUSION

In the light of the important case law of the European Court of Human Rights, the ambition and the need to make the EU into an area of freedom, security and justice, it is truly disappointing that the negotiations on the proposed Framework Decision after five years of consultations and deliberations finally collapsed in June 2007. In spite of renewed support for the Proposal from the European Parliament, important stakeholders such as NGOs and the Grotius-Agis project groups, arguing that the Proposal at least laid down minimum norms that could be implemented consistently and uniformly throughout the EU and hence would increase the trust in Member States' legal systems and improve mutual collaboration, six Member States remained adamant in their opposition to the Proposal on the grounds that ECHR and ECtHR case law were sufficient guiding principles to safeguard these rights, the implementation of which should be left to the Member States anyway on the grounds of the subsidiarity principle. There were also concerns that particularly the proposal to monitor the quality of the interpreting by means of audio or video tapes would lead to increased costs and a possible increase in litigation as well.

But of course, the needs and rationale for quality legal interpreting and translation remain the same. Issues and challenges such as mutual trust and judicial cooperation between the Member States, efficiency in the fight against crime, all ultimately rest on reliable communication channels and hence on reliable, quality legal interpreting and translation. On the other hand, there is the fundamental obligation of the EU to safeguard citizens' rights and hence guarantee a.o. access to justice across languages. However, the protection of the suspected citizen who does not speak the language of a prosecuting Member State is more than occasionally substandard. The measures now adopted by the European Union are still mainly of a repressive nature and create a semblance of first of all serving the interests of the State. It is not a superfluous luxury therefore when the EU, on its part, wants to counter this in the interest of the rights of the suspected citizen. This is why the continuation of the Grotius-Agis projects under the new Criminal Justice programme (2007–2013) must be welcomed and why the present questionnaire and study on the provision of legal interpreting and translation in the EU can make a worthwhile contribution to the ongoing effort to guarantee all EU citizens the right to access to justice across languages and culture.

REFERENCES

Agis Project Website. www.agisproject.com

European Judicial Systems. 2006. Council of Europe. Cepej Studies No.1.

Cape, E., J. Hodgson, T. Prakken and T. Spronken (eds.) 2007. *Suspects in Europe: Procedural Rights at the Investigative Stage of the Criminal Process in the European Union.* Antwerpen-Oxford: Intersentia.

De Wit, M. 2005. *Sign Language Interpreting in Europe.* Brussels: DG Justice, Freedom and Security.

Heres Diddens-Wischmeyer, J.G. 2005. *Tolken en vertalers in de EU.* Den Haag: Boom Juridische Uitgeverij.

Hertog, E. (ed.) 2001. *Aequitas. Access to Justice across Language and Culture in the EU.* Antwerpen: Lessius Hogeschool.

Hertog, E. (ed.) 2003. *Aequalitas: Equal Access to Justice across Language and Culture in the EU.* Antwerpen: Lessius Hogeschool.

Keijzer-Lambooy, H. and W.J. Gasille (eds.) 2005. *Aequilibrium. Instruments for Lifting Language Barriers in Intercultural Proceedings.* Utrecht: ITV Hogeschool.

Spronken, T. and M. Attinger (eds.) 2005. *Procedural Rights in Criminal Proceedings: Existing Level of Safeguards in the European Union.* Brussels: DG Justice, Freedom and Security.

CHAPTER II
METHODOLOGY

INTRODUCTION

This project sets out to establish the *status quaestionis* on the provision of legal interpreting and translation in the EU. The instrument that seemed most appropriate and efficient to do so was an EU-wide Questionnaire sent to all Member States and to both governmental as well as professional sources, so that as much information as possible might be collected and differences in policy and implementation of this procedural right could be ascertained.

PREVIOUS QUESTIONNAIRES

The Grotius 1997 Programme included a European Legal Interpreter Project for which Fair Trials Abroad ('FTA') issued a report based on a limited survey in a number of countries – Austria, Eire, France, Spain and Sweden – on the legislation governing the provision of interpreting and translation services, the administration of justice to non-native speakers, the ease of access to qualified translators and interpreters, the official standards of service provision and the availability of competent training programmes.[1]

In February 2002 the Commission sent out a Questionnaire to the Ministries of Justice and Home Affairs in the Member States in respect of existing criminal justice arrangements in the Member States on the following procedural rights:

1. the right to legal advice, including the level of legal aid;
2. the right to interpretation and translation for (non-native) defendants;
3. the right to specific attention for persons who cannot understand or follow the proceedings;
4. the right to communication and/or consular assistance;
5. the way in which the suspect or defendant is notified of his rights ('Letter of Rights').

---

[1]   Fair Trials Abroad 1999, Grotius Report 98/GR/003.

Professor Spronken and Ms Attinger collated and analysed the replies from these official sources in the Member States to the Questionnaire and did so with specific reference to the procedural rights as covered by the proposed Framework Decision.[2] The enlargement of the EU, the limitation of this survey to official sources and the need to gain a more thorough and focused understanding of the whole and complex issue of legal interpreting and translation are the rationale for our own questionnaire.

In 2003 the Green Paper on 'Procedural safeguards for suspects and defendants in criminal proceedings throughout the EU' also contained a list of questions on the above-mentioned rights. It is our feeling that this description, based as it was on a number of previous Grotius and Agis projects, is still the best framework for quality provision and the monitoring of legal interpreting and translation. Hence these Green Paper indicators provided a constant frame of reference when devising our Questionnaire.

A model survey carried out by Maya De Wit on the provision of sign language interpreting in the EU provides another interesting example.[3]

Other diverse EU questionnaires, e.g. on the legal framework conditions for information societies, on insolvency legislation, debt settlement and overindebtedness procedures, on the costs of justice, or a (Dutch) questionnaire by Euromos on the important and related issue of the European Arrest Warrant, provided other methodologically interesting models on how to actually set up the questionnaire.[4]

DRAFTING THE QUESTIONNAIRE

A number of salient points guided the drafting process of the questionnaire:

- To focus firmly on the (non-)compliance with the rights of suspects or defendants with regard to legal interpreting and translation
- To investigate not only the reality of existing provisions but also expectations and difficulties, i.e. to elucidate the tension between what Member States have and what they (and the EU) would want to have in a number of years

---

2   Spronken, T. and M. Attinger (eds.) 2005. *Procedural Rights in Criminal Proceedings: Existing Level of Safeguards in the European Union.* Brussels: DG Justice, Freedom and Security.

3   De Wit, M. 2005. *Sign Language Interpreting in Europe.* Brussels: DG Justice, Freedom and Security.

4   *http://www.costsofjustice.org/index.* by way of example.

- To focus on the pre-trial and trial stages, but not post-trial as that aspect was deemed to be a completely different issue
- To strike a balance between facts and figures, between closed multiple choice questions and items for qualitative analysis via comment or nuance
- To launch a pilot version in one language on a small but reliable sample in each of the four participants' countries to improve the efficiency of the questionnaire and responses
- To provide both a print and on-line version in order to reach a maximum number of respondents and facilitate the analysis of the statistical information
- To have the English source version of the questionnaire translated into French and German in order to maximize the response
- To query both 'official' governmental respondents in the Member States (as represented by the Ministry of Justice and the Permanent Representatives) and a whole range of professional stakeholders such as, the police, prosecution service, the judiciary, defence counsels, victims or witness support organizations, NGOs, interpreting or translation training institutes, professional associations of interpreters or translators, interpreters and translators themselves or providers thereof
- To approach professional respondents in Member States directly via a gathering of names of relevant and knowledgeable respondents, but to back this up by having a 'portal' name per Member State that would help provide more names and secure responses if needed.

The feedback and suggestions that emerged from the pilot version were incorporated and the improved version was then transformed by the Dutch company Intomart GfK into an efficient online version that could also, if need be, made available in print. The questionnaire was also translated into French and German by Intomart.[5]

Simultaneous with the preparation of the questionnaire, the project participants collated sufficient addresses in the 27 Member States of responsible, knowledgeable people from all judicial spheres who might act as respondents to fill out the questionnaire. Although there were significant problems in some Member States as such or in others to cover the whole range of judicial actors, every effort was made to try and fill the gaps. In the end a database was collected of over 1,000

---

[5]   In this respect, we want to express our deepest gratitude to the Raad voor Rechtsbijstand in 's Hertogenbosch who provided the additional funds for these two crucial procedures and particularly to Han von den Hoff for coordinating between the project and Intomart as well as to Peter van de Vijver and Nancy Vink of Intomart. It must be stressed that the quality of both the print and the electronic version was much appreciated.

respondents, which consisted for each Member State of the Ministry of Justice and the Permanent Representative as official, governmental sources, and a number of individual respondents from all walks of the judiciary. The European Criminal Bar Association (ECBA) and Council of Bars and Law Societies of Europe (CCBE) were invited as external partners into the project and agreed to send the questionnaire to a representative number of their colleagues in each Member State.

The questionnaire was sent out on 1st of September 2007. However, all respondents had been sent an advance email message in June (in English, German and French), alerting them to 'the coming' of the questionnaire in September. When it was put online, it was introduced to the respondents with an accompanying letter, again in three languages, setting out the purpose of the project and the questionnaire and providing a link to a contact person for either content or technical queries. Mid-September a reminder was sent to all those in the email database that had not yet responded. On the 24th September, another reminder was sent out, and a special and separate one on 1st October to all 'official', i.e. government sources that had not yet responded. Again all communication was done in three languages.

The questionnaire itself was to be opened with an individual link that was sent with the email. It could thus be opened and worked on but also left, to be picked up again at a later stage, and on completion it was sent off electronically to Intomart. The 'portals' or CCBE and ECBA could apply to Intomart for additional links to be sent to respondents of their choice.

The print version of the questionnaire can be consulted in Appendix I. The following are a couple of sample pages from the online version.

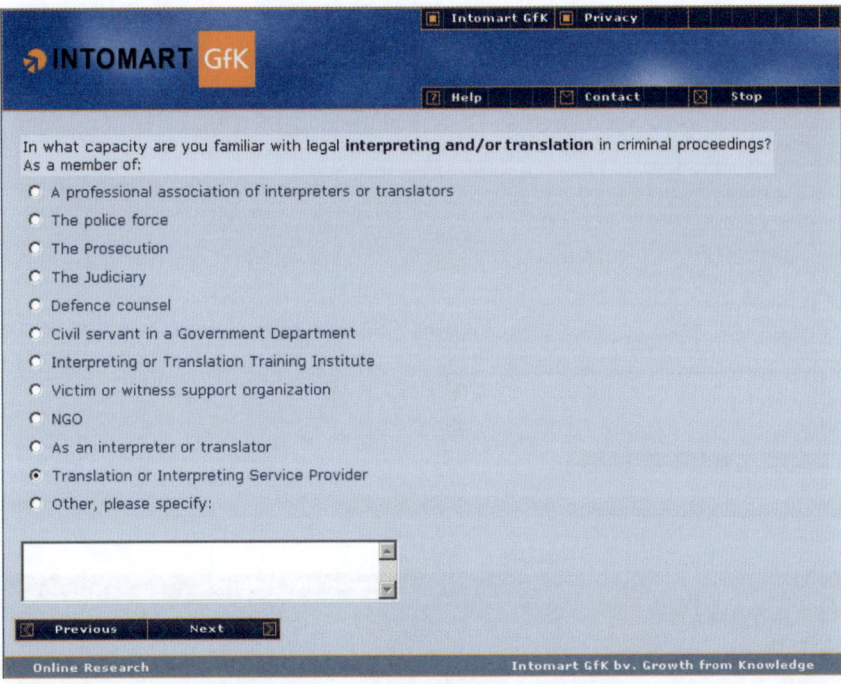

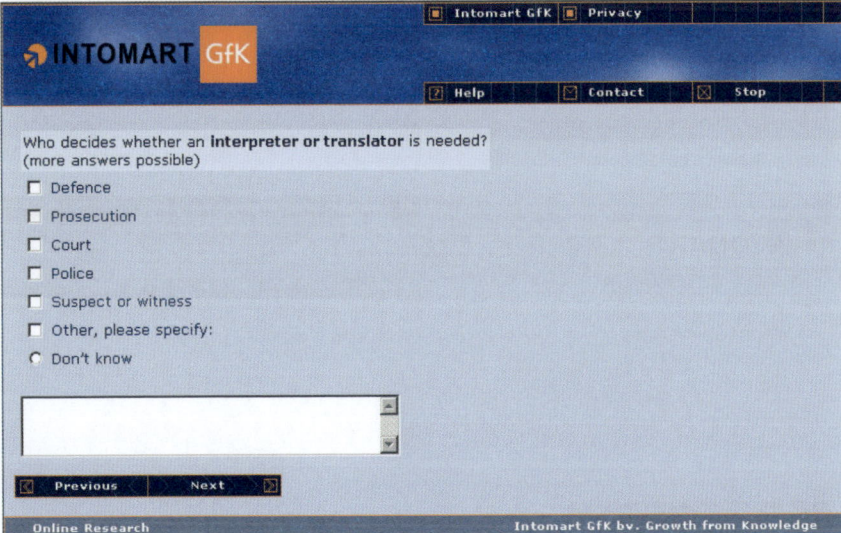

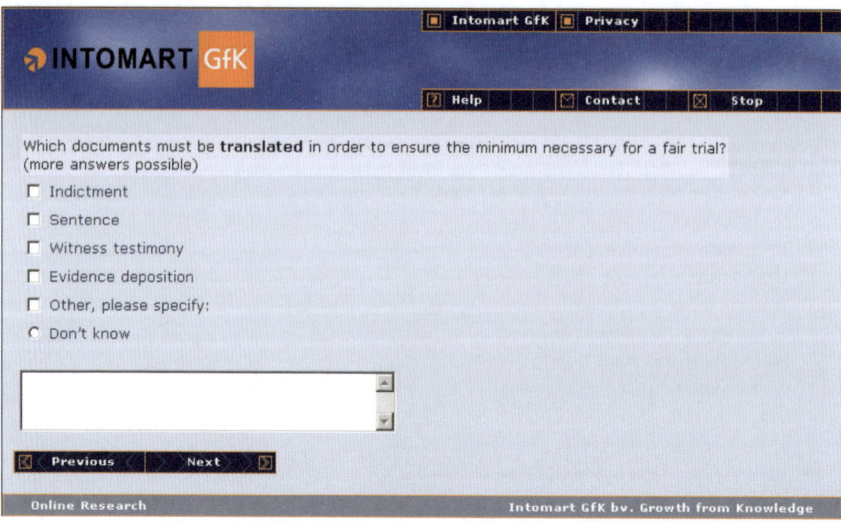

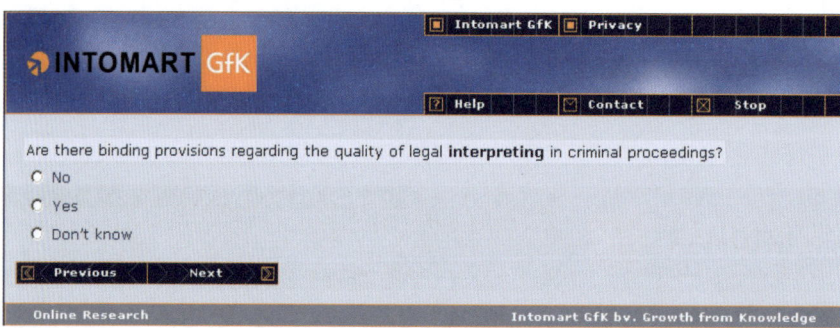

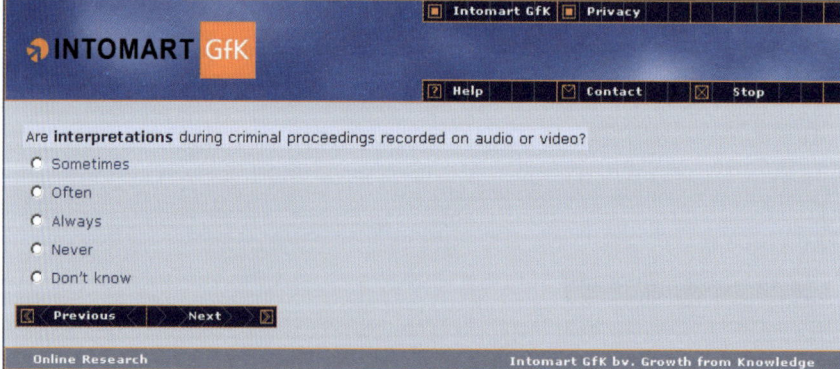

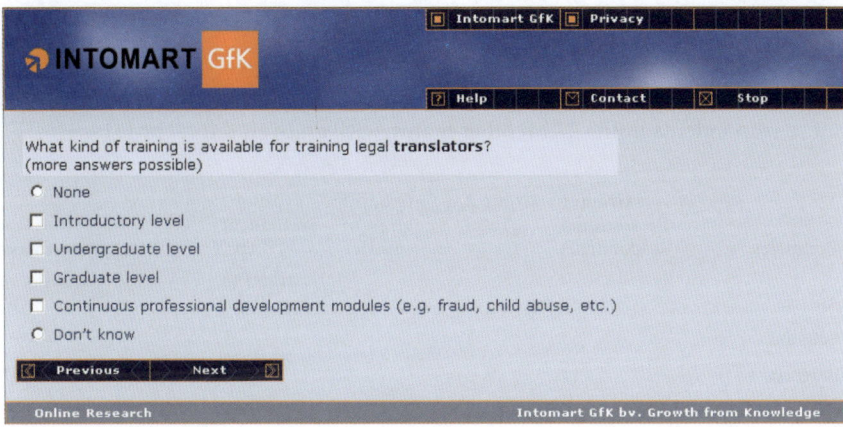

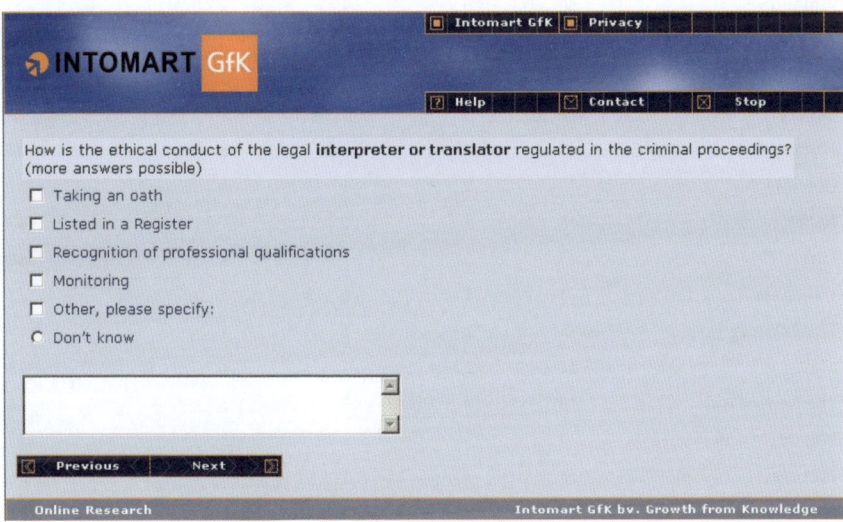

RESPONSE TO THE QUESTIONNAIRE

The following table provides an overview of the number of questionnaires sent out to respondents in the 27 Member States, with an overall total of 1119.

Countries	Group 1 Professional Respondents	Group 2 Total	Group 2 Mins. of Justice	Group 2 Permanent Reps.	Total per country
Austria	38	2	2	No access to Perm. Repr.	40
Belgium	53	3	2	1	56
Bulgaria	19	2	1	1	21
Cyprus	7	3	2	1	10
Czech Republic	21	5	4	1	26
Denmark	19	2	1	1	21
Estonia	16	2	1	1	18
Finland	30	3	1	2	33
France	35	3	1	2	38
Germany	43	6	1	5	49
Greece	22	3	1	2	25
Hungary	40	4	3	1	44
Ireland	50	2	1	1	52
Italy	45	3	2	1	48
Latvia	13	5	3	2	18
Lithuania	24	4	3	1	28
Luxembourg	5	2	1	1	7
Malta	11	2	1	1	13
The Netherlands	36	10	7	3	46
Poland	20	5	3	2	25
Portugal	13	3	1	2	16
Romania	17	4	3	1	21
Slovakia	38	4	3	1	42
Slovenia	23	5	3	2	28
Spain	35	5	3	2	40
Sweden	32	2	No access to Min. of Just.	2	34
United Kingdom	70	4	2	2	74
Total	775	98			873

112 additional logins sent to individual respondents
118 to ECBA
16 to CCBE

The following is a survey of the number of responses received per Member State divided into governmental and professional responses.

AUSTRIA Response:	2 governmental, 11 professional
BELGIUM Response:	1 governmental, 12 professional
BULGARIA Response:	1 governmental, 2 professional
CYPRUS Response:	0 governmental, 1 professional
CZECH REPUBLIC Response:	2 governmental, 4 professional
DENMARK Response:	0 governmental, 8 professional
ESTONIA Response:	0 governmental, 1 professional
FINLAND Response:	1 governmental, 10 professional
FRANCE Response:	0 governmental, 9 professional
GERMANY Response:	1 governmental, 7 professional
GREECE Response:	0 governmental, 5 professional
HUNGARY Response:	1 governmental, 8 professional
IRELAND Response:	1 governmental, 12 professional
ITALY Response:	0 governmental, 16 professional
LATVIA Response:	1 governmental, 2 professional
LITHUANIA Response:	1 governmental, 3 professional
MALTA Response:	0 governmental, 3 professional
THE NETHERLANDS Response:	1 governmental, 6 professional
POLAND Response:	0 governmental, 6 professional
PORTUGAL Response:	0 governmental, 3 professional
ROMANIA Response:	1 governmental, 4 professional
SLOVAKIA Response:	0 governmental, 5 professional
SLOVENIA Response:	2 governmental, 3 professional
SPAIN Response:	0 governmental, 8 professional
SWEDEN Response:	0 governmental, 6 professional
UNITED KINGDOM Response:	2 governmental, 21 professional

Of course, 194 responses, a roughly 20% overall return to a questionnaire is not bad. However, there are the striking features that from one Member State there were no replies at all, that there is a glaring lack of governmental response (only 13 out of 27 Member States), and a conspicuously low return from some Member States. It was decided to let these facts speak for themselves and make no attempt to launch a new effort to solicit more responses. As a matter of fact, these factual observations were to become part and parcel of the conclusions and recommendations.

PERFORMANCE INDICATORS

A comprehensive comparative analysis of EU Member States on all 97 questionnaire items is a rather impractical proposition. That is why a number of related key questions were clustered, on the basis of content analysis, in 14 basic level performance indicators[6], representing various aspects of the EU Green Paper. These indicators are to be seen as data-filters that show how a Member State is doing – 'performing' – on a particular issue.

Thus the set of questions 3+5+17+18, all about procedural guarantees, make up one indicator, which complemented with other related indicators (on the number of stages in the procedure where legal interpreting is needed or used, or the criteria for interpreting together with the issue of vulnerable groups) then constitute the overall higher category of 'procedural safeguards'. For an individual Member State, the result shown on these individual indicators might be a flashing or even warning light. All indicators were thus grouped in four higher level indicators and as a final bottom line, the four higher level indicators were consolidated into a single apex indicator. For the EU as a whole, this process allows for a ranking of countries according to their performance on the provision of legal interpreting and translation. Such analytical process has obviously the advantages and strength of comparison and ranking, but it also ultimately reduces the wealth of extra information that particular responses might contain, hence, as will be explained below, the suggestion to delve into the full potential of the materials in exhaustive country profiles.

The composition of all the performance indicators is shown hereafter:

Table 1: Hierarchy of indicators

Basic level indicators		Higher level indicators		Apex indicator	
I.1.1	Procedural guarantees	I.1	Procedural safeguards	AI	Overall ranking of Member State
I.1.2	Number of phases in the procedure				
I.1.3	Criteria for interpreting				
I.1.4	Vulnerable groups				
I.2.1	Protection and regulation	I.2	Regulation of the profession		
I.2.2	Accrediting body				
I.2.3	Register				
I.2.4	Code of conduct and disciplinary procedure				
I.3.1	Quality provisions	I.3	Quality provisions		
I.3.2	Training level				
I.3.3	Video taping				
I.3.4	Directives for magistrates				
I.3.5	Recruitment programme				
I.4.1	Percentage of cases	I.4	Quantitative provisions		

---

[6] Originally, a 15th basic level indicator quantifying the financial impact of LIT was proposed but only a small minority of respondents was able to provide the relevant financial information and even then only in a very fragmentary way.

INDICATOR 1: PROCEDURAL SAFEGUARDS

Indicator composition

Table 2: Composition of indicator I.1

Higher level indicator		Basic level indicators		Questions Interpreting	Questions Translation
I.1	Procedural safeguards	I.1.1	Procedural guarantees	Q3, 5, 17, 18	Q4, 5, 17, 18
		I.1.2	Number of phases in the procedure	Q10	Q11
		I.1.3	Criteria for interpreting	Q12	Q13
		I.1.4	Vulnerable groups	Q19	Q19

I.1.1 Procedural guarantees

3. Are there national or regional requirements concerning legal **interpreting** in criminal proceedings in your country?

   1 ☐ No
   2 ☐ Yes
   7 ☐ Don't know

   (selection: if V3 is 'yes')

3b. Which one(s)?
   (more answers possible)

   1 ☐ Legislation
   2 ☐ Government policy
   3 ☐ Agency or service provider regulations
   4 ☐ Ad hoc regulations
   6 ☐ Other: Please specify

4. Are there national or regional requirements concerning legal **translation** in criminal proceedings in your country?

   1 ☐ No
   2 ☐ Yes
   7 ☐ Don't know

   (selection: if V4 is 'yes')

4b. Which one(s)?
(more answers possible)

1 ☐ Legislation
2 ☐ Government policy
3 ☐ Agency or service provider regulations
4 ☐ Ad hoc regulations
6 ☐ Other: Please specify

5. In your country, is there any established procedure for ascertaining when there is a need for **translation or interpreting** in criminal proceedings or police investigations?

1 ☐ No
2 ☐ Yes
7 ☐ Don't know

17. Is there any monitoring of the provision of legal **interpreting or translation** in criminal proceedings?

1 ☐ No
2 ☐ Yes
7 ☐ Don't know

(selection: if V17 is 'yes')

17b. What kind of monitoring?
(more answers possible)

01 ☐ Through a controlling body
02 ☐ By lawyers in individual cases
03 ☐ By court officials in individual cases
04 ☐ Via a complaints procedure
05 ☐ Via budget management by the responsible authority
06 ☐ Not in an organized way
96 ☐ Other: Please specify

18. Are there national sanctions if the State fails to provide **interpretation and translation** when a person is entitled to it?

    1   ☐   No
    2   ☐   Yes
    7   ☐   Don't know

    (selection: if V18 is 'yes')

18b. Which national sanctions?
    (more answers possible)

    1   ☐   Retrial procedure
    2   ☐   Appeal procedure
    3   ☐   Reduction in budget allocation
    6   ☐   Other: Please specify

I.1.2 Number of phases in the procedure

10. At what stages of the criminal proceedings is **interpreting** provided?
    (more answers possible)

    01   ☐   Arrest
    02   ☐   Custody procedures (24 hrs)
    03   ☐   Investigation
    04   ☐   Detention
    05   ☐   Police interview/Pre-trial interrogation
    06   ☐   Preparation of a defence
    07   ☐   Court proceedings
    96   ☐   Other: Please specify
    97   ☐   Don't know

11. At what stages of the criminal proceedings is **translation** provided?
    (more answers possible)

    01   ☐   Arrest
    02   ☐   Custody procedures (24 hrs)
    03   ☐   Investigation
    04   ☐   Detention
    05   ☐   Police interview/Pre-trial interrogation
    06   ☐   Preparation of a defence

07 ☐ Court proceedings
96 ☐ Other: Please specify
97 ☐ Don't know

I.1.3 Criteria for interpreting

12. Are there any criteria that establish the extent to which the proceedings should be **interpreted**?

1 ☐ No
2 ☐ Yes
7 ☐ Don't know

(selection: if V12 is yes)

12b. Which criteria?
(more answers possible)

1 ☐ Nature of the communication
2 ☐ Time restrictions
3 ☐ Costs
6 ☐ Other: Please specify

13. Which documents must be **translated** in order to ensure the minimum necessary for a fair trial? *(more answers possible)*

1 ☐ Indictment
2 ☐ Sentence
3 ☐ Witness testimony
4 ☐ Evidence deposition
6 ☐ Other: Please specify
7 ☐ Don't know

I.1.4 Vulnerable groups

19. Are suspects from the following categories classified as particularly vulnerable in criminal proceedings?

19a. Foreign nationals

1 ☐ No
2 ☐ Yes

7   ☐   Don't know

(selection: if V19a is 'yes)

19a2. What protection is provided for them in criminal proceedings?

19b. The visually or hearing impaired

1   ☐   No
2   ☐   Yes
7   ☐   Don't know

(selection: if V19b is 'yes)

19b2. What protection is provided for them in criminal proceedings?

19c. Individuals with insufficient proficiency in the necessary language

1   ☐   No
2   ☐   Yes
7   ☐   Don't know

(selection: if V19c is 'yes)

19c2. What protection is provided for them in criminal proceedings?

INDICATOR 2: REGULATION OF THE PROFESSION

Table 3: Composition of indicator I.2

Higher level indicator		Basic level indicators		Questions Interpreting	Questions Translation
I.2	Regulation of the profession	I.2.1	Protection and regulation	Q21, 22	Q23, 24
		I.2.2	Accrediting body	Q44	Q45
		I.2.3	Register	Q50	Q46
		I.2.4	Code of conduct and procedure	Q58, 62	Q59, 63

21. Is the title of legal **interpreter** protected?

    1 ☐ No
    2 ☐ Yes
    7 ☐ Don't know

22. Is the profession of legal **interpreter** regulated?

    1 ☐ No
    2 ☐ Yes, partially
    3 ☐ Yes, fully
    7 ☐ Don't know

23. Is the title of legal **translator** protected?

    1 ☐ No
    2 ☐ Yes
    7 ☐ Don't know

24. Is the profession of legal **translator** regulated?

    1 ☐ No
    2 ☐ Yes, partially
    3 ☐ Yes, fully
    7 ☐ Don't know

44. Is there an accrediting body for the accreditation of legal **interpreters**?

    1 ☐ No
    2 ☐ Yes
    7 ☐ Don't know

45. Is there an accrediting body for the accreditation of legal **translators**?

    1 ☐ No
    2 ☐ Yes
    7 ☐ Don't know

46 Is there a national register of legal **translators**?

    1 ☐ No

2 ☐ Yes
7 ☐ Don't know

50. Is there a national register of legal **interpreters**?

1 ☐ No
2 ☐ Yes
7 ☐ Don't know

58. Is there a national or regional Code of Conduct for legal **interpreters** in your country?

1 ☐ No
2 ☐ Yes
7 ☐ Don't know

59. Is there a national or regional Code of Conduct for legal **translators** in your country?

1 ☐ No
2 ☐ Yes
7 ☐ Don't know

62. Is there a disciplinary procedures system in relation to legal **interpreters** in your country?

1 ☐ There is no disciplinary procedures system
2 ☐ There are different disciplinary procedures systems
2 ☐ There is a national procedure
6 ☐ Other: Please specify
7 ☐ Don't know

63. Is there a disciplinary procedures system in relation to legal **translators** in your country?

1 ☐ There is no disciplinary procedures system
2 ☐ There are different disciplinary procedures systems
3 ☐ There is a national procedure
6 ☐ Other: Please specify
7 ☐ Don't know

INDICATOR 3: QUALITY PROVISIONS

Table 4: Composition of indicator I.3

Higher level indicator		Basic level indicators		Questions Interpreting	Questions Translation
I.3	Quality provisions	I.3.1	Quality provisions	Q27, 67	Q27, 67
		I.3.2	Training level	Q42	Q42
		I.3.3	Video taping	Q70, 71	
		I.3.4	Directives for magistrates	Q72	Q72
		I.3.5	Recruitment programme	Q73	Q73

67. Is the quality of practice of legal **interpreting or translation** in criminal proceedings monitored?

   for interpreters

   1   ☐   No
   2   ☐   Yes
   7   ☐   Don't know

   for translators

   1   ☐   No
   2   ☐   Yes
   7   ☐   Don't know

70. Are **interpretations** during criminal proceedings recorded on audio or video?

   1   ☐   Sometimes
   2   ☐   Often
   3   ☐   Always
   4   ☐   Never
   7   ☐   Don't know

71. At which stage are **interpretations** during criminal proceedings recorded on audio or video? (more answers possible)

   1   ☐   Police questioning
   2   ☐   Investigation
   3   ☐   Court hearings

6 ☐ Other: Please specify

7 ☐ Don't know

72. What good practice guidelines exist for members of the legal services such as lawyers, judges, the police etc. on how to work with legal **interpreters or translators?**

1 ☐ None

2 ☐ In-service training

3 ☐ Courses

4 ☐ Documents

6 ☐ Other: Please specify

7 ☐ Don't know

73. Is there a national or regional programme to increase numbers and quality of legal **interpreters and translators** to meet demand and demographic changes?

Interpreters:

1 ☐ No

2 ☐ Yes

7 ☐ Don't know

Translators:

1 ☐ No

2 ☐ Yes

7 ☐ Don't know

INDICATOR 4: QUANTITATIVE PROVISIONS

Table 5: Composition of indicator I.4

Higher level indicator		Basic level indicators		Questions Interpreting	Questions Translation
I.4	Quantitative provisions	I.4.1	Ratio interpreted cases/ total	Q75	Q76

74. How many criminal proceedings are there currently in your country?

    1   ☐ Precise number:
    2   ☐ Approximate number:
    3   ☐ No records kept
    7   ☐ Don't know

75. In how many cases is a legal **interpreter** currently required?

    1   ☐ Precise percentage:
    2   ☐ Approximate percentage:
    3   ☐ No records kept
    7   ☐ Don't know

76. In how many cases is a legal **translator** currently required?

    1   ☐ Precise percentage:
    2   ☐ Approximate percentage:
    3   ☐ No records kept
    7   ☐ Don't know

ANALYSIS AND PRESENTATION FORMAT

T-SCORES

For the purpose of a comparative analysis of EU Member States on different performance indicators or for comparison of different indicators within a same country, the indicators were converted to T-scores, following the formula:

$$10 * (x - \mu)/\sigma + 50$$

Where: x is the raw score to be standardised
                μ is the population mean
                σ is the standard deviation of the population

T-scores are dimensionless quantities that always have a mean of 50 and a standard deviation of 10 and express how many standard deviations an observation is above or below the population mean.

The data are presented in the form of both bar and radial or 'spider' graphs, always using the same corresponding colours to indicate the level of performance, from poor to excellent, thus making visible where a Member State situates itself on a particular category and vis-à-vis other Member States on an again correspondingly coloured EU map.

Table 6: colour coding and interpretation of T-scores

T – score	Category
91 to 100	High (high)
81 to 90	High (low)
71 to 80	Above average (High)
61 to 70	Above average (Low)
51 to 60	Average (High)
41 to 50	Average (Low)
31 to 40	Sub average (High)
21 to 30	Sub average (Low)
11 to 20	Low (High)
0 to 10	Low (low)

CONTRASTING GOVERNMENT AND PROFESSIONALS' PERSPECTIVES

In order to compare governmental responses to the day to day practice in a Member State, at least as seen and experienced by a number of knowledgeable respondents, in this study the responses of the respective national Ministries of Justice and Permanent Representatives were systematically compared to those of the other key informer categories.

INDIVIDUAL COUNTRY PROFILES

The individual country profile presents an executive overview of all the performance indicators of a Member State, whereby it is relatively situated in comparison to the respective EU averages.

The full set of data on the Member States are made available on the *www. agisproject.com* website. They allow interested parties to carry out further statistical as well as qualitative analysis on each Member State by studying in detail all responses including any written comments, and to structure a country profile in depth by looking at all questions on the basic as well as on the intermediate level of the indicators.

In Appendix II one will find additional data on the Member States derived from the Council of Europe Cepej study on European Judicial Systems (2006) and from the Spronken-Attinger survey.[7]

SAMPLE EXTENDED COUNTRY PROFILE

As was mentioned before, the basic level, higher level and apex performance indicators are based on a selection of relevant questions in the questionnaire. For one sample Member State[8], the underlying questions are also presented in greater detail in Chapter IV. From a prospective point of view, in this profile, the indicators and sub-questions depicting the current state of affairs are also contrasted with the corresponding desired developments.

For ease of reference, the underlying questions and prospective elements are colour coded in different hues (in purple and blue respectively).

The reader should note that even this extended profile does not even by far represent the full potential of the entire questionnaire material. For a more in-depth analysis of the participating countries, as said, full country data sets are available on the website.

EU TOPOGRAPHICAL MAPS OF LINGUISTIC ASSISTANCE

For the purpose of inter-Member State comparisons, topographical EU maps are drawn up for each of the main performance indicators. For this particular analysis, the aspects of legal interpreting and legal translation were consolidated into a singe 'linguistic assistance' bottom line factor.

EU TOPOGRAPHICAL MAPS OF GREEN PAPER INDICATORS

It should not come as a surprise that the five basic level indicators, i.e. 'protection of vulnerable groups', 'accreditation body', 'register', 'code of conduct and disciplinary procedure' and 'training level', correspond exactly with the quality vectors mentioned in the EU Green Paper. A sixth quality concern of the Green

---

[7]   See also *http://www.intersentia.be/zoekdetail.asp?pid=1426).*
[8]   To avoid any possible selection bias in picking the sample country, the first country in alphabetical order i.e. Austria was chosen.

Paper, the need for interdisciplinary quality systems, was inserted transversally by consolidating the governmental and professional responses.

CHAPTER III
EU MEMBER STATES PROFILES

INTRODUCTION

In this chapter, an individual overview of all the performance indicators is presented for each of the 26 participating EU Member States.

Every profile is made up out of two radar diagrams and their corresponding data tables. The first diagram in the profile shows an overview of the country's relative performance in the field of legal interpreting, whereas the second concerns legal translation. Whenever possible, the radar diagrams present both the government and the professional sources' evaluation.

To facilitate comparisons between Member States or between different indicators within one country profile, the results have been converted to T-scores. By means of this data conversion technique, a country's score on any given performance indicator is essentially expressed in comparison with the EU average for that indicator. A score of 50 always corresponds with the EU average and every increment of 10 represents a distance of one standard deviation. This allows us to stratify the results in 10 point-bands that may be interpreted as shown in the following table:

Table: interpretation of T-scores

T – score	Category
91 to 100	High (high)
81 to 90	High (low)
71 to 80	Above average (High)
61 to 70	Above average (Low)
51 to 60	Average (High)
41 to 50	Average (Low)
31 to 40	Sub average (High)
21 to 30	Sub average (Low)
11 to 20	Low (High)
0 to 10	Low (low)

The colour coding will be used in later chapters to represent a Member State's score in topographical maps.

1. GENERAL OBSERVATIONS

1.1. SAMPLE COMPOSITION

Respondent Profile

A total of 194 respondents from 26 EU Member States participated in this study. Among these, 18 represented government sources and 176 participated in an individual professional capacity[1].

Table 1a: sample composition

Capacity of the respondent	Number	Percentage
Professional association of interpreters or translators	17	8.76%
Police force	7	3.61%
Prosecution	6	3.09%
Judiciary	17	8.76%
Defence counsel	18	9.28%
Civil servant	18	9.28%
Interpreting /Translation Training Institute	30	15.46%
Victim / witness support organisation	1	0.52%
NGO	5	2.58%
Interpreter or translator	54	27.84%
Translation / Interpreting Service Provider	9	4.64%
Other	12	6.19%

---

[1]   Please refer to the methodology chapter for a more thorough analysis of the composition of the respondents.

Member State participation:
Response of governmental sources

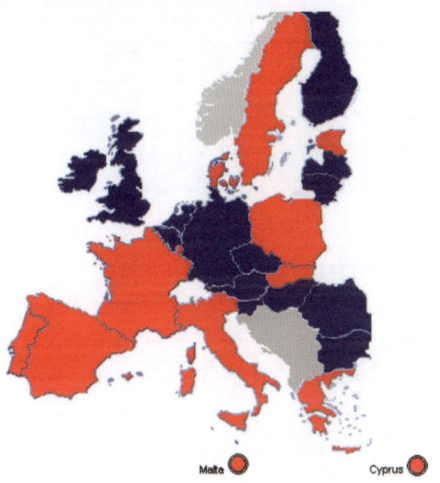

Government officials of the following EU Member States have participated in the study: Austria, Belgium, Bulgaria, Czech Republic, Finland, Germany, Hungary, Ireland, Latvia, Lithuania, Netherlands, Romania, Slovenia, United Kingdom.

Member State participation:
Response of professional sources

With the exception of Luxemburg, professional experts from all EU Member States have participated in this study.

Table 1b: sample composition of respondents

COUNTRY	GOVERNTMENTAL	PROFESSIONAL
AUSTRIA	2	11
BELGIUM	1	12
BULGARIA	1	2
CYPRUS	0	1
CZECH REPUBLIC	2	4
DENMARK	0	8
ESTONIA	0	1
FINLAND	1	10
FRANCE	0	9
GERMANY	1	7
GREECE	0	5
HUNGARY	1	8
IRELAND	1	12
ITALY	0	16
LATVIA	1	2
LITHUANIA	1	3
MALTA	0	3
THE NETHERLANDS	1	6
POLAND	0	6
PORTUGAL	0	3
ROMANIA	1	4
SLOVAKIA	0	5
SLOVENIA	2	3
SPAIN	0	8
SWEDEN	0	6
UK	2	21

1.2. INDICATOR COMPOSITION

Table 2: Hierarchy of indicators

Basic level indicators		Intermediate level indicators		Apex indicator	
I.1.1	Procedural guarantees	I.1	Procedural safeguards	AI	Overall ranking
I.1.2	Number of phases in the procedure				
I.1.3	Criteria for interpreting				
I.1.4	Vulnerable groups				
I.2.1	Protection and regulation	I.2	Regulation of the profession		
I.2.2	Accrediting body				
I.2.3	Register				
I.2.4	Code of conduct and procedure				
I.3.1	Quality provisions	I.3	Quality provisions		
I.3.2	Training level				
I.3.3	Video taping				
I.3.4	Directives for magistrates				
I.3.5	Recruitment programme				
I.4.1	Percentage of cases	I.4	Quantitative provisions		

Table 2 shows an overview of the basic level, intermediate level and apex indicators[2], as well as the way in which they interrelate.

1.3. GENERAL OBSERVATIONS

With the exception of the basic level indicators 2.1 'Protection and regulation of the profession', 2.2 'Accrediting body' and 2.3 'Register', the response patterns of the governmental sources are only weakly correlated with those of the professional sources. This implies that, rather than a mere tendency for one group to systematically overrate or underrate in comparison to the other, both respondent categories have a different outlook on the current state of affairs in their countries.

Moreover, in those countries where more than one governmental source has responded, these sources gave different, and sometimes contradictory information on several indicators.

Another noteworthy observation is that ten in fourteen governmental sources were unable to provide information on the state of affairs with regard to the training of legal interpreters and translators. Likewise, only four governmental sources were able to produce an estimate national percentage of cases in which legal interpreters or translators are used. Only one civil servant provided some national budgetary information.

---

[2] Please refer to the methodology chapter for a more thorough analysis of the composition of these indicators.

2. MEMBER STATE INDICATOR PROFILES

2.1. AUSTRIA

AUSTRIA : INDICATOR PROFILE INTERPRETING

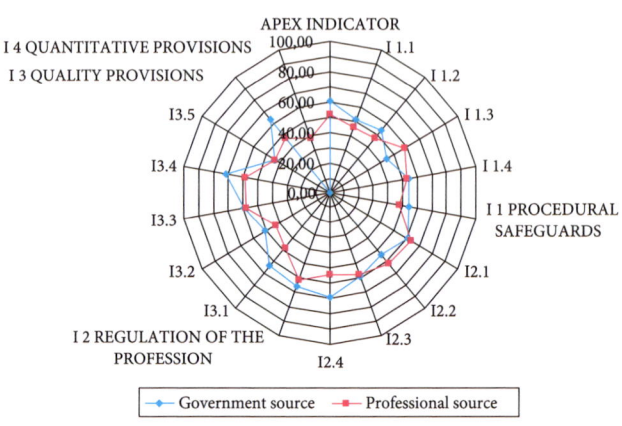

	T-SCORE GVT	T-SCORE PROF		T-SCORE GVT	T-SCORE PROF
APEX INDICATOR	60,61	51,61	**I 2 REGULATION OF THE PROFESSION**	65,19	60,90
I 1.1 Procedural Guarantees	51,22	45,89	I3.1 Quality provisions	63,33	47,27
I 1.2 Number of phases in procedure	53,94	46,90	I3.2 Training level	50,71	42,59
I 1.3 Criteria for interpretation	44,00	58,00	I3.3 Video taping	58,85	57,50
I 1.4 Vulnerable groups	53,62	52,71	I3.4 Directives for magistrates	72,00	58,18
I 1 PROCEDURAL SAFEGUARDS	54,27	47,41	I3.5 Recruitment programme	43,44	43,08
I2.1 Protection and regulation	60,30	63,10	**I 3 QUALITY PROVISIONS**	62,39	46,54
I2.2 Accreditation body	54,19	60,98	**I 4 QUANTITATIVE PROVISIONS**	0,00	38,45
I2.3 Register	58,85	57,50			
I2.4 Code of conduct and procedure	69,21	53,91			

General situation

According to governmental sources, Austria's overall score is situated in the lower above average range, whereas according to the professional sources the country scores in the upper above average range.

Salient features

There are notable differences between the governmental and professional sources for the main indicator 'Quality provisions', as well as for the following basic level indicators: 'Criteria for interpretation', 'Code of conduct and procedure', 'Quality provisions' and 'Directives for magistrates'.

AUSTRIA : INDICATOR PROFILE TRANSLATION

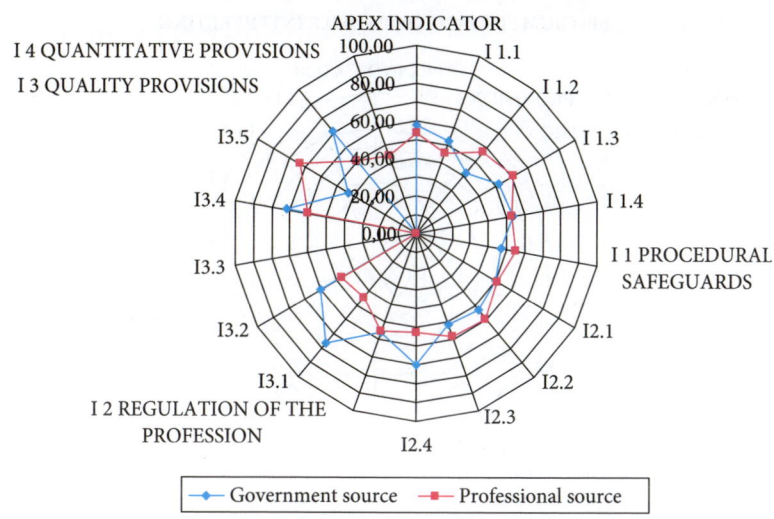

	T-SCORE GVT	T-SCORE PROF		T-SCORE GVT	T-SCORE PROF
APEX INDICATOR	58.21	53.83	**I 2 REGULATION OF THE PROFESSION**	56.14	55.45
I 1.1 Procedural Guarantees	51.94	45.56	I3.1 Quality provisions	76.58	45.00
I 1.2 Number of phases in procedure	41.88	56.20	I3.2 Training level	60.00	46.86
I 1.3 Criteria for translation	52.13	60.61	I3.3 Video taping	0.00	0.00
I 1.4 Vulnerable groups	53.62	52.71	I3.4 Directives for magistrates	72.00	59.71
I 1 PROCEDURAL SAFEGUARDS	47.44	55.35	I3.5 Recruitment programme	42.93	73.48
I2.1 Protection and regulation	50.00	51.51	**I 3 QUALITY PROVISIONS**	71.06	50.71
I2.2 Accreditation body	53.83	58.97	**I 4 QUANTITATIVE PROVISIONS**	0.00	44.23
I2.3 Register	51.60	58.75			
I2.4 Code of conduct and procedure	70.31	53.04			

General situation

According to both governmental and professional sources, Austria's overall score is situated in the upper average range.

Salient features

There are notable differences between the governmental and professional sources for the main indicator 'Quality provisions', as well as for the following basic level indicators: 'Number of phases in the procedure', 'Code of conduct and procedure', and all indicators regarding quality provisions.

2.2. BELGIUM

BELGIUM : INDICATOR PROFILE INTERPRETING

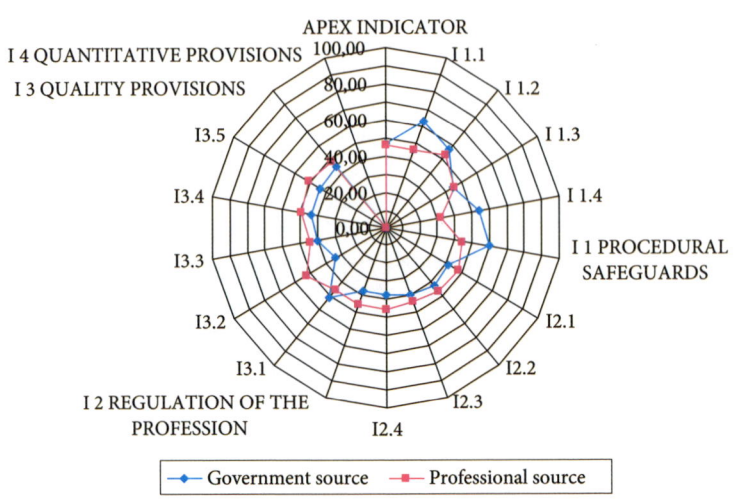

	T-SCORE GVT	T-SCORE PROF		T-SCORE GVT	T-SCORE PROF
APEX INDICATOR	46.81	45.88	**I 2 REGULATION OF THE PROFESSION**	37.15	45.56
I 1.1 Procedural Guarantees	62.33	45.89	I3.1 Quality provisions	50.51	45.45
I 1.2 Number of phases in procedure	56.35	52.21	I3.2 Training level	32.86	52.47
I 1.3 Criteria for interpretation	44.00	44.67	I3.3 Video taping	39.62	43.86
I 1.4 Vulnerable groups	53.62	31.88	I3.4 Directives for magistrates	43.43	49.09
I 1 PROCEDURAL SAFEGUARDS	59.53	43.61	I3.5 Recruitment programme	43.44	50.77
I2.1 Protection and regulation	41.36	47.62	**I 3 QUALITY PROVISIONS**	43.76	48.49
I2.2 Accreditation body	42.56	46.34	**I 4 QUANTITATIVE PROVISIONS**		
I2.3 Register	39.62	43.86			
I2.4 Code of conduct and procedure	37.46	45.22			

General situation

According to both governmental and professional sources, Belgium's overall score is situated in the lower average range.

Salient features

There are notable differences between the governmental and professional sources for the main indicator 'Procedural safeguards' and for the following basic level indicators: 'Procedural guarantees', 'Vulnerable groups' and 'Training level'.

BELGIUM : INDICATOR PROFILE TRANSLATION

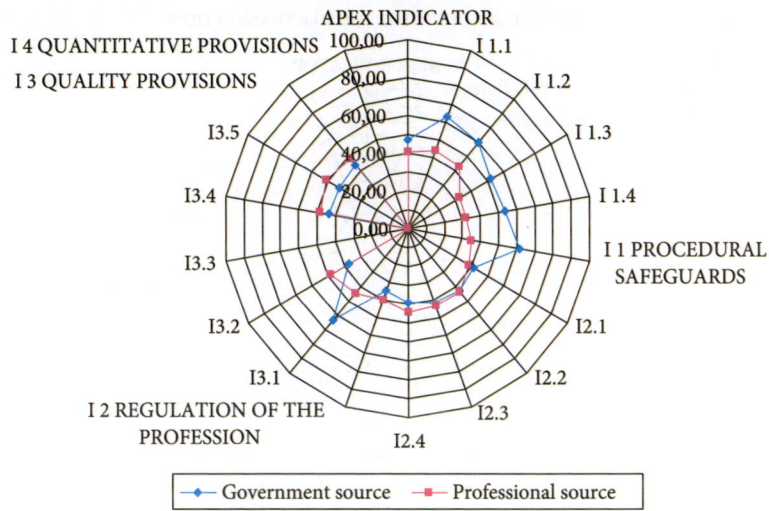

	T-SCORE GVT	T-SCORE PROF		T-SCORE GVT	T-SCORE PROF
APEX INDICATOR	47.08	40.99	I 2 REGULATION OF THE PROFESSION	56.14	55.45
I 1.1 Procedural Guarantees	51.94	45.56	I3.1 Quality provisions	76.58	45.00
I 1.2 Number of phases in procedure	41.88	56.20	I3.2 Training level	60.00	46.86
I 1.3 Criteria for translation	52.13	60.61	I3.3 Video taping	0.00	0.00
I 1.4 Vulnerable groups	53.62	52.71	I3.4 Directives for magistrates	72.00	59.71
I 1 PROCEDURAL SAFEGUARDS	47.44	55.35	I3.5 Recruitment programme	42.93	73.48
I2.1 Protection and regulation	50.00	51.51	I 3 QUALITY PROVISIONS	71.06	50.71
I2.2 Accreditation body	53.83	58.97	I 4 QUANTITATIVE PROVISIONS		
I2.3 Register	51.60	58.75			
I2.4 Code of conduct and procedure	70.31	53.04			

General situation

According to both governmental and professional sources, Belgium's overall score is situated in the lower average range.

Salient features

There are notable differences between the governmental and professional sources for the main indicators 'Quality provisions' and 'Quantitative provisions' and for the following basic level indicators: 'Code of conduct and procedure', as well as for all basic indicators pertaining to quality provisions.

2.3. BULGARIA

BULGARIA : INDICATOR PROFILE TRANSLATION

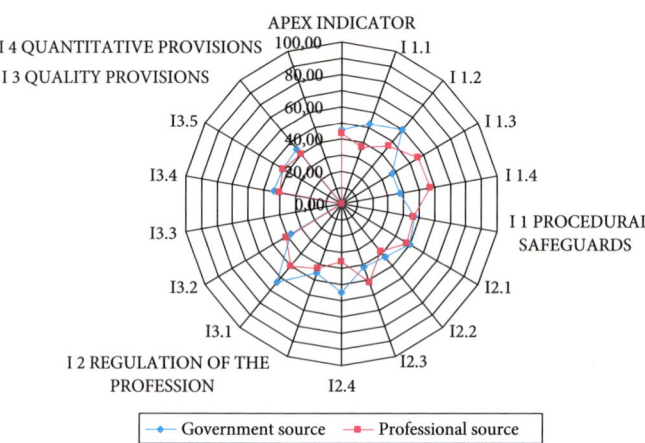

	T-SCORE GVT	T-SCORE PROF		T-SCORE GVT	T-SCORE PROF
APEX INDICATOR	48.49	42.26	**I 2 REGULATION OF THE PROFESSION**	46.50	42.91
I 1.1 Procedural Guarantees	51.22	36.30	I3.1 Quality provisions	50.51	49.09
I 1.2 Number of phases in procedure	56.35	37.17	I3.2 Training level	32.86	48.77
I 1.3 Criteria for interpretation	44.00	38.00	I3.3 Video taping	39.62	50.68
I 1.4 Vulnerable groups	37.87	56.88	I3.4 Directives for magistrates	43.43	42.27
I 1 PROCEDURAL SAFEGUARDS	49.00	35.38	I3.5 Recruitment programme	43.44	43.08
I2.1 Protection and regulation	48.94	47.62	**I 3 QUALITY PROVISIONS**	49.97	48.49
I2.2 Accreditation body	42.56	39.02	**I 4 QUANTITATIVE PROVISIONS**	0.00	0.00
I2.3 Register	39.62	50.68			
I2.4 Code of conduct and procedure	53.33	34.35			

General situation
According to both governmental and professional sources, Bulgaria's overall score is situated in the lower average range.

Salient features
There are notable differences between the governmental and professional sources for the main indicator 'Procedural safeguards' and for the following basic level indicators: 'Procedural guarantees', 'Number of phases in the procedure', Vulnerable groups', 'Register', 'Code of conduct and procedure', 'Training level' and 'Video taping'.

BULGARIA : INDICATOR PROFILE TRANSLATION

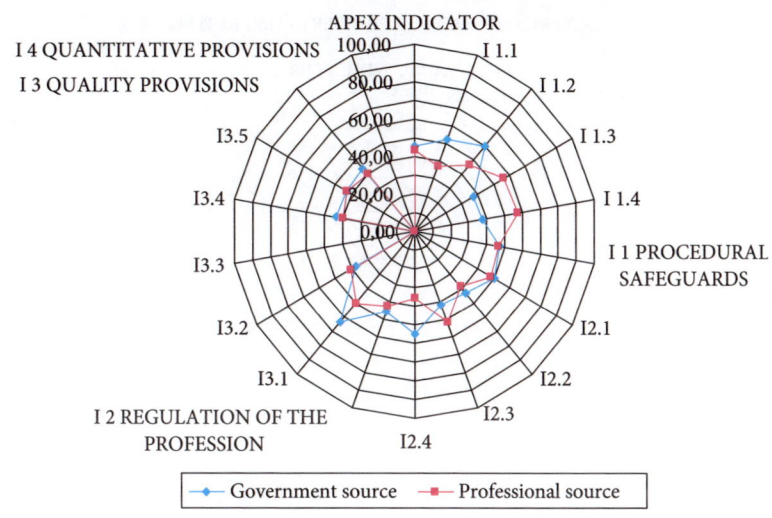

	T-SCORE GVT	T-SCORE PROF		T-SCORE GVT	T-SCORE PROF
APEX INDICATOR	45.83	43.29	**I 2 REGULATION OF THE PROFESSION**	45.56	43.09
I 1.1 Procedural Guarantees	51.94	37.22	I3.1 Quality provisions	63.42	50.26
I 1.2 Number of phases in procedure	59.73	46.28	I3.2 Training level	36.92	40.95
I 1.3 Criteria for translation	37.43	56.53	I3.3 Video taping	0.00	0.00
I 1.4 Vulnerable groups	37.87	56.88	I3.4 Directives for magistrates	43.43	39.71
I 1 PROCEDURAL SAFEGUARDS	47.44	46.44	I3.5 Recruitment programme	42.93	43.04
I2.1 Protection and regulation	50.00	48.02	**I 3 QUALITY PROVISIONS**	44.49	40.33
I2.2 Accreditation body	43.19	38.46	**I 4 QUANTITATIVE PROVISIONS**	0.00	0.00
I2.3 Register	41.60	51.25			
I2.4 Code of conduct and procedure	54.92	35.65			

General situation

According to both governmental and professional sources, Bulgaria's overall score is situated in the lower average range.

Salient features

There are notable differences between the governmental and professional sources for the basic level indicators 'Procedural guarantees', 'Number of phases in the procedure', 'Criteria for translation', Vulnerable groups', 'Code of conduct and procedure' and 'Quality provisions'.

2.4. CYPRUS

CYPRUS : INDICATOR PROFILE INTERPRETING

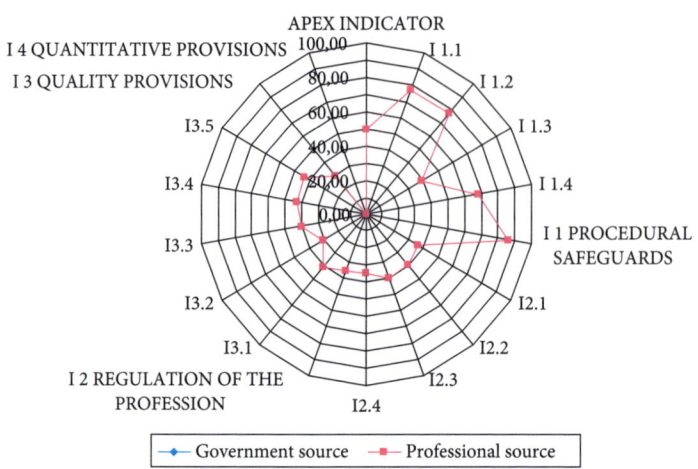

	T-SCORE GVT	T-SCORE PROF		T-SCORE GVT	T-SCORE PROF
APEX INDICATOR	0.00	49.99	**I 2 REGULATION OF THE PROFESSION**	0.00	34.97
I 1.1 Procedural Guarantees	0.00	77.40	I3.1 Quality provisions	0.00	40.00
I 1.2 Number of phases in procedure	0.00	76.99	I3.2 Training level	0.00	30.25
I 1.3 Criteria for interpretation	0.00	38.00	I3.3 Video taping	0.00	39.32
I 1.4 Vulnerable groups	0.00	67.29	I3.4 Directives for magistrates	0.00	42.27
I 1 PROCEDURAL SAFEGUARDS	0.00	86.01	I3.5 Recruitment programme	0.00	43.08
I2.1 Protection and regulation	0.00	35.71	**I 3 QUALITY PROVISIONS**	0.00	28.98
I2.2 Accreditation body	0.00	39.02	**I 4 QUANTITATIVE PROVISIONS**	0.00	0.00
I2.3 Register	0.00	39.32			
I2.4 Code of conduct and procedure	0.00	34.35			

General situation

According to the professional sources, Cyprus' overall score is situated in the lower average range.

Salient features

Along with the basic level indicators 'Procedural guarantees', 'Number of phases in the procedure' and 'Vulnerable groups', the intermediate level indicator 'Procedural safeguards' stands out as significantly increased (lower high range), whereas, at the other end, the intermediate level indicator 'Quality provisions' only scores in the lower sub-average band.

CYPRUS : INDICATOR PROFILE TRANSLATION

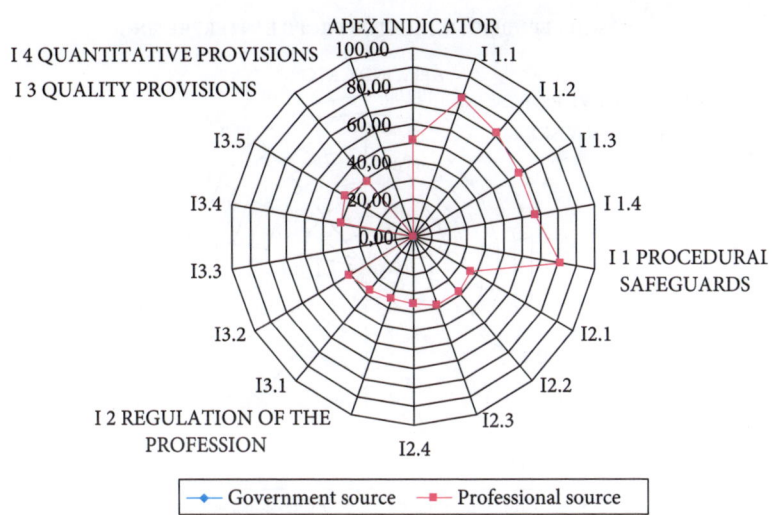

	T-SCORE GVT	T-SCORE PROF		T-SCORE GVT	T-SCORE PROF
			I 2 REGULATION OF THE PROFESSION	0.00	34.66
APEX INDICATOR	0.00	51.34			
I 1.1 Procedural Guarantees	0.00	78.89	I3.1 Quality provisions	0.00	37.11
I 1.2 Number of phases in procedure	0.00	71.07	I3.2 Training level	0.00	40.95
I 1.3 Criteria for translation	0.00	66.73	I3.3 Video taping	0.00	0.00
I 1.4 Vulnerable groups	0.00	67.29	I3.4 Directives for magistrates	0.00	39.71
I 1 PROCEDURAL SAFEGUARDS	0.00	81.09	I3.5 Recruitment programme	0.00	43.04
I2.1 Protection and regulation	0.00	36.40	**I 3 QUALITY PROVISIONS**	0.00	38.26
I2.2 Accreditation body	0.00	38.46	**I 4 QUANTITATIVE PROVISIONS**	0.00	0.00
I2.3 Register	0.00	38.75			
I2.4 Code of conduct and procedure	0.00	35.65			

General situation

According to the professional sources, Cyprus' overall score is situated in the upper average range.

Salient features

Along with the basic level indicators 'Procedural guarantees', 'Number of phases in the procedure', 'Criteria' and 'Vulnerable groups', the intermediate level indicator 'Procedural safeguards' stands out as elevated (lower high range).

2.5. CZECH REPUBLIC

CZECH REPUBLIC : INDICATOR PROFILE INTERPRETING

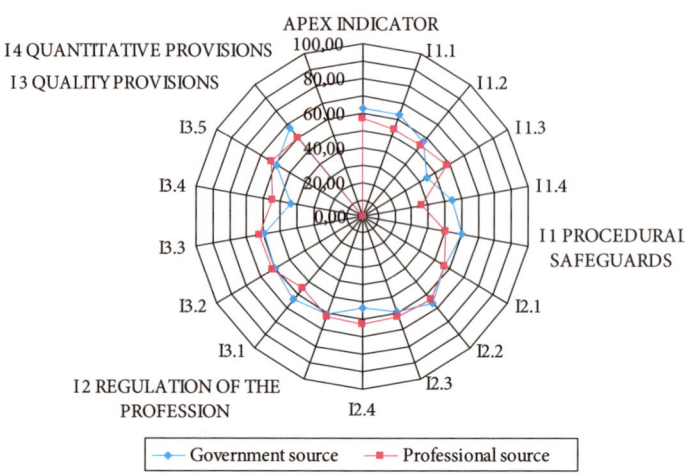

	T-SCORE GVT	T-SCORE PROF		T-SCORE GVT	T-SCORE PROF
APEX INDICATOR	62.37	57.09	**I 2 REGULATION OF THE PROFESSION**	60.51	61.96
I 1.1 Procedural Guarantees	62.33	54.11	I3.1 Quality provisions	63.33	54.55
I 1.2 Number of phases in procedure	56.35	53.10	I3.2 Training level	59.64	61.11
I 1.3 Criteria for interpretation	44.00	58.00	I3.3 Video taping	58.85	62.05
I 1.4 Vulnerable groups	53.62	36.04	I3.4 Directives for magistrates	43.43	53.64
I 1 PROCEDURAL SAFEGUARDS	59.53	50.57	I3.5 Recruitment programme	59.06	62.31
I2.1 Protection and regulation	56.52	57.14	**I 3 QUALITY PROVISIONS**	67.05	58.73
I2.2 Accreditation body	65.81	63.41	**I 4 QUANTITATIVE PROVISIONS**	0.00	0.00
I2.3 Register	58.85	62.05			
I2.4 Code of conduct and procedure	53.33	62.61			

General situation

According to governmental sources, the Czech Republic's overall score is situated in the lower above average range, whereas according to the professional sources, the country scores in the upper above average range.

Salient features

The only notable discrepancy between the governmental and professional sources is found in the basic level indicator 'Directives for magistrates'. On the whole, this profile stands out as well rounded and generally positive (upper average to lower above average range).

CZECH REPUBLIC : INDICATOR PROFILE TRANSLATION

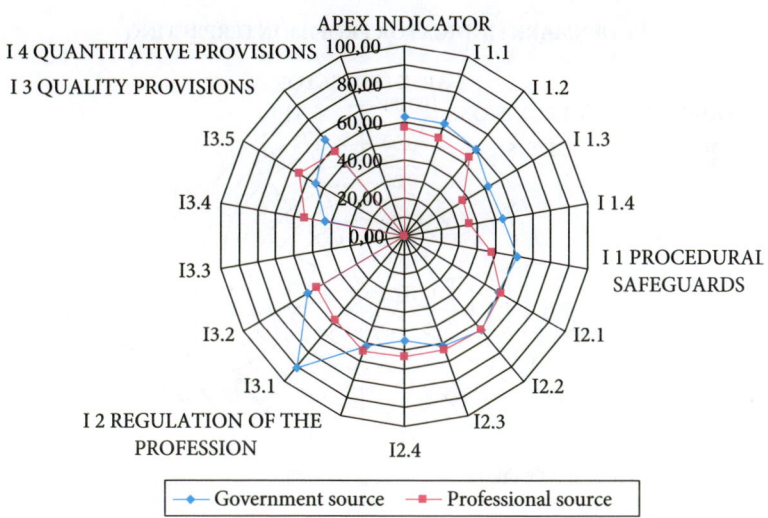

	T-SCORE GVT	T-SCORE PROF		T-SCORE GVT	T-SCORE PROF
APEX INDICATOR	63.15	56.84	**I 2 REGULATION OF THE PROFESSION**	61.43	64.44
I 1.1 Procedural Guarantees	62.69	55.28	I3.1 Quality provisions	89.74	58.16
I 1.2 Number of phases in procedure	59.73	54.55	I3.2 Training level	60.00	54.59
I 1.3 Criteria for tranlation	52.13	36.12	I3.3 Video taping	0.00	0.00
I 1.4 Vulnerable groups	53.62	36.04	I3.4 Directives for magistrates	43.43	54.00
I 1 PROCEDURAL SAFEGUARDS	61.78	47.92	I3.5 Recruitment programme	55.12	64.78
I2.1 Protection and regulation	58.70	59.65	**I 3 QUALITY PROVISIONS**	66.23	58.17
I2.2 Accreditation body	64.47	64.10	**I 4 QUANTITATIVE PROVISIONS**	0.00	0.00
I2.3 Register	61.60	63.75			
I2.4 Code of conduct and procedure	54.92	63.91			

General situation

According to governmental sources, the Czech Republic's overall score is situated in the lower above average range, whereas according to the professional sources, the country scores in the upper above average range.

Salient features

There are notable differences between the governmental and professional sources for the main indicator 'Procedural safeguards', as well as for the following basic level indicators: 'Criteria for interpretation', 'Vulnerable groups' and 'Quality provisions'.

2.6. DENMARK

DENMARK : INDICATOR PROFILE INTERPRETING

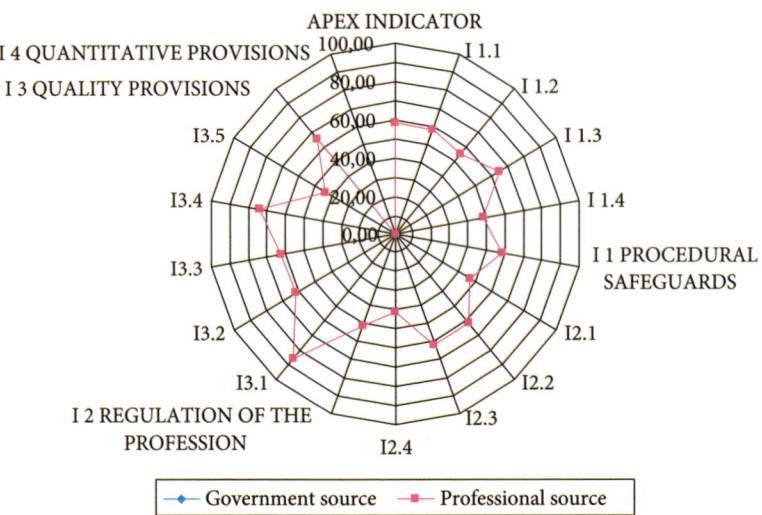

	T-SCORE GVT	T-SCORE PROF		T-SCORE GVT	T-SCORE PROF
APEX INDICATOR	0.00	58.04	I 2 REGULATION OF THE PROFESSION	0.00	51.38
I 1.1 Procedural Guarantees	0.00	58.22	I3.1 Quality provisions	0.00	85.45
I 1.2 Number of phases in procedure	0.00	54.87	I3.2 Training level	0.00	61.11
I 1.3 Criteria for interpretation	0.00	64.67	I3.3 Video taping	0.00	62.05
I 1.4 Vulnerable groups	0.00	48.54	I3.4 Directives for magistrates	0.00	74.09
I 1 PROCEDURAL SAFEGUARDS	0.00	58.16	I3.5 Recruitment programme	0.00	43.08
I2.1 Protection and regulation	0.00	46.43	I 3 QUALITY PROVISIONS	0.00	64.59
I2.2 Accreditation body	0.00	60.98	I 4 QUANTITATIVE PROVISIONS	0.00	0.00
I2.3 Register	0.00	62.05			
I2.4 Code of conduct and procedure	0.00	40.87			

General situation

According to the professional sources, Denmark's overall score is situated in the upper average range.

Salient features

The basic level indicators 'Quality provisions' (lower high range) and 'Directives for magistrates' (upper above average range) stand out as elevated.

DENMARK : INDICATOR PROFILE TRANSLATION

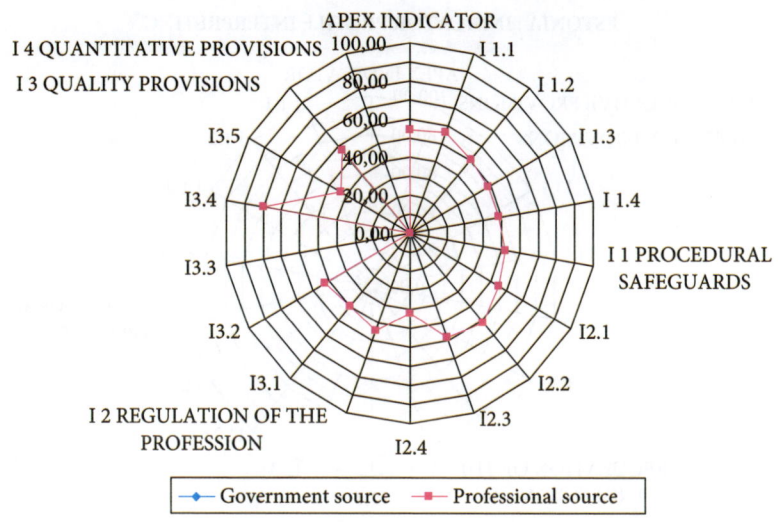

	T-SCORE GVT	T-SCORE PROF		T-SCORE GVT	T-SCORE PROF
APEX INDICATOR	0.00	54.57	**I 2 REGULATION OF THE PROFESSION**	0.00	54.89
I 1.1 Procedural Guarantees	0.00	56.67	I3.1 Quality provisions	0.00	50.26
I 1.2 Number of phases in procedure	0.00	50.41	I3.2 Training level	0.00	52.77
I 1.3 Criteria for translation	0.00	48.37	I3.3 Video taping	0.00	0.00
I 1.4 Vulnerable groups	0.00	48.54	I3.4 Directives for magistrates	0.00	79.71
I 1 PROCEDURAL SAFEGUARDS	0.00	51.88	I3.5 Recruitment programme	0.00	43.04
I2.1 Protection and regulation	0.00	55.00	**I 3 QUALITY PROVISIONS**	0.00	56.93
I2.2 Accreditation body	0.00	61.54	**I 4 QUANTITATIVE PROVISIONS**	0.00	0.00
I2.3 Register	0.00	58.75			
I2.4 Code of conduct and procedure	0.00	42.17			

General situation
According to the professional sources, Denmark's overall score is situated in the upper average range.

Salient features
The basic level indicator 'Directives for magistrates' (upper above average range) stands out as elevated.

2.7. ESTONIA

ESTONIA : INDICATOR PROFILE INTERPRETING

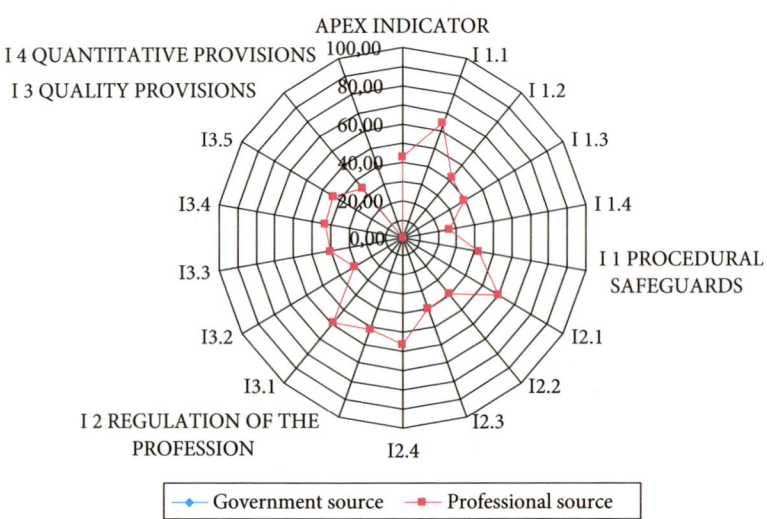

	T-SCORE GVT	T-SCORE PROF		T-SCORE GVT	T-SCORE PROF
APEX INDICATOR	0.00	42.14	**I 2 REGULATION OF THE PROFESSION**	0.00	50.85
I 1.1 Procedural Guarantees	0.00	63.70	I3.1 Quality provisions	0.00	58.18
I 1.2 Number of phases in procedure	0.00	41.59	I3.2 Training level	0.00	30.25
I 1.3 Criteria for interpretation	0.00	38.00	I3.3 Video taping	0.00	39.32
I 1.4 Vulnerable groups	0.00	25.63	I3.4 Directives for magistrates	0.00	42.27
I 1 PROCEDURAL SAFEGUARDS	0.00	41.71	I3.5 Recruitment programme	0.00	43.08
I2.1 Protection and regulation	0.00	59.52	**I 3 QUALITY PROVISIONS**	0.00	33.85
I2.2 Accreditation body	0.00	39.02	**I 4 QUANTITATIVE PROVISIONS**	0.00	0.00
I2.3 Register	0.00	39.32			
I2.4 Code of conduct and procedure	0.00	56.09			

General situation

According to the professional sources, Estonia's overall score is situated in the lower average range.

Salient features

The basic level indicator 'Procedural guarantees' (lower above average range) stands out as relatively elevated, whereas 'Vulnerable groups' (lower sub average range) is situated at the other extreme.

ESTONIA : INDICATOR PROFILE TRANSLATION

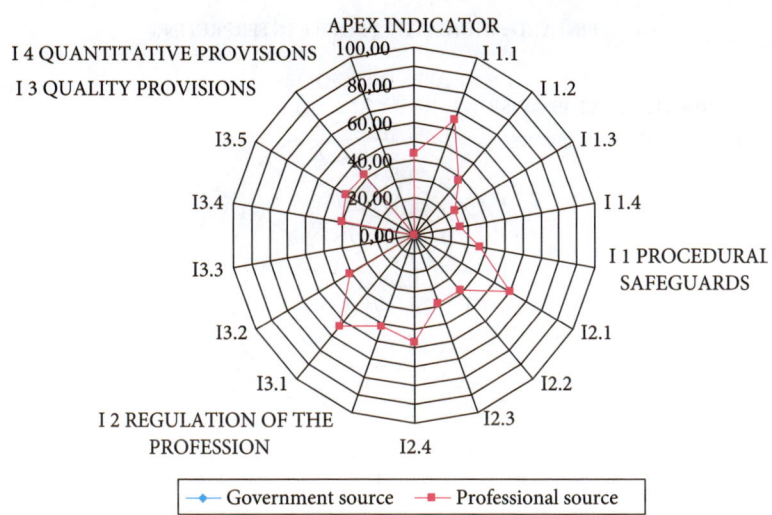

	T-SCORE GVT	T-SCORE PROF		T-SCORE GVT	T-SCORE PROF
APEX INDICATOR	0.00	43.49	**I 2 REGULATION OF THE PROFESSION**	0.00	51.52
I 1.1 Procedural Guarantees	0.00	65.00	I3.1 Quality provisions	0.00	63.42
I 1.2 Number of phases in procedure	0.00	38.02	I3.2 Training level	0.00	40.95
I 1.3 Criteria for translation	0.00	25.92	I3.3 Video taping	0.00	0.00
I 1.4 Vulnerable groups	0.00	25.63	I3.4 Directives for magistrates	0.00	39.71
I 1 PROCEDURAL SAFEGUARDS	0.00	36.53	I3.5 Recruitment programme	0.00	43.04
I2.1 Protection and regulation	0.00	59.65	**I 3 QUALITY PROVISIONS**	0.00	42.41
I2.2 Accreditation body	0.00	38.46	**I 4 QUANTITATIVE PROVISIONS**	0.00	0.00
I2.3 Register	0.00	38.75			
I2.4 Code of conduct and procedure	0.00	57.39			

General situation

According to the professional sources, Estonia's overall score is situated in the lower average range.

Salient features

The basic level indicators 'Procedural guarantees' and 'Quality provisions' (both lower above average range) stand out as relatively elevated, whereas 'Criteria for interpretation' and 'Vulnerable groups' (both lower sub average range) stand out at the low end.

2.8. FINLAND

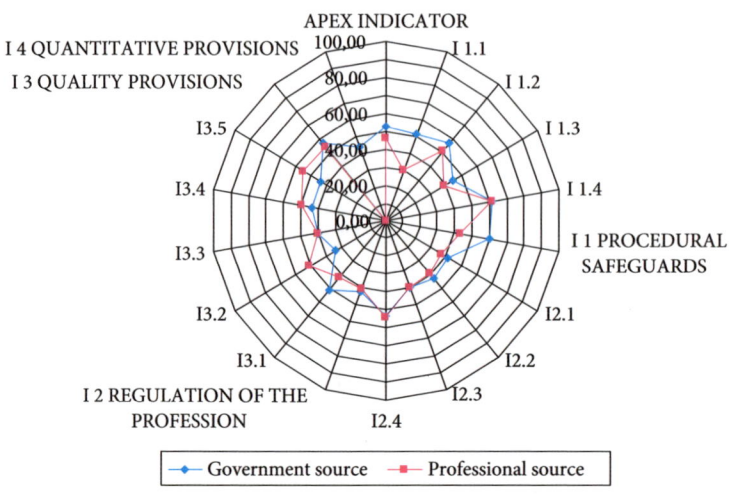

FINLAND : INDICATOR PROFILE INTERPRETING

APEX INDICATOR

→ Government source   ─■─ Professional source

	T-SCORE GVT	T-SCORE PROF		T-SCORE GVT	T-SCORE PROF
APEX INDICATOR	52.51	45.70	**I 2 REGULATION OF THE PROFESSION**	41.82	40.26
I 1.1 Procedural Guarantees	51.22	29.45	I3.1 Quality provisions	50.51	41.82
I 1.2 Number of phases in procedure	56.35	50.44	I3.2 Training level	32.86	50.00
I 1.3 Criteria for interpretation	44.00	38.00	I3.3 Video taping	39.62	39.32
I 1.4 Vulnerable groups	61.50	61.04	I3.4 Directives for magistrates	43.43	49.09
I 1 PROCEDURAL SAFEGUARDS	59.53	42.97	I3.5 Recruitment programme	43.44	54.62
I2.1 Protection and regulation	41.36	36.90	**I 3 QUALITY PROVISIONS**	56.18	53.85
I2.2 Accreditation body	42.56	39.02	**I 4 QUANTITATIVE PROVISIONS**	43.91	0.00
I2.3 Register	39.62	39.32			
I2.4 Code of conduct and procedure	53.33	53.91			

General situation

According to governmental sources, Finland's overall score is situated in the upper average range, whereas according to the professional sources the country scores in the lower average range.

Salient features

There are notable differences between the governmental and professional sources for the main indicator 'Procedural safeguards' and the basic level indicators 'Procedural guarantees' and 'Training level'.

FINLAND : INDICATOR PROFILE TRANSLATION

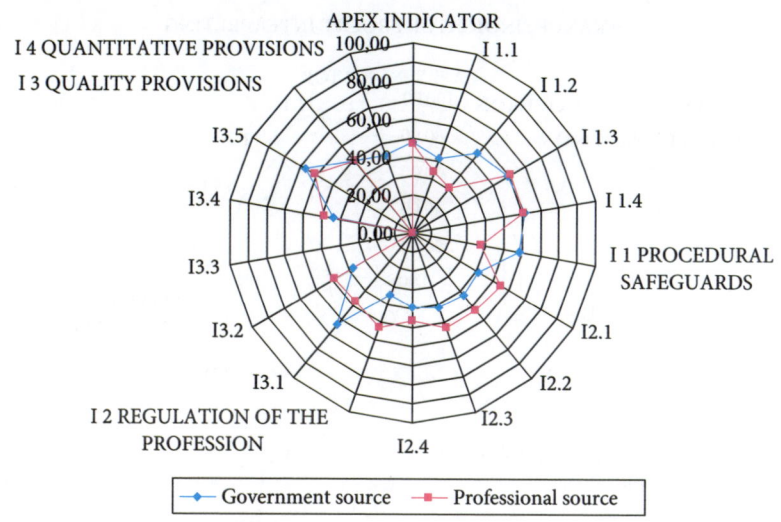

	T-SCORE GVT	T-SCORE PROF		T-SCORE GVT	T-SCORE PROF
APEX INDICATOR	47.74	46.89	I 2 REGULATION OF THE PROFESSION	34.97	53.20
I 1.1 Procedural Guarantees	41.18	34.44	I3.1 Quality provisions	63.42	47.63
I 1.2 Number of phases in procedure	55.27	30.58	I3.2 Training level	36.92	48.23
I 1.3 Criteria for translation	59.49	60.61	I3.3 Video taping	0.00	0.00
I 1.4 Vulnerable groups	61.50	61.04	I3.4 Directives for magistrates	43.43	48.29
I 1 PROCEDURAL SAFEGUARDS	58.91	38.02	I3.5 Recruitment programme	67.32	60.43
I2.1 Protection and regulation	41.30	55.00	I 3 QUALITY PROVISIONS	49.32	49.46
I2.2 Accreditation body	43.19	53.85	I 4 QUANTITATIVE PROVISIONS	43.91	0.00
I2.3 Register	41.60	53.75			
I2.4 Code of conduct and procedure	39.54	46.52			

General situation

According to governmental sources and professional sources, Finland's overall score is situated in the lower average range.

Salient features

There are notable differences between the governmental and professional sources for the main indicators 'Procedural safeguards' and 'Regulation of the profession' as well as for the basic level indicators 'Number of phases in the procedure', 'Protection and regulation', 'Accrediting body', 'register' and 'Quality provisions'.

2.9. FRANCE

FRANCE : INDICATOR PROFILE INTERPRETING

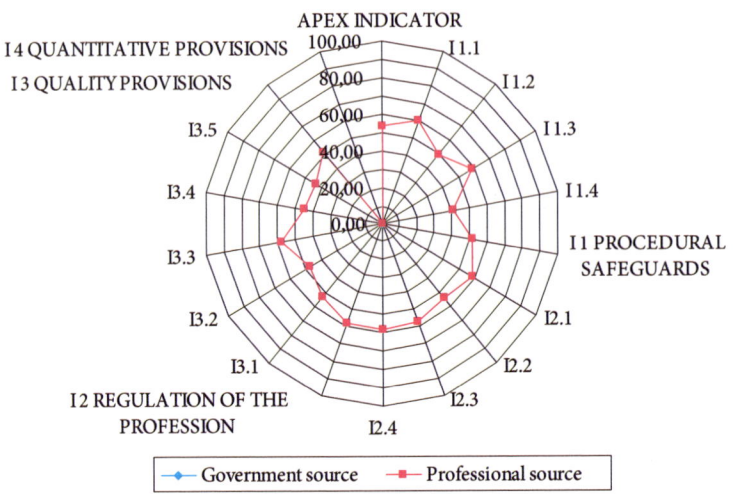

	T-SCORE GVT	T-SCORE PROF		T-SCORE GVT	T-SCORE PROF
APEX INDICATOR	0.00	53.46	**I 2 REGULATION OF THE PROFESSION**	0.00	58.25
I 1.1 Procedural Guarantees	0.00	59.59	I3.1 Quality provisions	0.00	52.73
I 1.2 Number of phases in procedure	0.00	48.67	I3.2 Training level	0.00	47.53
I 1.3 Criteria for interpretation	0.00	58.00	I3.3 Video taping	0.00	57.50
I 1.4 Vulnerable groups	0.00	40.21	I3.4 Directives for magistrates	0.00	44.55
I 1 PROCEDURAL SAFEGUARDS	0.00	51.20	I3.5 Recruitment programme	0.00	43.08
I2.1 Protection and regulation	0.00	58.33	**I 3 QUALITY PROVISIONS**	0.00	50.93
I2.2 Accreditation body	0.00	53.66	**I 4 QUANTITATIVE PROVISIONS**	0.00	0.00
I2.3 Register	0.00	57.50			
I2.4 Code of conduct and procedure	0.00	58.26			

General situation

According to the professional sources, France's overall score is situated in the upper average range.

Salient features

On the whole, this profile stands out as well rounded and generally average to above average.

FRANCE : INDICATOR PROFILE TRANSLATION

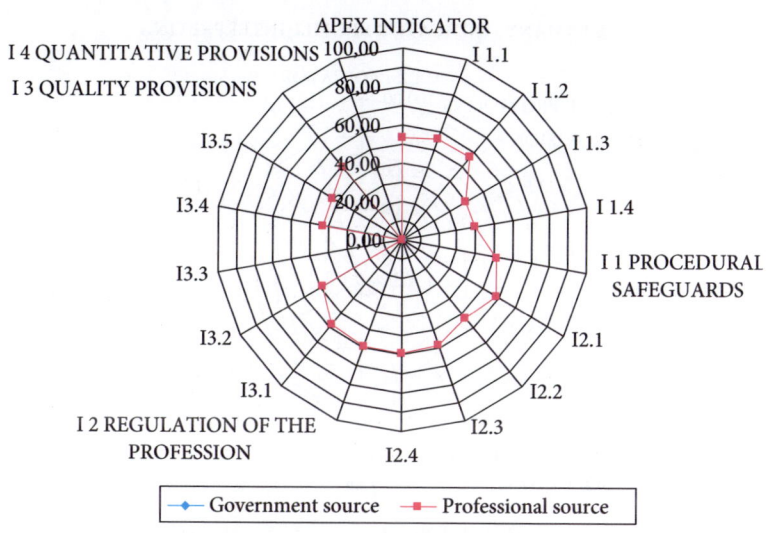

APEX INDICATOR

	T-SCORE GVT	T-SCORE PROF		T-SCORE GVT	T-SCORE PROF
APEX INDICATOR	0.00	53.27	**I 2 REGULATION OF THE PROFESSION**	0.00	59.38
I 1.1 Procedural Guarantees	0.00	56.67	I3.1 Quality provisions	0.00	58.16
I 1.2 Number of phases in procedure	0.00	56.20	I3.2 Training level	0.00	48.68
I 1.3 Criteria for translation	0.00	40.20	I3.3 Video taping	0.00	0.00
I 1.4 Vulnerable groups	0.00	40.21	I3.4 Directives for magistrates	0.00	42.57
I 1 PROCEDURAL SAFEGUARDS	0.00	51.39	I3.5 Recruitment programme	0.00	43.04
I2.1 Protection and regulation	0.00	58.49	**I 3 QUALITY PROVISIONS**	0.00	49.05
I2.2 Accreditation body	0.00	53.85	**I 4 QUANTITATIVE PROVISIONS**	0.00	0.00
I2.3 Register	0.00	58.75			
I2.4 Code of conduct and procedure	0.00	59.57			

General situation

According to the professional sources, France's overall score is situated in the upper average range.

Salient features

On the whole, this profile stands out as well rounded and generally positive (average to above average range).

2.10. GERMANY

GERMANY : INDICATOR PROFILE INTERPRETING

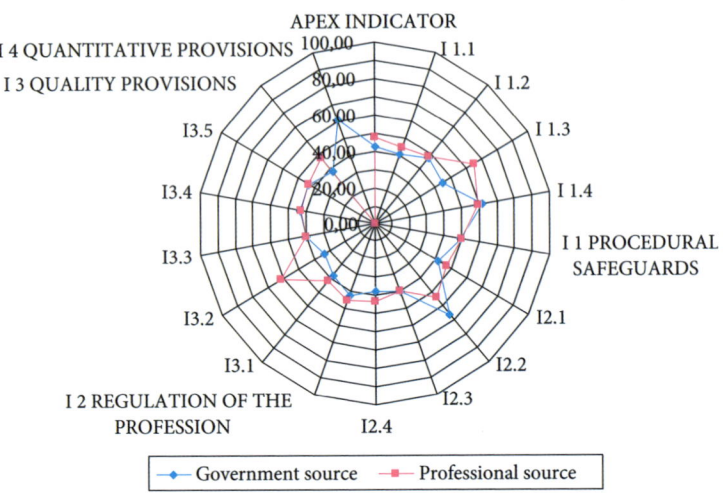

	T-SCORE GVT	T-SCORE PROF		T-SCORE GVT	T-SCORE PROF
			I 2 REGULATION OF THE PROFESSION	41.82	45.03
APEX INDICATOR	42.79	47.17			
I 1.1 Procedural Guarantees	40.11	44.52	I3.1 Quality provisions	37.69	41.82
I 1.2 Number of phases in procedure	46.73	47.79	I3.2 Training level	32.86	61.11
I 1.3 Criteria for interpretation	44.00	64.67	I3.3 Video taping	39.62	39.32
I 1.4 Vulnerable groups	61.50	58.96	I3.4 Directives for magistrates	43.43	42.27
I 1 PROCEDURAL SAFEGUARDS	49.00	49.94	I3.5 Recruitment programme	43.44	43.08
I2.1 Protection and regulation	41.36	46.43	**I 3 QUALITY PROVISIONS**	37.55	46.54
I2.2 Accreditation body	65.81	53.66	**I 4 QUANTITATIVE PROVISIONS**	61.21	0.00
I2.3 Register	39.62	39.32			
I2.4 Code of conduct and procedure	37.46	43.04			

General situation

According to both governmental and professional sources, Germany's overall score is situated in the lower average range.

Salient features

There are notable differences between the governmental and professional sources for the basic level indicators 'Criteria for interpretation', 'Accrediting Body' and 'Training Level'.

GERMANY : INDICATOR PROFILE INTERPRETING

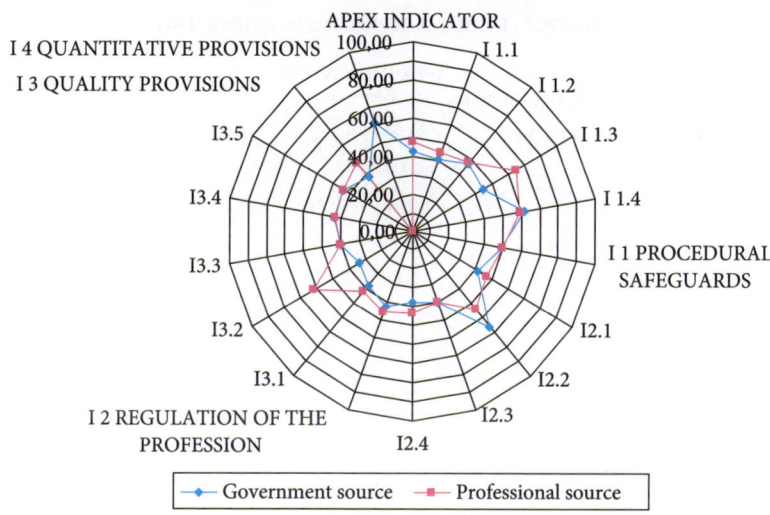

	T-SCORE GVT	T-SCORE PROF		T-SCORE GVT	T-SCORE PROF
APEX INDICATOR	42.79	47.17	I 2 REGULATION OF THE PROFESSION	41.82	45.03
I 1.1 Procedural Guarantees	40.11	44.52	I3.1 Quality provisions	37.69	41.82
I 1.2 Number of phases in procedure	46.73	47.79	I3.2 Training level	32.86	61.11
I 1.3 Criteria for translation	44.00	64.67	I3.3 Video taping	39.62	39.32
I 1.4 Vulnerable groups	61.50	58.96	I3.4 Directives for magistrates	43.43	42.27
I 1 PROCEDURAL SAFEGUARDS	49.00	49.94	I3.5 Recruitment programme	43.44	43.08
I2.1 Protection and regulation	41.36	46.43	I 3 QUALITY PROVISIONS	37.55	46.54
I2.2 Accreditation body	65.81	53.66	I 4 QUANTITATIVE PROVISIONS	61.21	0.00
I2.3 Register	39.62	39.32			
I2.4 Code of conduct and procedure	37.46	43.04			

General situation

According to both governmental and professional sources, Germany's overall score is situated in the lower average range.

Salient features

There are notable differences between the governmental and professional sources for the basic level indicators 'Criteria for translation', 'Accrediting Body' and 'Training Level'.

2.11. GREECE

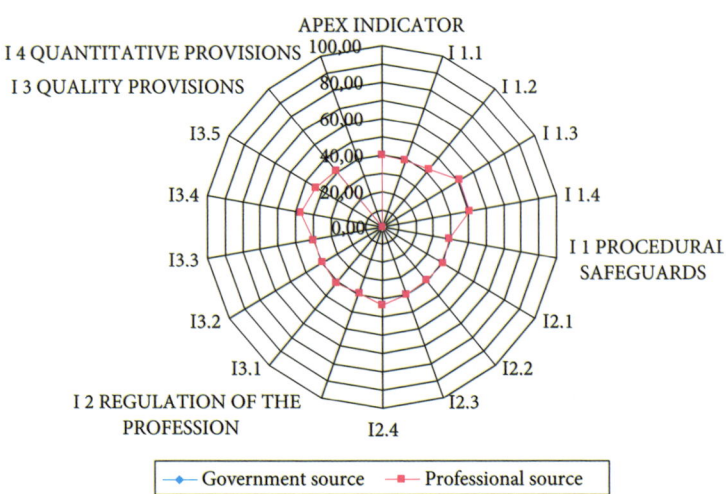

GREECE : INDICATOR PROFILE INTERPRETING

	T-SCORE GVT	T-SCORE PROF		T-SCORE GVT	T-SCORE PROF
APEX INDICATOR	0.00	39.53	**I 2 REGULATION OF THE PROFESSION**	0.00	39.21
I 1.1 Procedural Guarantees	0.00	39.04	I3.1 Quality provisions	0.00	40.00
I 1.2 Number of phases in procedure	0.00	41.59	I3.2 Training level	0.00	38.89
I 1.3 Criteria for interpretation	0.00	51.33	I3.3 Video taping	0.00	39.32
I 1.4 Vulnerable groups	0.00	50.63	I3.4 Directives for magistrates	0.00	46.82
I 1 PROCEDURAL SAFEGUARDS	0.00	39.18	I3.5 Recruitment programme	0.00	43.08
I2.1 Protection and regulation	0.00	40.48	**I 3 QUALITY PROVISIONS**	0.00	40.20
I2.2 Accreditation body	0.00	39.02	**I 4 QUANTITATIVE PROVISIONS**	0.00	0.00
I2.3 Register	0.00	39.32			
I2.4 Code of conduct and procedure	0.00	43.04			

General situation

According to the professional sources, Greece's overall score is situated in the upper sub average range.

Salient features

On the whole, this profile stands out as consistent in the average and sub average range.

GREECE : INDICATOR PROFILE TRANSLATION

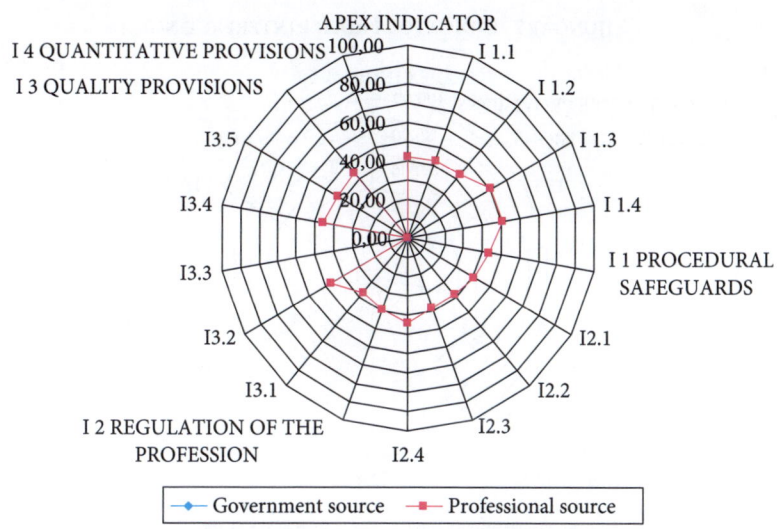

	T-SCORE GVT	T-SCORE PROF		T-SCORE GVT	T-SCORE PROF
APEX INDICATOR	0.00	42.37	**I 2 REGULATION OF THE PROFESSION**	0.00	39.16
I 1.1 Procedural Guarantees	0.00	42.78	I3.1 Quality provisions	0.00	37.11
I 1.2 Number of phases in procedure	0.00	42.98	I3.2 Training level	0.00	46.86
I 1.3 Criteria for translation	0.00	50.41	I3.3 Video taping	0.00	0.00
I 1.4 Vulnerable groups	0.00	50.63	I3.4 Directives for magistrates	0.00	45.43
I 1 PROCEDURAL SAFEGUARDS	0.00	43.47	I3.5 Recruitment programme	0.00	43.04
I2.1 Protection and regulation	0.00	41.05	**I 3 QUALITY PROVISIONS**	0.00	44.48
I2.2 Accreditation body	0.00	38.46	**I 4 QUANTITATIVE PROVISIONS**	0.00	0.00
I2.3 Register	0.00	38.75			
I2.4 Code of conduct and procedure	0.00	44.35			

General situation

According to the professional sources, Greece's overall score is situated in the upper sub average range.

Salient features

On the whole, this profile stands out as consistent in the average and sub average range.

2.12. HUNGARY

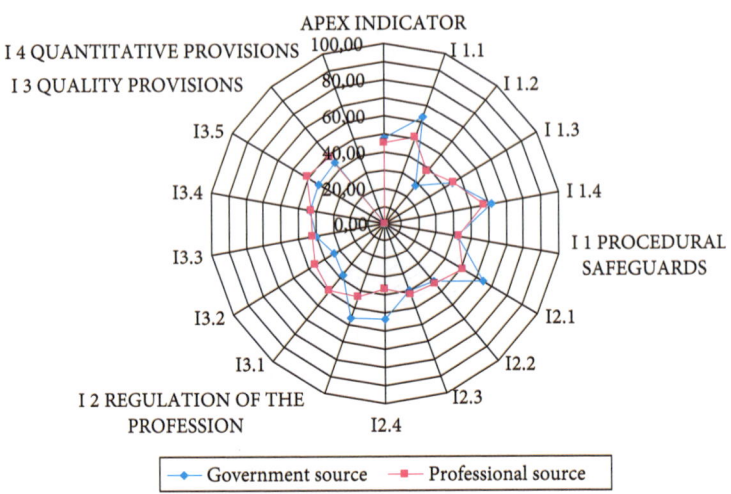

HUNGARY : INDICATOR PROFILE INTERPRETING

	T-SCORE GVT	T-SCORE PROF		T-SCORE GVT	T-SCORE PROF
APEX INDICATOR	47.19	44.77	**I 2 REGULATION OF THE PROFESSION**	55.84	43.97
I 1.1 Procedural Guarantees	62.33	50.00	I3.1 Quality provisions	37.69	49.09
I 1.2 Number of phases in procedure	27.50	37.17	I3.2 Training level	32.86	45.06
I 1.3 Criteria for interpretation	44.00	44.67	I3.3 Video taping	39.62	41.59
I 1.4 Vulnerable groups	61.50	56.88	I3.4 Directives for magistrates	43.43	42.27
I 1 PROCEDURAL SAFEGUARDS	41.97	42.34	I3.5 Recruitment programme	43.44	50.77
I2.1 Protection and regulation	64.09	51.19	**I 3 QUALITY PROVISIONS**	43.76	48.00
I2.2 Accreditation body	42.56	43.90	**I 4 QUANTITATIVE PROVISIONS**	0.00	0.00
I2.3 Register	39.62	41.59			
I2.4 Code of conduct and procedure	53.33	36.52			

General situation

According to both governmental and professional sources, Hungary's overall score is situated in the lower average range.

Salient features

There are notable differences between the governmental and professional sources for the main indicator 'Regulation of the profession', as well as for the following basic level indicators: 'Procedural guarantees', 'Protection and regulation', 'Code of conduct and procedure', 'Quality provisions' and 'Training level'.

HUNGARY : INDICATOR PROFILE TRANSLATION

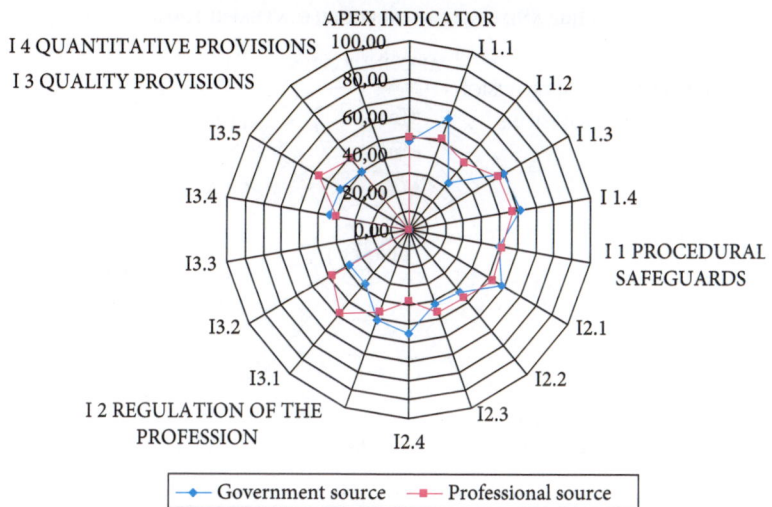

	T-SCORE GVT	T-SCORE PROF		T-SCORE GVT	T-SCORE PROF
APEX INDICATOR	46.94	48.96	I 2 REGULATION OF THE PROFESSION	50.85	46.46
I 1.1 Procedural Guarantees	62.69	51.11	I3.1 Quality provisions	37.11	58.16
I 1.2 Number of phases in procedure	32.95	46.28	I3.2 Training level	36.92	47.77
I 1.3 Criteria for translation	59.49	56.53	I3.3 Video taping	0.00	0.00
I 1.4 Vulnerable groups	61.50	56.88	I3.4 Directives for magistrates	43.43	39.71
I 1 PROCEDURAL SAFEGUARDS	50.31	51.39	I3.5 Recruitment programme	42.93	56.09
I2.1 Protection and regulation	58.70	52.67	I 3 QUALITY PROVISIONS	39.66	49.05
I2.2 Accreditation body	43.19	46.15	I 4 QUANTITATIVE PROVISIONS	0.00	0.00
I2.3 Register	41.60	46.25			
I2.4 Code of conduct and procedure	54.92	37.83			

General situation

According to both governmental and professional sources, Hungary's overall score is situated in the lower average range.

Salient features

There are notable differences between the governmental and professional sources for the basic level indicators 'Procedural guarantees', 'Number of phases in the procedure', 'Code of conduct and procedure', 'Quality provisions', 'Training level' and 'Recruitment programme'.

2.13.   IRELAND

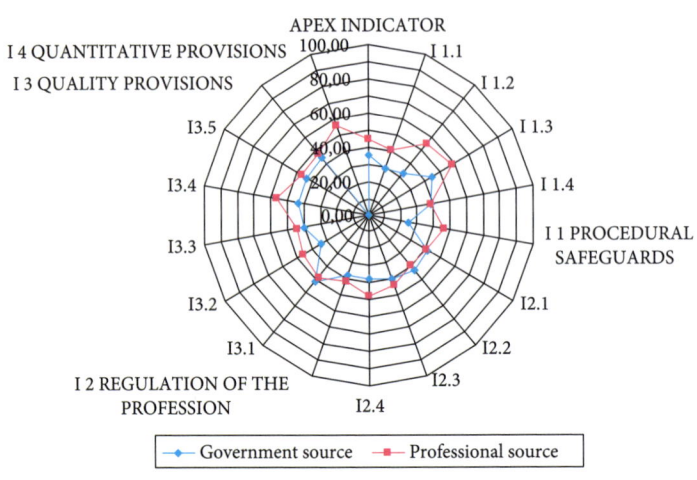

IRELAND : INDICATOR PROFILE INTERPRETING

	T-SCORE GVT	T-SCORE PROF		T-SCORE GVT	T-SCORE PROF
APEX INDICATOR	35.10	44.49	**I 2 REGULATION OF THE PROFESSION**	37.15	40.79
I 1.1 Procedural Guarantees	29.00	40.41	I3.1 Quality provisions	50.51	47.27
I 1.2 Number of phases in procedure	32.31	54.87	I3.2 Training level	32.86	45.06
I 1.3 Criteria for interpretation	44.00	58.00	I3.3 Video taping	39.62	43.86
I 1.4 Vulnerable groups	37.87	38.13	I3.4 Directives for magistrates	43.43	55.91
I 1 PROCEDURAL SAFEGUARDS	24.41	46.14	I3.5 Recruitment programme	43.44	46.92
I2.1 Protection and regulation	41.36	39.29	**I 3 QUALITY PROVISIONS**	43.76	46.54
I2.2 Accreditation body	42.56	39.02	**I 4 QUANTITATIVE PROVISIONS**	0.00	55.77
I2.3 Register	39.62	43.86			
I2.4 Code of conduct and procedure	37.46	47.39			

General situation

According to governmental sources, Ireland's overall score is situated in the lower average range. According to the professional sources, the country scores in the upper sub average band.

Salient features

There are notable differences between the governmental and professional sources for the main indicator 'Procedural safeguards', as well as for the following basic level indicators: 'Procedural guarantees', 'Number of phases in the procedure', 'Criteria for interpretation', 'Training level' and 'Directives for magistrates'.

IRELAND : INDICATOR PROFILE TRANSLATION

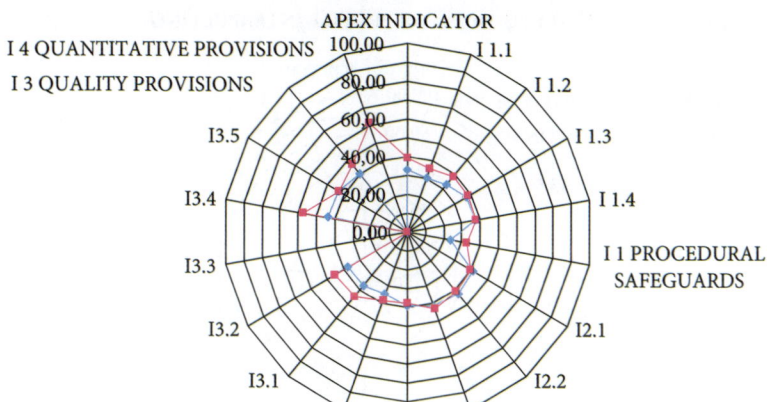

	T-SCORE GVT	T-SCORE PROF		T-SCORE GVT	T-SCORE PROF
APEX INDICATOR	33.04	39.24	**I 2 REGULATION OF THE PROFESSION**	34.97	38.60
I 1.1 Procedural Guarantees	30.43	35.83	I3.1 Quality provisions	37.11	45.00
I 1.2 Number of phases in procedure	32.95	38.84	I3.2 Training level	36.92	45.95
I 1.3 Criteria for translation	37.43	38.16	I3.3 Video taping	0.00	0.00
I 1.4 Vulnerable groups	37.87	38.13	I3.4 Directives for magistrates	43.43	56.86
I 1 PROCEDURAL SAFEGUARDS	24.50	32.57	I3.5 Recruitment programme	42.93	43.04
I2.1 Protection and regulation	41.30	39.88	**I 3 QUALITY PROVISIONS**	39.66	46.56
I2.2 Accreditation body	43.19	41.03	**I 4 QUANTITATIVE PROVISIONS**	0.00	61.56
I2.3 Register	41.60	43.75			
I2.4 Code of conduct and procedure	39.54	37.83			

General situation

According to both governmental and professional sources, Ireland's overall score is situated in the upper sub average band.

Salient features

The only notable difference between the governmental and professional sources is in the basic level indicator 'Directives for magistrates'.

2.14. ITALY

ITALY : INDICATOR PROFILE INTERPRETING

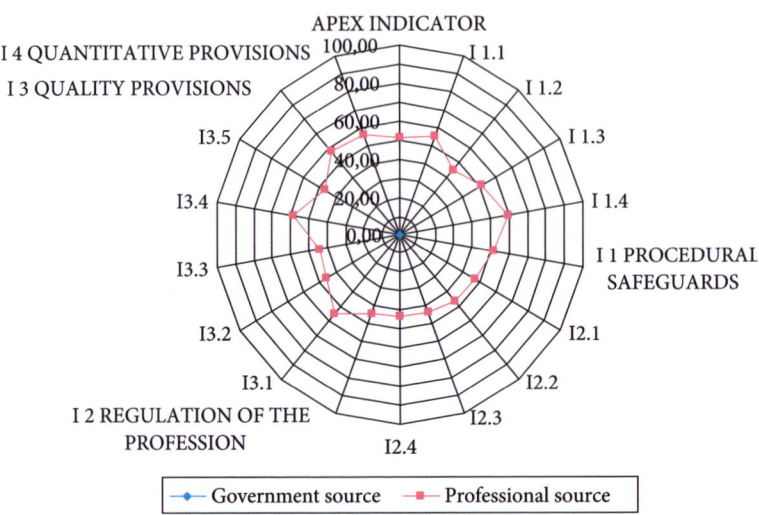

	T-SCORE GVT	T-SCORE PROF		T-SCORE GVT	T-SCORE PROF
APEX INDICATOR	0.00	51.15	**I 2 REGULATION OF THE PROFESSION**	0.00	44.50
I 1.1 Procedural Guarantees	0.00	55.48	I3.1 Quality provisions	0.00	54.55
I 1.2 Number of phases in procedure	0.00	44.25	I3.2 Training level	0.00	46.30
I 1.3 Criteria for interpretation	0.00	51.33	I3.3 Video taping	0.00	43.86
I 1.4 Vulnerable groups	0.00	58.96	I3.4 Directives for magistrates	0.00	58.18
I 1 PROCEDURAL SAFEGUARDS	0.00	51.20	I3.5 Recruitment programme	0.00	46.92
I2.1 Protection and regulation	0.00	46.43	**I 3 QUALITY PROVISIONS**	0.00	57.76
I2.2 Accreditation body	0.00	46.34	**I 4 QUANTITATIVE PROVISIONS**	0.00	55.77
I2.3 Register	0.00	43.86			
I2.4 Code of conduct and procedure	0.00	43.04			

General situation

According to the professional sources, Italy's overall score is situated in the upper average range.

Salient features

On the whole, this profile stands out as well rounded and generally average (upper and lower average range).

ITALY : INDICATOR PROFILE TRANSLATION

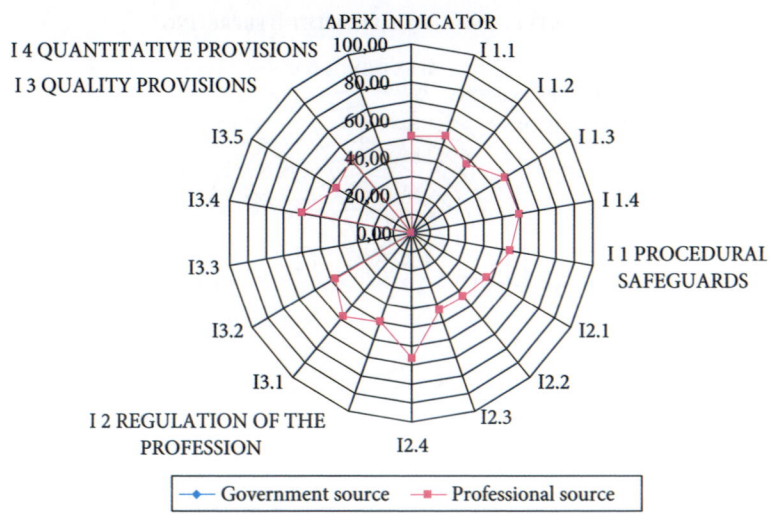

	T-SCORE GVT	T-SCORE PROF		T-SCORE GVT	T-SCORE PROF
APEX INDICATOR	0.00	51.77	**I 2 REGULATION OF THE PROFESSION**	0.00	49.83
I 1.1 Procedural Guarantees	0.00	55.28	I3.1 Quality provisions	0.00	58.16
I 1.2 Number of phases in procedure	0.00	47.11	I3.2 Training level	0.00	47.77
I 1.3 Criteria for translation	0.00	58.57	I3.3 Video taping	0.00	0.00
I 1.4 Vulnerable groups	0.00	58.96	I3.4 Directives for magistrates	0.00	59.71
I 1 PROCEDURAL SAFEGUARDS	0.00	54.36	I3.5 Recruitment programme	0.00	47.39
I2.1 Protection and regulation	0.00	46.86	**I 3 QUALITY PROVISIONS**	0.00	51.12
I2.2 Accreditation body	0.00	43.59	**I 4 QUANTITATIVE PROVISIONS**	0.00	0.00
I2.3 Register	0.00	43.75			
I2.4 Code of conduct and procedure	0.00	66.09			

General situation

According to the professional sources, Italy's overall score is situated in the upper average range.

Salient features

On the whole, this profile stands out as well rounded and generally average (upper and lower average range), with the score for 'Code of conduct and procedure' as the only relative elevation.

2.15. LATVIA

LATVIA : INDICATOR PROFILE INTERPRETING

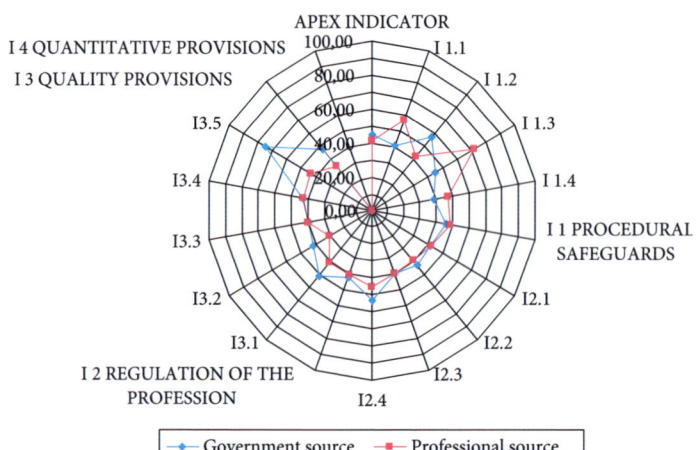

	T-SCORE GVT	T-SCORE PROF		T-SCORE GVT	T-SCORE PROF
APEX INDICATOR	44.72	40.72	**I 2 REGULATION OF THE PROFESSION**	41.82	40.26
I 1.1 Procedural Guarantees	40.11	56.85	I3.1 Quality provisions	50.51	40.00
I 1.2 Number of phases in procedure	56.35	41.59	I3.2 Training level	41.79	30.25
I 1.3 Criteria for interpretation	44.00	71.33	I3.3 Video taping	39.62	39.32
I 1.4 Vulnerable groups	37.87	46.46	I3.4 Directives for magistrates	43.43	42.27
I 1 PROCEDURAL SAFEGUARDS	45.48	48.04	I3.5 Recruitment programme	74.69	43.08
I2.1 Protection and regulation	41.36	41.67	**I 3 QUALITY PROVISIONS**	46.86	33.85
I2.2 Accreditation body	42.56	39.02	**I 4 QUANTITATIVE PROVISIONS**	0.00	0.00
I2.3 Register	39.62	39.32			
I2.4 Code of conduct and procedure	53.33	45.22			

General situation
According to both governmental and professional sources, Latvia's overall score is situated in the lower average range.

Salient features
There are notable differences between the governmental and professional sources for the intermediate level indicator 'Quality provisions' and the basic level indicators 'Procedural guarantees', 'Number of phases in the procedure', 'Criteria for interpretation', 'Quality provisions', 'Training level' and 'Recruitment programme'.

LATVIA : INDICATOR PROFILE TRANSLATION

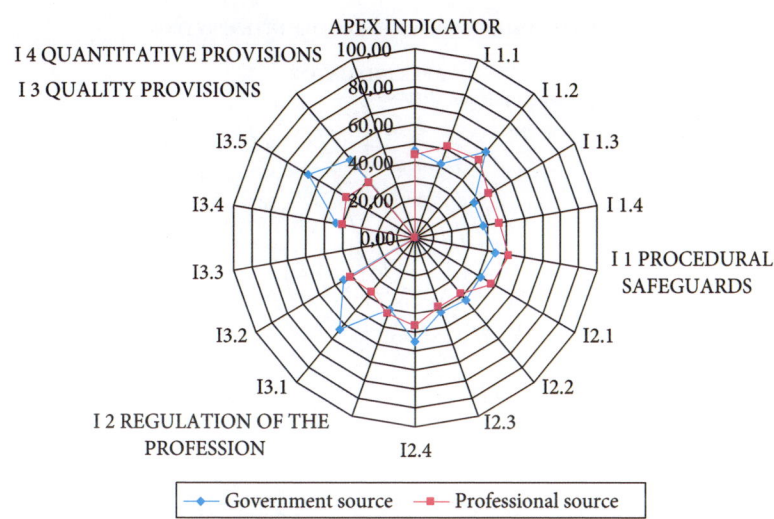

	T-SCORE GVT	T-SCORE PROF		T-SCORE GVT	T-SCORE PROF
APEX INDICATOR	46.33	44.24	**I 2 REGULATION OF THE PROFESSION**	40.26	43.09
I 1.1 Procedural Guarantees	41.18	51.11	I3.1 Quality provisions	63.42	37.11
I 1.2 Number of phases in procedure	59.73	54.55	I3.2 Training level	44.62	40.95
I 1.3 Criteria for translation	37.43	46.33	I3.3 Video taping	0.00	0.00
I 1.4 Vulnerable groups	37.87	46.46	I3.4 Directives for magistrates	43.43	39.71
I 1 PROCEDURAL SAFEGUARDS	44.57	51.39	I3.5 Recruitment programme	67.32	43.04
I2.1 Protection and regulation	41.30	48.02	**I 3 QUALITY PROVISIONS**	54.15	38.26
I2.2 Accreditation body	43.19	38.46	**I 4 QUANTITATIVE PROVISIONS**	0.00	0.00
I2.3 Register	41.60	38.75			
I2.4 Code of conduct and procedure	54.92	46.52			

General situation

According to both governmental and professional sources, Latvia's overall score is situated in the lower average range.

Salient features

There are notable differences between the governmental and professional sources for the intermediate level indicator 'Quality provisions' and the basic level indicators 'Quality provisions' and 'Recruitment programme'.

2.16. LITHUANIA

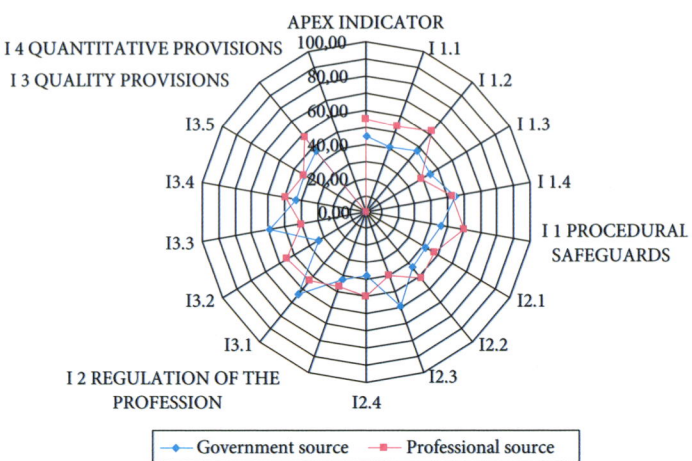

LITHUANIA : INDICATOR PROFILE INTERPRETING

	T-SCORE GVT	T-SCORE PROF		T-SCORE GVT	T-SCORE PROF
APEX INDICATOR	44.72	54.49	**I 2 REGULATION OF THE PROFESSION**	41.82	46.61
I 1.1 Procedural Guarantees	40.11	54.11	I3.1 Quality provisions	63.33	52.73
I 1.2 Number of phases in procedure	46.73	61.95	I3.2 Training level	32.86	54.94
I 1.3 Criteria for interpretation	44.00	38.00	I3.3 Video taping	58.85	39.32
I 1.4 Vulnerable groups	53.62	52.71	I3.4 Directives for magistrates	43.43	49.09
I 1 PROCEDURAL SAFEGUARDS	45.48	60.06	I3.5 Recruitment programme	43.44	43.08
I2.1 Protection and regulation	41.36	47.62	**I 3 QUALITY PROVISIONS**	46.86	56.78
I2.2 Accreditation body	42.56	51.22	**I 4 QUANTITATIVE PROVISIONS**	0.00	0.00
I2.3 Register	58.85	39.32			
I2.4 Code of conduct and procedure	37.46	49.57			

General situation

According to governmental sources, Lithuania's overall score is situated in the lower average range, whereas professional sources situate it in the upper average band.

Salient features

There are notable differences between the governmental and professional sources for the intermediate level indicators 'Procedural safeguards' and 'Quality provisions' as well as in the basic level indicators 'Procedural guarantees', 'Number of phases in the procedure', 'Register', 'Quality provisions' and 'Training level'.

LITHUANIA : INDICATOR PROFILE TRANSLATION

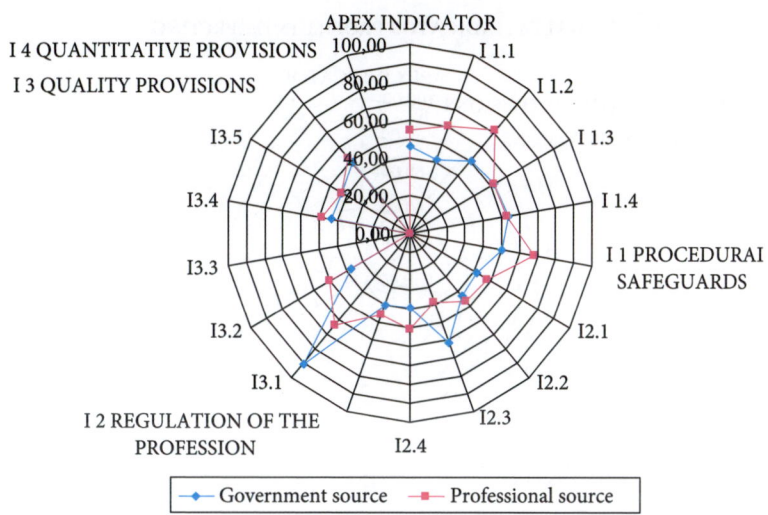

	T-SCORE GVT	T-SCORE PROF		T-SCORE GVT	T-SCORE PROF
APEX INDICATOR	46.63	55.19	**I 2 REGULATION OF THE PROFESSION**	40.26	45.90
I 1.1 Procedural Guarantees	41.18	60.83	I3.1 Quality provisions	89.74	63.42
I 1.2 Number of phases in procedure	50.80	71.07	I3.2 Training level	36.92	50.05
I 1.3 Criteria for translation	52.13	52.45	I3.3 Video taping	0.00	0.00
I 1.4 Vulnerable groups	53.62	52.71	I3.4 Directives for magistrates	43.43	48.29
I 1 PROCEDURAL SAFEGUARDS	50.31	67.72	I3.5 Recruitment programme	42.93	43.04
I2.1 Protection and regulation	41.30	48.02	**I 3 QUALITY PROVISIONS**	49.32	51.95
I2.2 Accreditation body	43.19	46.15	**I 4 QUANTITATIVE PROVISIONS**	0.00	0.00
I2.3 Register	61.60	38.75			
I2.4 Code of conduct and procedure	39.54	50.87			

General situation

According to governmental sources, Lithuania's overall score is situated in the lower average range, whereas professional sources situate it in the lower above average band.

Salient features

There are notable differences between the governmental and professional sources for the Apex indicator and the intermediate level indicator 'Procedural safeguards' as well as in the basic level indicators 'Procedural guarantees', 'Number of phases in the procedure', 'Register', 'Quality provisions' and 'Training level'.

2.17. MALTA

MALTA : INDICATOR PROFILE INTERPRETING

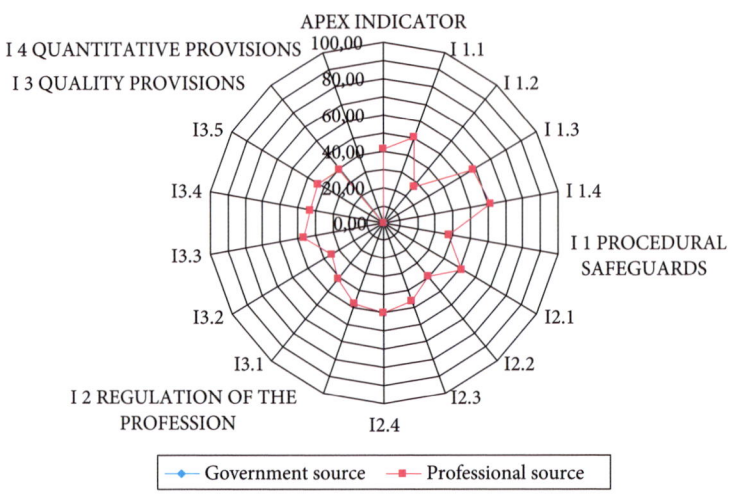

	T-SCORE GVT	T-SCORE PROF		T-SCORE GVT	T-SCORE PROF
APEX INDICATOR	0.00	41.05	**I 2 REGULATION OF THE PROFESSION**	0.00	47.14
I 1.1 Procedural Guarantees	0.00	50.00	I3.1 Quality provisions	0.00	40.00
I 1.2 Number of phases in procedure	0.00	26.55	I3.2 Training level	0.00	33.95
I 1.3 Criteria for interpretation	0.00	58.00	I3.3 Video taping	0.00	46.14
I 1.4 Vulnerable groups	0.00	61.04	I3.4 Directives for magistrates	0.00	42.27
I 1 PROCEDURAL SAFEGUARDS	0.00	37.28	I3.5 Recruitment programme	0.00	43.08
I2.1 Protection and regulation	0.00	51.19	**I 3 QUALITY PROVISIONS**	0.00	38.73
I2.2 Accreditation body	0.00	39.02	**I 4 QUANTITATIVE PROVISIONS**	0.00	0.00
I2.3 Register	0.00	46.14			
I2.4 Code of conduct and procedure	0.00	49.57			

General situation

According to the professional sources, Malta's overall score is situated in the lower average range.

Salient features

On the high end, the score for the intermediate level indicator 'Vulnerable groups' (lower above average range) stands out, while 'Number of phases in the procedures' (lower sub average band) stands out as the lower extreme.

MALTA : INDICATOR PROFILE TRANSLATION

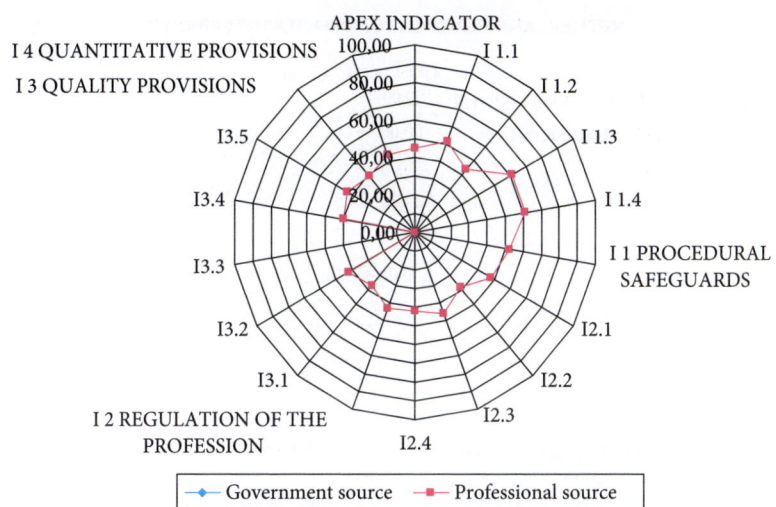

<table>
<thead>
<tr><th></th><th>T-SCORE GVT</th><th>T-SCORE PROF</th><th></th><th>T-SCORE GVT</th><th>T-SCORE PROF</th></tr>
</thead>
<tbody>
<tr><td>APEX INDICATOR</td><td>0.00</td><td>45.01</td><td>I 2 REGULATION OF THE PROFESSION</td><td>0.00</td><td>43.65</td></tr>
<tr><td>I 1.1 Procedural Guarantees</td><td>0.00</td><td>51.11</td><td>I3.1 Quality provisions</td><td>0.00</td><td>37.11</td></tr>
<tr><td>I 1.2 Number of phases in procedure</td><td>0.00</td><td>43.80</td><td>I3.2 Training level</td><td>0.00</td><td>42.32</td></tr>
<tr><td>I 1.3 Criteria for interpretation</td><td>0.00</td><td>60.61</td><td>I3.3 Video taping</td><td>0.00</td><td>0.00</td></tr>
<tr><td>I 1.4 Vulnerable groups</td><td>0.00</td><td>61.04</td><td>I3.4 Directives for magistrates</td><td>0.00</td><td>39.71</td></tr>
<tr><td>I 1 PROCEDURAL SAFEGUARDS</td><td>0.00</td><td>51.88</td><td>I3.5 Recruitment programme</td><td>0.00</td><td>43.04</td></tr>
<tr><td>I2.1 Protection and regulation</td><td>0.00</td><td>48.02</td><td>I 3 QUALITY PROVISIONS</td><td>0.00</td><td>39.50</td></tr>
<tr><td>I2.2 Accreditation body</td><td>0.00</td><td>38.46</td><td>I 4 QUANTITATIVE PROVISIONS</td><td>0.00</td><td>44.23</td></tr>
<tr><td>I2.3 Register</td><td>0.00</td><td>46.25</td><td></td><td></td><td></td></tr>
<tr><td>I2.4 Code of conduct and procedure</td><td>0.00</td><td>42.17</td><td></td><td></td><td></td></tr>
</tbody>
</table>

General situation

According to the professional sources, Malta's overall score is situated in the lower average range.

Salient features

The intermediate level indicators 'Vulnerable groups' and 'Criteria for translation' (lower above average range) stand out as elevated.

2.18. THE NETHERLANDS

NETHERLANDS : INDICATOR PROFILE INTERPRETING

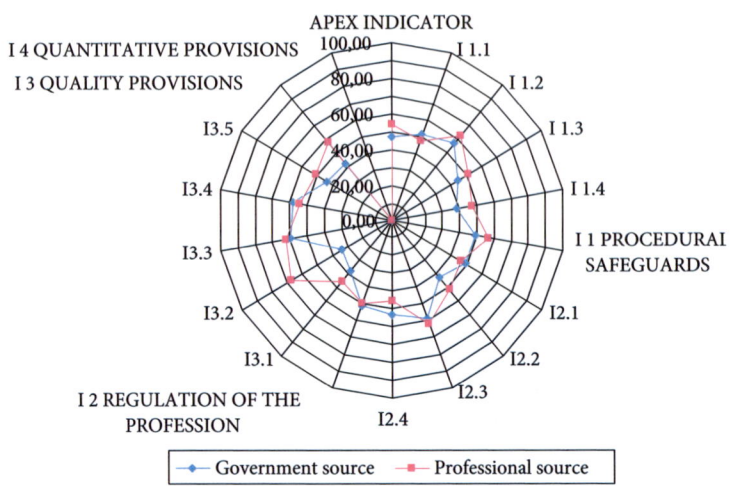

	T-SCORE GVT	T-SCORE PROF		T-SCORE GVT	T-SCORE PROF
APEX INDICATOR	46.94	54.28	**I 2 REGULATION OF THE PROFESSION**	51.17	49.79
I 1.1 Procedural Guarantees	51.22	47.26	I3.1 Quality provisions	37.69	45.45
I 1.2 Number of phases in procedure	56.35	61.95	I3.2 Training level	32.86	67.28
I 1.3 Criteria for interpretation	44.00	51.33	I3.3 Video taping	58.85	62.05
I 1.4 Vulnerable groups	37.87	46.46	I3.4 Directives for magistrates	57.71	53.64
I 1 PROCEDURAL SAFEGUARDS	49.00	56.27	I3.5 Recruitment programme	43.44	50.77
I2.1 Protection and regulation	48.94	45.24	**I 3 QUALITY PROVISIONS**	40.65	56.78
I2.2 Accreditation body	42.56	51.22	**I 4 QUANTITATIVE PROVISIONS**	0.00	0.00
I2.3 Register	58.85	62.05			
I2.4 Code of conduct and procedure	53.33	45.22			

General situation

According to governmental sources, the Netherlands' overall score is situated in the lower average range, whereas professional sources situate it in the upper average band.

Salient features

The only divergence of note between the governmental and professional sources is in the basic level indicator 'Training level'.

NETHERLANDS : INDICATOR PROFILE TRANSLATION

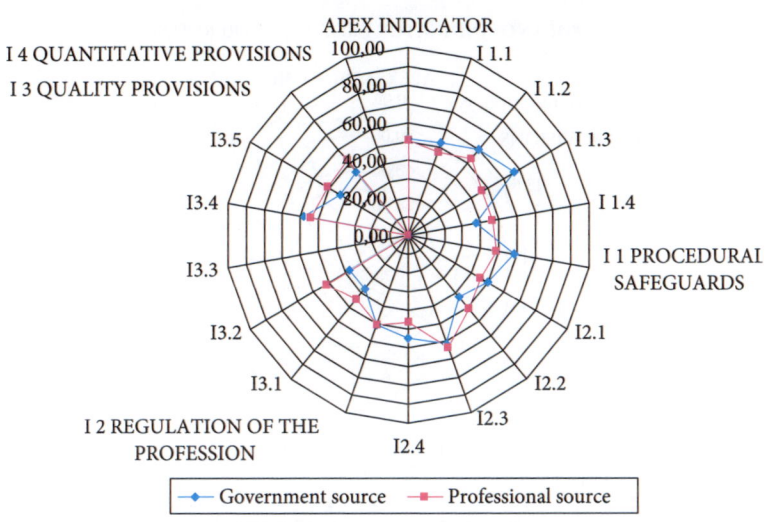

	T-SCORE GVT	T-SCORE PROF		T-SCORE GVT	T-SCORE PROF
APEX INDICATOR	51.42	50.56	I 2 REGULATION OF THE PROFESSION	50.85	50.39
I 1.1 Procedural Guarantees	51.94	46.94	I3.1 Quality provisions	37.11	45.00
I 1.2 Number of phases in procedure	59.73	52.89	I3.2 Training level	36.92	51.86
I 1.3 Criteria for translation	66.84	46.33	I3.3 Video taping	0.00	0.00
I 1.4 Vulnerable groups	37.87	46.46	I3.4 Directives for magistrates	57.71	54.00
I 1 PROCEDURAL SAFEGUARDS	58.91	48.91	I3.5 Recruitment programme	42.93	51.74
I2.1 Protection and regulation	50.00	45.70	I 3 QUALITY PROVISIONS	44.49	52.37
I2.2 Accreditation body	43.19	51.28	I 4 QUANTITATIVE PROVISIONS	0.00	0.00
I2.3 Register	61.60	63.75			
I2.4 Code of conduct and procedure	54.92	46.52			

General situation

According to both governmental and professional sources, the Netherlands' overall score is situated in the upper average band.

Salient features

There are notable differences between the governmental and professional sources in the intermediate level indicator 'Procedural safeguards' and the basic level indicators 'Criteria for translation' and 'Training level'.

2.19. POLAND

POLAND : INDICATOR PROFILE INTERPRETING

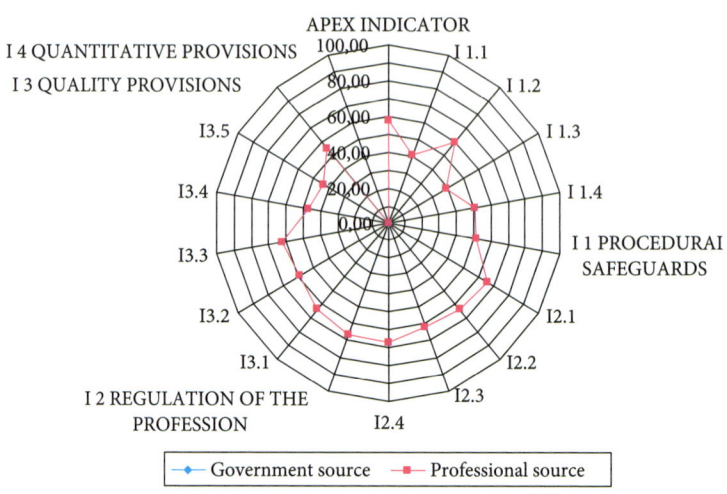

	T-SCORE GVT	T-SCORE PROF		T-SCORE GVT	T-SCORE PROF
APEX INDICATOR	0.00	57.58	**I 2 REGULATION OF THE PROFESSION**	0.00	66.72
I 1.1 Procedural Guarantees	0.00	40.41	I3.1 Quality provisions	0.00	63.64
I 1.2 Number of phases in procedure	0.00	59.29	I3.2 Training level	0.00	58.64
I 1.3 Criteria for interpretation	0.00	38.00	I3.3 Video taping	0.00	62.05
I 1.4 Vulnerable groups	0.00	50.63	I3.4 Directives for magistrates	0.00	46.82
I 1 PROCEDURAL SAFEGUARDS	0.00	51.20	I3.5 Recruitment programme	0.00	43.08
I2.1 Protection and regulation	0.00	65.48	**I 3 QUALITY PROVISIONS**	0.00	54.83
I2.2 Accreditation body	0.00	63.41	**I 4 QUANTITATIVE PROVISIONS**	0.00	0.00
I2.3 Register	0.00	62.05			
I2.4 Code of conduct and procedure	0.00	66.96			

General situation

According to the professional sources, Poland's overall score is situated in the upper average range.

Salient features

The intermediate level indicator 'Criteria for interpretation' (upper sub average range) stands out as decreased.

POLAND : INDICATOR PROFILE TRANSLATION

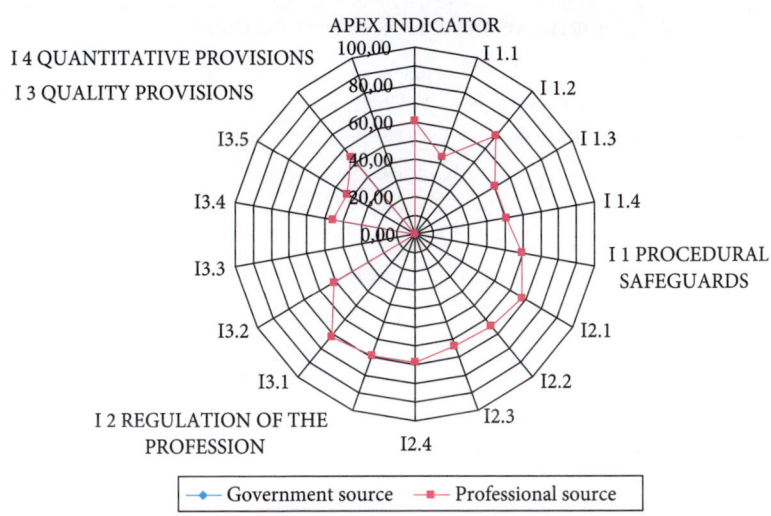

	T-SCORE GVT	T-SCORE PROF		T-SCORE GVT	T-SCORE PROF
APEX INDICATOR	0.00	60.94	**I 2 REGULATION OF THE PROFESSION**	0.00	69.49
I 1.1 Procedural Guarantees	0.00	44.17	I3.1 Quality provisions	0.00	71.32
I 1.2 Number of phases in procedure	0.00	68.60	I3.2 Training level	0.00	51.41
I 1.3 Criteria for translation	0.00	50.41	I3.3 Video taping	0.00	0.00
I 1.4 Vulnerable groups	0.00	50.63	I3.4 Directives for magistrates	0.00	45.43
I 1 PROCEDURAL SAFEGUARDS	0.00	59.31	I3.5 Recruitment programme	0.00	43.04
I2.1 Protection and regulation	0.00	67.79	**I 3 QUALITY PROVISIONS**	0.00	54.02
I2.2 Accreditation body	0.00	64.10	**I 4 QUANTITATIVE PROVISIONS**	0.00	0.00
I2.3 Register	0.00	63.75			
I2.4 Code of conduct and procedure	0.00	68.26			

General situation

According to the professional sources, Poland's overall score is situated in the lower above average range.

Salient features

The intermediate level indicator 'Quality provisions' (upper sub average range) stands out as elevated.

2.20. PORTUGAL

PORTUGAL : INDICATOR PROFILE INTERPRETING

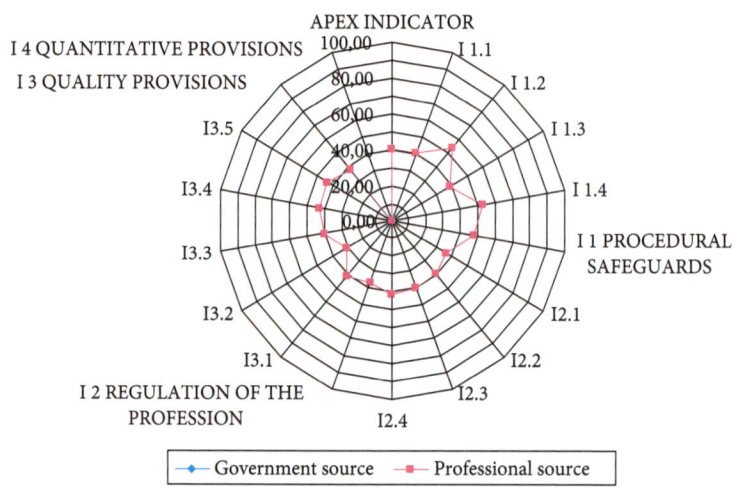

	T-SCORE GVT	T-SCORE PROF		T-SCORE GVT	T-SCORE PROF
APEX INDICATOR	0.00	40.41	**I 2 REGULATION OF THE PROFESSION**	0.00	36.56
I 1.1 Procedural Guarantees	0.00	40.41	I3.1 Quality provisions	0.00	40.00
I 1.2 Number of phases in procedure	0.00	53.10	I3.2 Training level	0.00	30.25
I 1.3 Criteria for interpretation	0.00	38.00	I3.3 Video taping	0.00	39.32
I 1.4 Vulnerable groups	0.00	52.71	I3.4 Directives for magistrates	0.00	42.27
I 1 PROCEDURAL SAFEGUARDS	0.00	47.41	I3.5 Recruitment programme	0.00	43.08
I2.1 Protection and regulation	0.00	35.71	**I 3 QUALITY PROVISIONS**	0.00	37.27
I2.2 Accreditation body	0.00	39.02	**I 4 QUANTITATIVE PROVISIONS**	0.00	0.00
I2.3 Register	0.00	39.32			
I2.4 Code of conduct and procedure	0.00	40.87			

General situation

According to the professional sources, Portugal's overall score is situated in the lower average range.

Salient features

With the exception of the indicators 'Number of phases in the procedure' and 'Vulnerable groups' (both in the upper average range), the profile stands out as consistently sub average to lower average.

PORTUGAL : INDICATOR PROFILE TRANSLATION

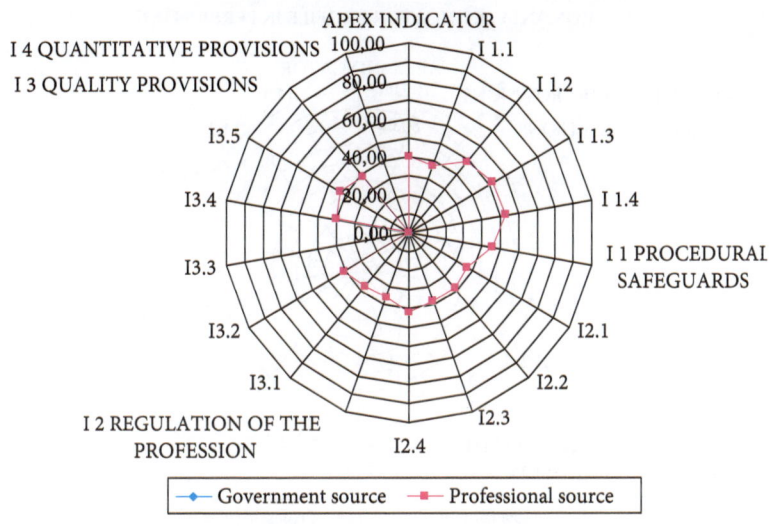

	T-SCORE GVT	T-SCORE PROF		T-SCORE GVT	T-SCORE PROF
APEX INDICATOR	0.00	40.18	**I 2 REGULATION OF THE PROFESSION**	0.00	36.35
I 1.1 Procedural Guarantees	0.00	37.22	I3.1 Quality provisions	0.00	37.11
I 1.2 Number of phases in procedure	0.00	48.76	I3.2 Training level	0.00	40.95
I 1.3 Criteria for translation	0.00	52.45	I3.3 Video taping	0.00	0.00
I 1.4 Vulnerable groups	0.00	52.71	I3.4 Directives for magistrates	0.00	39.71
I 1 PROCEDURAL SAFEGUARDS	0.00	45.94	I3.5 Recruitment programme	0.00	43.04
I2.1 Protection and regulation	0.00	36.40	**I 3 QUALITY PROVISIONS**	0.00	38.26
I2.2 Accreditation body	0.00	38.46	**I 4 QUANTITATIVE PROVISIONS**	0.00	0.00
I2.3 Register	0.00	38.75			
I2.4 Code of conduct and procedure	0.00	42.17			

General situation

According to the professional sources, Portugal's overall score is situated in the lower average range.

Salient features

With the exception of the indicators 'Criteria for translation' and 'Vulnerable groups' (both in the upper average range), the profile stands out as consistently sub average to lower average.

2.21.   ROMANIA

ROMANIA : INDICATOR PROFILE INTERPRETING

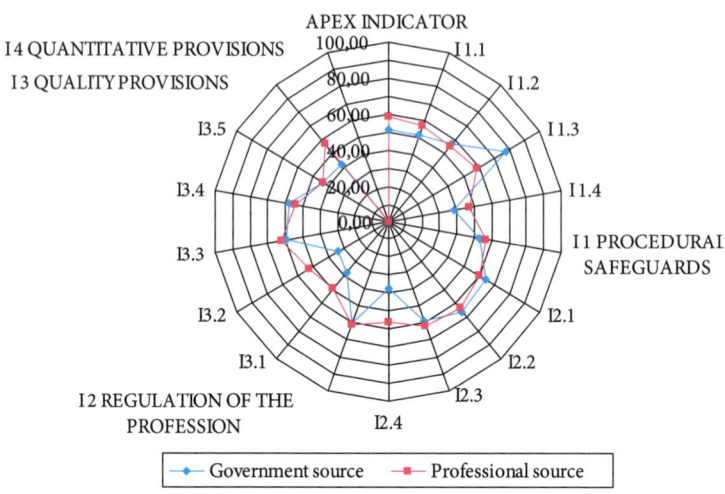

	T-SCORE GVT	T-SCORE PROF		T-SCORE GVT	T-SCORE PROF
			I 2 REGULATION OF THE PROFESSION		
APEX INDICATOR	51.23	58.00		60.51	61.43
I 1.1 Procedural Guarantees	51.22	56.85	I3.1 Quality provisions	37.69	49.09
I 1.2 Number of phases in procedure	56.35	54.87	I3.2 Training level	32.86	52.47
I 1.3 Criteria for interpretation	77.33	58.00	I3.3 Video taping	58.85	62.05
I 1.4 Vulnerable groups	37.87	46.46	I3.4 Directives for magistrates	57.71	53.64
I 1 PROCEDURAL SAFEGUARDS	52.51	56.27	I3.5 Recruitment programme	43.44	43.08
I2.1 Protection and regulation	64.09	59.52	**I 3 QUALITY PROVISIONS**	40.65	56.29
I2.2 Accreditation body	65.81	63.41	**I 4 QUANTITATIVE PROVISIONS**	0.00	0.00
I2.3 Register	58.85	62.05			
I2.4 Code of conduct and procedure	37.46	56.09			

General situation

According to both governmental and professional sources, Romania's overall score is situated in the upper average range.

Salient features

There are notable differences between the governmental and professional sources for the intermediate level indicator 'Quality provisions' as well as for the basic level indicators 'Criteria for interpretation', 'Code of conduct and procedure and 'Quality provisions'.

ROMANIA : INDICATOR PROFILE TRANSLATION

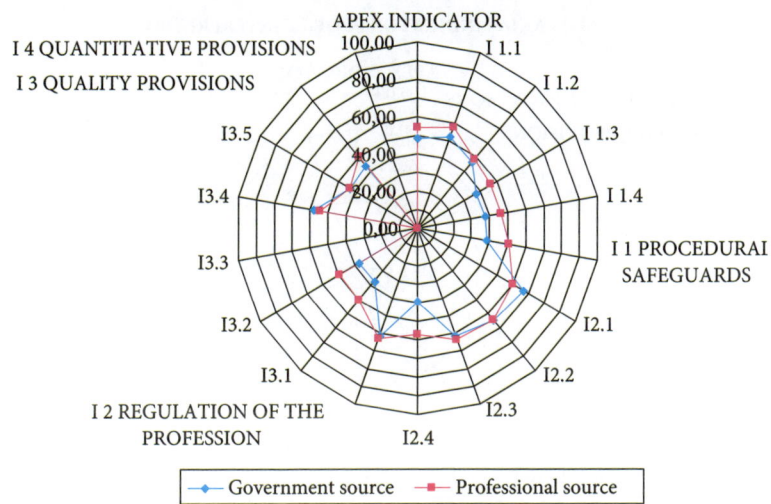

	T-SCORE GVT	T-SCORE PROF		T-SCORE GVT	T-SCORE PROF
APEX INDICATOR	48.25	54.34	I 2 REGULATION OF THE PROFESSION	61.43	62.75
I 1.1 Procedural Guarantees	51.94	58.06	I3.1 Quality provisions	37.11	50.26
I 1.2 Number of phases in procedure	46.34	48.76	I3.2 Training level	36.92	49.14
I 1.3 Criteria for translation	37.43	46.33	I3.3 Video taping	0.00	0.00
I 1.4 Vulnerable groups	37.87	46.46	I3.4 Directives for magistrates	57.71	54.00
I 1 PROCEDURAL SAFEGUARDS	38.84	50.40	I3.5 Recruitment programme	42.93	43.04
I2.1 Protection and regulation	67.39	59.65	I 3 QUALITY PROVISIONS	44.49	49.88
I2.2 Accreditation body	64.47	64.10	I 4 QUANTITATIVE PROVISIONS	0.00	0.00
I2.3 Register	61.60	63.75			
I2.4 Code of conduct and procedure	39.54	57.39			

General situation

According to governmental sources, Romania's overall score is situated in the lower average range, while professional sources situate the country in the upper average range.

Salient features

There are notable differences between the governmental and professional sources for the intermediate level indicator 'Procedural safeguards' as well as for the basic level indicators, 'Code of conduct and procedure', 'Quality provisions' and 'Training level'.

2.22. SLOVAKIA

SLOVAKIA : INDICATOR PROFILE INTERPRETING

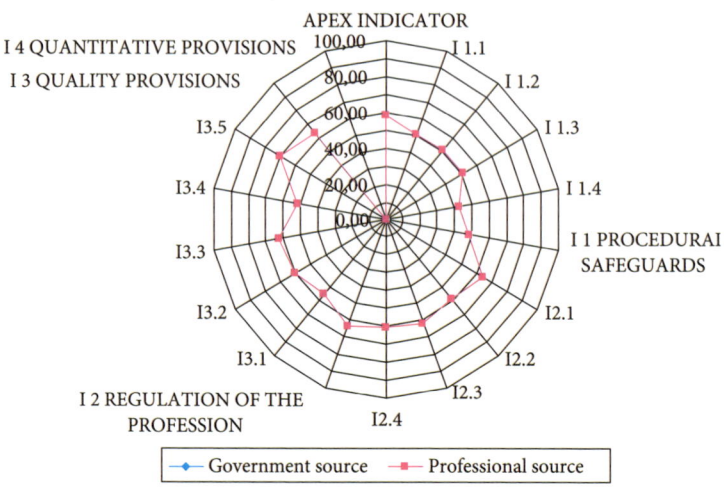

	T-SCORE GVT	T-SCORE PROF		T-SCORE GVT	T-SCORE PROF
APEX INDICATOR	0.00	58.07	**I 2 REGULATION OF THE PROFESSION**	0.00	63.54
I 1.1 Procedural Guarantees	0.00	50.00	I3.1 Quality provisions	0.00	54.55
I 1.2 Number of phases in procedure	0.00	50.44	I3.2 Training level	0.00	59.88
I 1.3 Criteria for interpretation	0.00	51.33	I3.3 Video taping	0.00	62.05
I 1.4 Vulnerable groups	0.00	42.29	I3.4 Directives for magistrates	0.00	51.36
I 1 PROCEDURAL SAFEGUARDS	0.00	48.04	I3.5 Recruitment programme	0.00	70.00
I2.1 Protection and regulation	0.00	64.29	**I 3 QUALITY PROVISIONS**	0.00	62.63
I2.2 Accreditation body	0.00	58.54	**I 4 QUANTITATIVE PROVISIONS**	0.00	0.00
I2.3 Register	0.00	62.05			
I2.4 Code of conduct and procedure	0.00	60.43			

General situation

According to the professional sources, Slovakia's overall score is situated in the upper average range.

Salient features

With the exception of the indicator 'Recruitment programme' (upper above average range), the profile stands out as consistently average to lower above average.

SLOVAKIA : INDICATOR PROFILE TRANSLATION

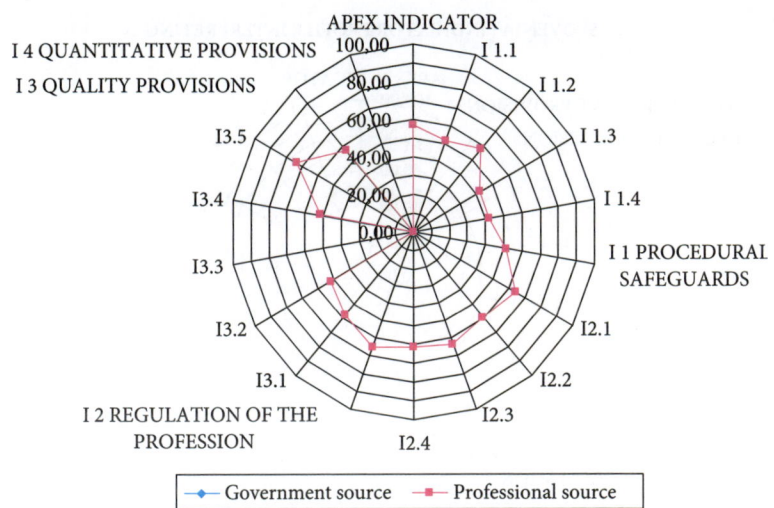

	T-SCORE GVT	T-SCORE PROF		T-SCORE GVT	T-SCORE PROF
APEX INDICATOR	0.00	57.50	**I 2 REGULATION OF THE PROFESSION**	0.00	65.00
I 1.1 Procedural Guarantees	0.00	51.11	I3.1 Quality provisions	0.00	58.16
I 1.2 Number of phases in procedure	0.00	57.85	I3.2 Training level	0.00	51.86
I 1.3 Criteria for translation	0.00	42.24	I3.3 Video taping	0.00	0.00
I 1.4 Vulnerable groups	0.00	42.29	I3.4 Directives for magistrates	0.00	51.14
I 1 PROCEDURAL SAFEGUARDS	0.00	51.39	I3.5 Recruitment programme	0.00	73.48
I2.1 Protection and regulation	0.00	64.30	**I 3 QUALITY PROVISIONS**	0.00	56.10
I2.2 Accreditation body	0.00	58.97	**I 4 QUANTITATIVE PROVISIONS**	0.00	0.00
I2.3 Register	0.00	63.75			
I2.4 Code of conduct and procedure	0.00	61.74			

General situation

According to the professional sources, Slovakia's overall score is situated in the upper average range.

Salient features

With the exception of the indicator 'Recruitment programme' (upper above average range), the profile stands out as consistently average to lower above average.

2.23.   SLOVENIA

SLOVENIA : INDICATOR PROFILE INTERPRETING

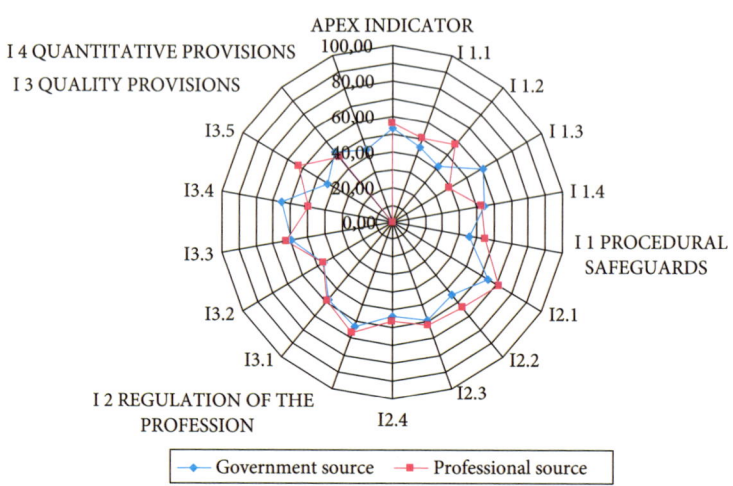

	T-SCORE GVT	T-SCORE PROF		T-SCORE GVT	T-SCORE PROF
APEX INDICATOR	53.49	56.20	**I 2 REGULATION OF THE PROFESSION**	62.85	66.72
I 1.1 Procedural Guarantees	45.67	50.00	I3.1 Quality provisions	56.92	58.18
I 1.2 Number of phases in procedure	41.92	56.64	I3.2 Training level	46.25	46.30
I 1.3 Criteria for interpretation	60.67	38.00	I3.3 Video taping	58.85	62.05
I 1.4 Vulnerable groups	53.62	52.71	I3.4 Directives for magistrates	64.86	49.09
I 1 PROCEDURAL SAFEGUARDS	45.48	54.37	I3.5 Recruitment programme	43.44	62.31
I2.1 Protection and regulation	64.09	71.43	**I 3 QUALITY PROVISIONS**	52.14	47.51
I2.2 Accreditation body	54.19	63.41	**I 4 QUANTITATIVE PROVISIONS**	43.91	0.00
I2.3 Register	58.85	62.05			
I2.4 Code of conduct and procedure	53.33	56.09			

General situation
According to both governmental and professional sources, Slovenia's overall score is situated in the upper average range.

Salient features
There are notable differences between the governmental and professional sources for the basic level indicators, 'Criteria for interpretation' and 'Recruitment programme'.

SLOVENIA : INDICATOR PROFILE TRANSLATION

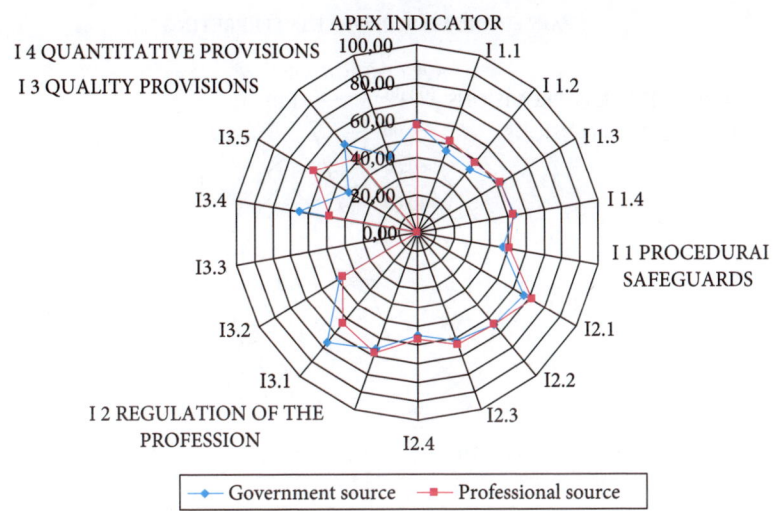

	T-SCORE GVT	T-SCORE PROF		T-SCORE GVT	T-SCORE PROF
APEX INDICATOR	58.52	56.79	**I 2 REGULATION OF THE PROFESSION**	66.72	68.37
I 1.1 Procedural Guarantees	46.56	51.11	I3.1 Quality provisions	76.58	63.42
I 1.2 Number of phases in procedure	44.11	48.76	I3.2 Training level	48.46	46.86
I 1.3 Criteria for translation	52.13	52.45	I3.3 Video taping	0.00	0.00
I 1.4 Vulnerable groups	53.62	52.71	I3.4 Directives for magistrates	64.86	48.29
I 1 PROCEDURAL SAFEGUARDS	47.44	50.89	I3.5 Recruitment programme	42.93	64.78
I2.1 Protection and regulation	67.39	71.28	**I 3 QUALITY PROVISIONS**	61.40	51.12
I2.2 Accreditation body	64.47	64.10	**I 4 QUANTITATIVE PROVISIONS**	43.91	0.00
I2.3 Register	61.60	63.75			
I2.4 Code of conduct and procedure	54.92	57.39			

General situation

According to both governmental and professional sources, Slovenia's overall score is situated in the upper average range.

Salient features

There are notable differences between the governmental and professional sources for the basic level indicators 'Quality provisions', 'Directives for magistrates' and 'Recruitment programme'.

2.24. SPAIN

SPAIN : INDICATOR PROFILE INTERPRETING

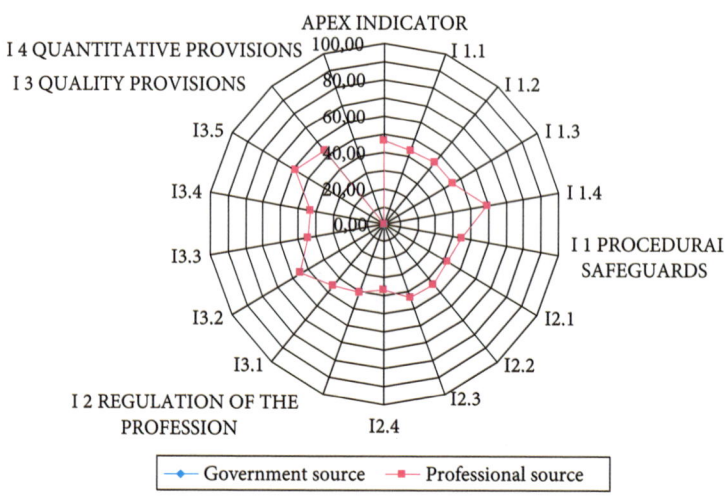

	T-SCORE GVT	T-SCORE PROF		T-SCORE GVT	T-SCORE PROF
			I 2 REGULATION OF THE PROFESSION	0.00	40.26
APEX INDICATOR	0.00	45.84			
I 1.1 Procedural Guarantees	0.00	43.15	I3.1 Quality provisions	0.00	45.45
I 1.2 Number of phases in procedure	0.00	44.25	I3.2 Training level	0.00	54.94
I 1.3 Criteria for interpretation	0.00	44.67	I3.3 Video taping	0.00	43.86
I 1.4 Vulnerable groups	0.00	58.96	I3.4 Directives for magistrates	0.00	42.27
I 1 PROCEDURAL SAFEGUARDS	0.00	44.87	I3.5 Recruitment programme	0.00	58.46
I2.1 Protection and regulation	0.00	41.67	**I 3 QUALITY PROVISIONS**	0.00	52.39
I2.2 Accreditation body	0.00	43.90	**I 4 QUANTITATIVE PROVISIONS**	0.00	0.00
I2.3 Register	0.00	43.86			
I2.4 Code of conduct and procedure	0.00	36.52			

General situation

According to the professional sources, Spain's overall score is situated in the lower average range.

Salient features

With the exception of the indicator 'Code of conduct and procedure' (upper sub average range), Spain's profile stands out as consistently average.

SPAIN : INDICATOR PROFILE TRANSLATION

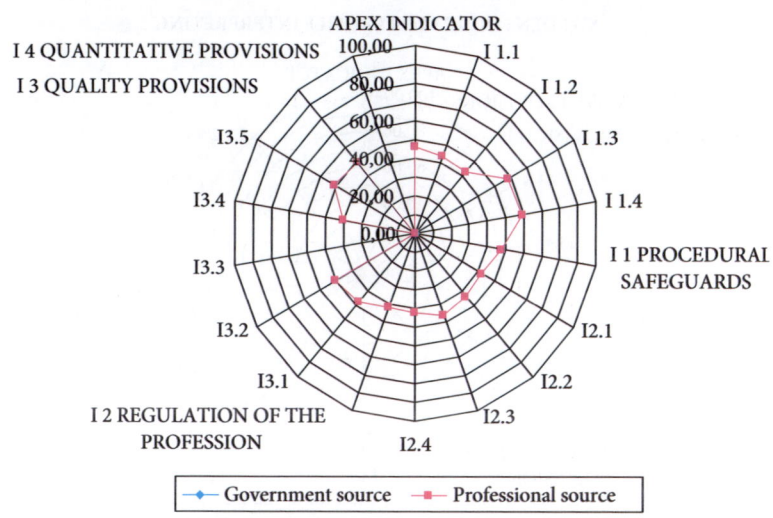

	T-SCORE GVT	T-SCORE PROF		T-SCORE GVT	T-SCORE PROF
APEX INDICATOR	0.00	46.31	**I 2 REGULATION OF THE PROFESSION**	0.00	41.97
I 1.1 Procedural Guarantees	0.00	44.17	I3.1 Quality provisions	0.00	47.63
I 1.2 Number of phases in procedure	0.00	42.98	I3.2 Training level	0.00	50.05
I 1.3 Criteria for translation	0.00	58.57	I3.3 Video taping	0.00	0.00
I 1.4 Vulnerable groups	0.00	58.96	I3.4 Directives for magistrates	0.00	39.71
I 1 PROCEDURAL SAFEGUARDS	0.00	47.92	I3.5 Recruitment programme	0.00	51.74
I2.1 Protection and regulation	0.00	42.21	**I 3 QUALITY PROVISIONS**	0.00	49.05
I2.2 Accreditation body	0.00	43.59	**I 4 QUANTITATIVE PROVISIONS**	0.00	0.00
I2.3 Register	0.00	46.25			
I2.4 Code of conduct and procedure	0.00	42.17			

General situation

According to the professional sources, Spain's overall score is situated in the lower average range.

Salient features

With the exception of the indicator 'Directives for magistrates' (upper sub average range), Spain's profile stands out as consistently average.

2.25. SWEDEN

SWEDEN : INDICATOR PROFILE INTERPRETING

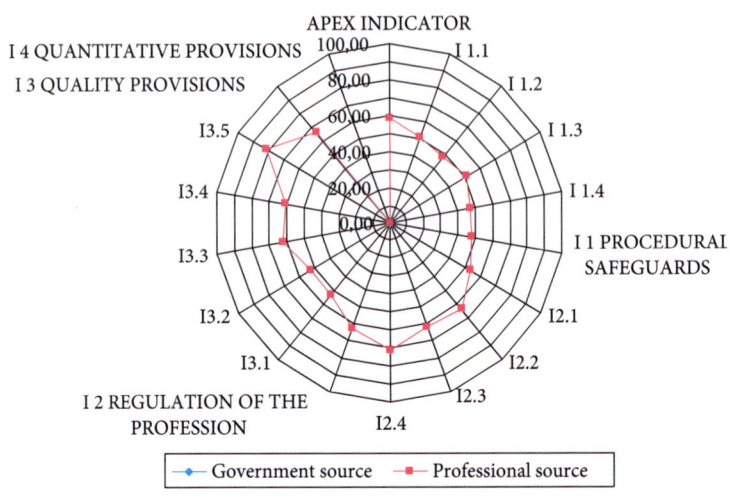

	T-SCORE GVT	T-SCORE PROF		T-SCORE GVT	T-SCORE PROF
APEX INDICATOR	0.00	58.48	I 2 REGULATION OF THE PROFESSION	0.00	62.49
I 1.1 Procedural Guarantees	0.00	50.00	I3.1 Quality provisions	0.00	52.73
I 1.2 Number of phases in procedure	0.00	47.79	I3.2 Training level	0.00	52.47
I 1.3 Criteria for interpretation	0.00	51.33	I3.3 Video taping	0.00	62.05
I 1.4 Vulnerable groups	0.00	46.46	I3.4 Directives for magistrates	0.00	60.45
I 1 PROCEDURAL SAFEGUARDS	0.00	47.41	I3.5 Recruitment programme	0.00	81.54
I2.1 Protection and regulation	0.00	53.57	I 3 QUALITY PROVISIONS	0.00	65.56
I2.2 Accreditation body	0.00	63.41	I 4 QUANTITATIVE PROVISIONS	0.00	0.00
I2.3 Register	0.00	62.05			
I2.4 Code of conduct and procedure	0.00	71.30			

General situation

According to the professional sources, Sweden's overall score is situated in the upper average range.

Salient features

With the exception of the indicator 'Recruitment programme' (lower high range), Sweden's profile stands out as consistently average to above average.

SWEDEN : INDICATOR PROFILE TRANSLATION

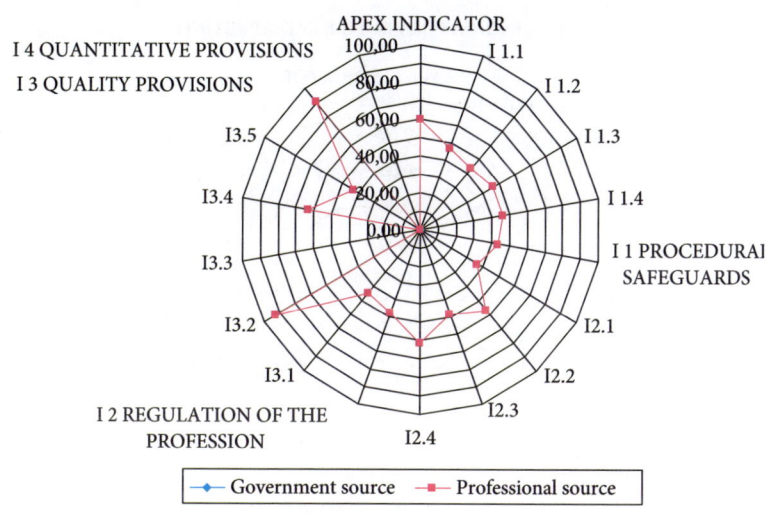

	T-SCORE GVT	T-SCORE PROF		T-SCORE GVT	T-SCORE PROF
APEX INDICATOR	0.00	60.25	**I 2 REGULATION OF THE PROFESSION**	0.00	47.58
I 1.1 Procedural Guarantees	0.00	46.94	I3.1 Quality provisions	0.00	45.00
I 1.2 Number of phases in procedure	0.00	43.80	I3.2 Training level	0.00	92.32
I 1.3 Criteria for translation	0.00	46.33	I3.3 Video taping	0.00	0.00
I 1.4 Vulnerable groups	0.00	46.46	I3.4 Directives for magistrates	0.00	62.57
I 1 PROCEDURAL SAFEGUARDS	0.00	43.47	I3.5 Recruitment programme	0.00	43.04
I2.1 Protection and regulation	0.00	36.40	**I 3 QUALITY PROVISIONS**	0.00	89.71
I2.2 Accreditation body	0.00	56.41	**I 4 QUANTITATIVE PROVISIONS**	0.00	0.00
I2.3 Register	0.00	48.75			
I2.4 Code of conduct and procedure	0.00	61.74			

General situation

According to the professional sources, Sweden's overall score is situated in the lower above average range.

Salient features

This profile is predominantly average, except for a number of extreme scores with a very wide range: 'Protection and regulation' (upper sub average), 'Training level' (upper high band) and 'Quality provisions' (lower high band).

2.26. UNITED KINGDOM

UK : INDICATOR PROFILE INTERPRETING

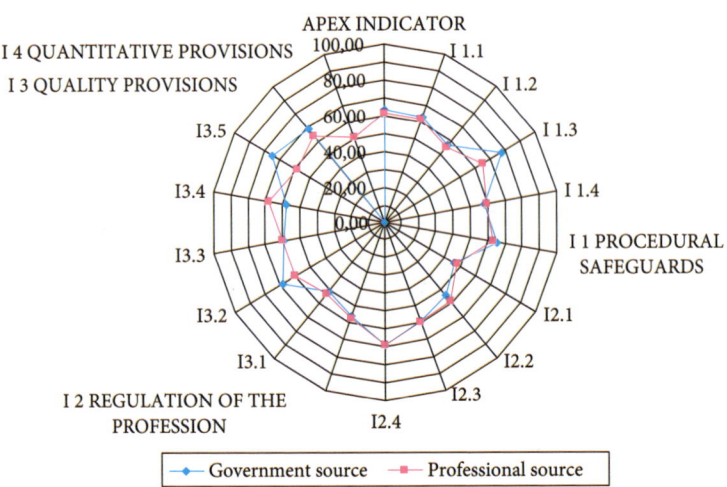

	T-SCORE GVT	T-SCORE PROF		T-SCORE GVT	T-SCORE PROF
			I 2 REGULATION OF THE		
APEX INDICATOR	63.08	61.31	**PROFESSION**	55.84	57.72
I 1.1 Procedural Guarantees	62.33	60.96	I3.1 Quality provisions	50.51	52.73
I 1.2 Number of phases in procedure	56.35	54.87	I3.2 Training level	68.57	59.88
I 1.3 Criteria for interpretation	77.33	64.67	I3.3 Video taping	58.85	59.77
I 1.4 Vulnerable groups	57.56	58.96	I3.4 Directives for magistrates	57.71	67.27
I 1 PROCEDURAL SAFEGUARDS	64.80	62.59	I3.5 Recruitment programme	74.69	58.46
I2.1 Protection and regulation	45.15	47.62	**I 3 QUALITY PROVISIONS**	68.60	63.61
I2.2 Accreditation body	54.19	58.54	**I 4 QUANTITATIVE PROVISIONS**	0.00	50.00
I2.3 Register	58.85	59.77			
I2.4 Code of conduct and procedure	69.21	69.13			

General situation

According to both governmental and professional sources, the United Kingdom's overall score is situated in the lower above average range.

Salient features

There are notable differences between the governmental and professional sources in the basic level indicators 'Criteria for interpretation', and 'Recruitment programme', but the overall image is one of consistency between both sources. The UK stands out as a well-rounded average to above average profile.

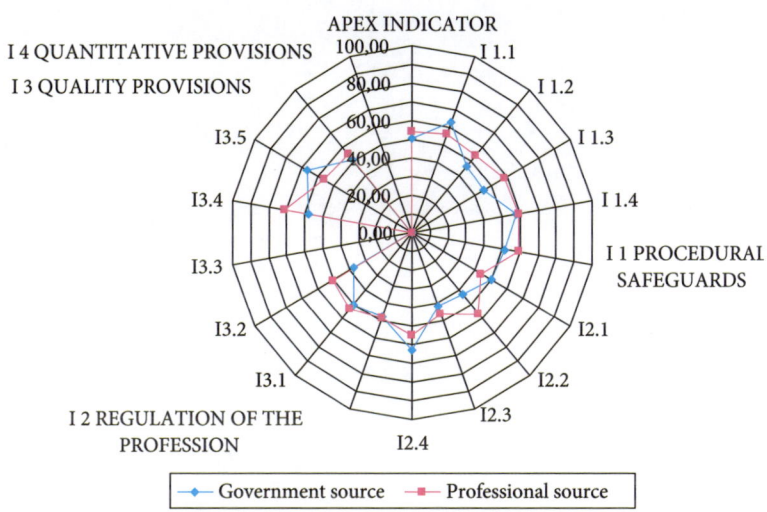

UK : INDICATOR PROFILE TRANSLATION

	T-SCORE GVT	T-SCORE PROF		T-SCORE GVT	T-SCORE PROF
APEX INDICATOR	50.56	54.43	I 2 REGULATION OF THE PROFESSION	48.20	48.71
I 1.1 Procedural Guarantees	62.69	56.67	I3.1 Quality provisions	50.26	52.89
I 1.2 Number of phases in procedure	46.34	54.55	I3.2 Training level	36.92	50.50
I 1.3 Criteria for translation	44.78	58.57	I3.3 Video taping	0.00	0.00
I 1.4 Vulnerable groups	57.56	58.96	I3.4 Directives for magistrates	57.71	71.14
I 1 PROCEDURAL SAFEGUARDS	51.74	59.31	I3.5 Recruitment programme	67.32	56.09
I2.1 Protection and regulation	50.00	43.37	I 3 QUALITY PROVISIONS	51.74	55.27
I2.2 Accreditation body	43.19	56.41	I 4 QUANTITATIVE PROVISIONS	0.00	0.00
I2.3 Register	41.60	46.25			
I2.4 Code of conduct and procedure	62.62	55.22			

General situation

According to both governmental and professional sources, the United Kingdom's overall score is situated in the upper average range.

Salient features

There are notable differences between the governmental and professional sources in the basic level indicators 'Training level', 'Directives for magistrates' and 'Recruitment programme', but the overall image is one of consistency between both sources. The UK stands out as a well-rounded average to above average profile.

CHAPTER IV
SAMPLE COUNTRY PROFILE: AUSTRIA

INTRODUCTION

In this chapter, by way of illustration, a profile of results for the sub-questions underlying the basic level performance indicators is presented for one sample member state. In order to avoid any possible bias in the selection, the first participating country in alphabetical order, Austria, was selected for the purpose of this example.

The full country profile is divided into four sections.

The first section presents the performance indicators and underlying questions concerning the field of legal interpreting.

For each higher level indicator, topographical maps situating Austria's assessment by both governmental and professional sources in the EU are presented. Subsequently, the higher level indicator and its component basic level indicators are presented in bar charts, using the same colour coding as the topographical maps. Finally, the national response frequencies for the underlying items of the questionnaire are shown. To avoid any confusion with the indicator level, expressed by way of T-scores, these graphs have a different colour coding.

The second section, concerning legal translation, is essentially organised in the same way as the first section.

In the third section, the sub-questions concerning future developments are clustered and presented in categories corresponding with Austria's higher level indicators. Again, these graphs are colour coded differently to avoid any confusion with previous sections.

Finally, in a fourth section, some additional information from the Cepej and Spronken-Attinger surveys is presented.

T-scores

To facilitate comparisons between member states or between different indicators within this country profile, the results have been converted to T-scores.

By means of this data conversion technique, a country's score on any given performance indicator is essentially expressed in comparison with the EU average for that indicator. A score of 50 always corresponds with the EU average and every increment of 10 represents a distance of one standard deviation. This allows the stratification of the results in 10 point-bands that may be interpreted as shown in the following table:

Table: interpretation of T-scores

T – score	Category
91 to 100	High (high)
81 to 90	High (low)
71 to 80	Above average (High)
61 to 70	Above average (Low)
51 to 60	Average (High)
41 to 50	Average (Low)
31 to 40	Sub average (High)
21 to 30	Sub average (Low)
11 to 20	Low (High)
0 to 10	Low (low)

This colour coding is used to represent Austria's score on the performance indicators in the topographical maps and bar charts.

1. LEGAL INTERPRETING

INDICATOR 1   PROCEDURAL SAFEGUARDS EU CONTEXTUAL INFORMATION

Procedural safeguards interpreting: government sources

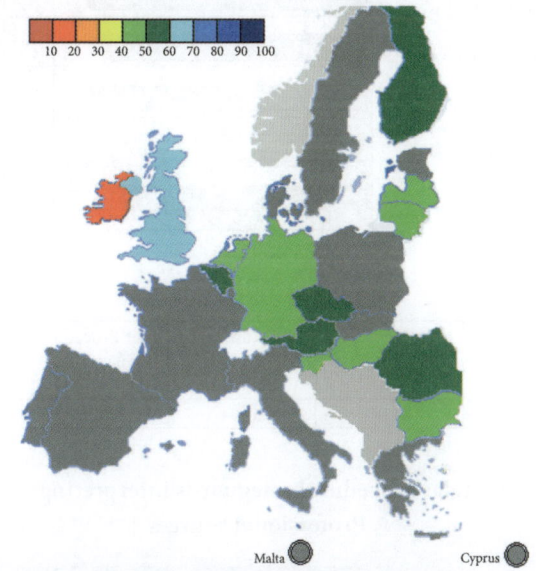

Procedural safeguards interpreting: professional sources

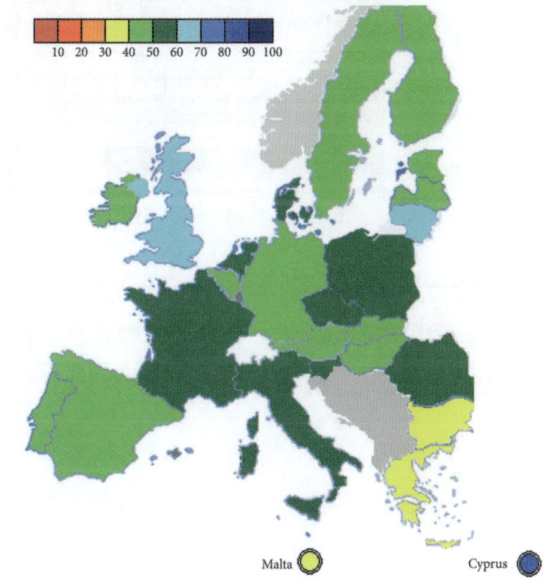

INDICATOR 1   PROCEDURAL SAFEGUARDS

Austria: Procedural safeguards interpreting Government sources

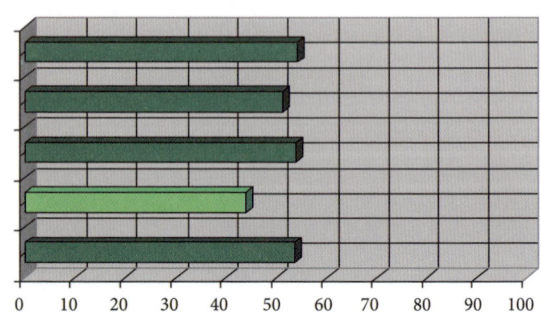

	I 1.4 Vulnerable groups	I 1.3 Criteria for interpretation	I 1.2 Number of phases in procedure	I 1.1 Procedural Guarantees	I 1 PROCEDURAL SAFEGUARDS
T Score	53,62	44,00	53,94	51,22	54,27

Austria: Procedural safeguards interpreting Professional sources

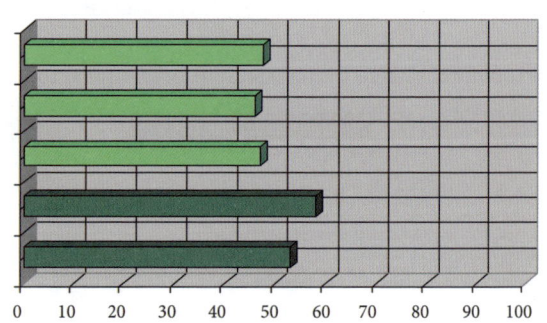

	I 1.4 Vulnerable groups	I 1.3 Criteria for interpretation	I 1.2 Number of phases in procedure	I 1.1 Procedural Guarantees	I 1 PROCEDURAL SAFEGUARDS
T Score	52,71	58,00	46,90	45,89	47,41

INDICATOR 1   PROCEDURAL SAFEGUARDS

General situation

According to governmental sources, Austria's score is situated in the upper average range, whereas according to the professional sources the country scores in the lower average range.

Salient features

For the basic level indicators 'Procedural guarantees', 'Number of phases in the procedure' and 'Criteria for interpretation', both respondent groups seem to have an inverted scoring pattern.

BASIC LEVEL INDICATOR 1 PROCEDURAL SAFEGUARDS UNDERLYING QUESTION PROFILES

I1.1 Procedural guarantees

3. National or regional requirements concerning legal interpreting (Professional sources)

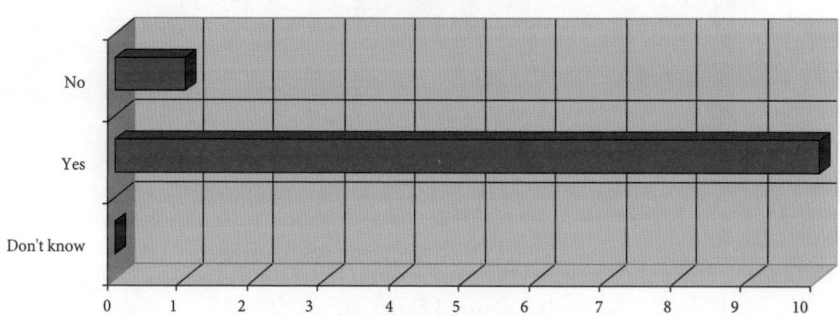

3. National or regional requirements concerning legal interpreting (Government sources)

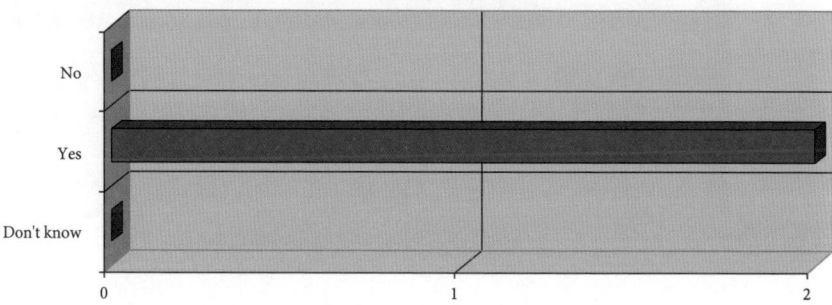

5. Existence of established procedure for ascertaining when there is a need for
translation or interpreting in criminal proceedings
(Professional sources)

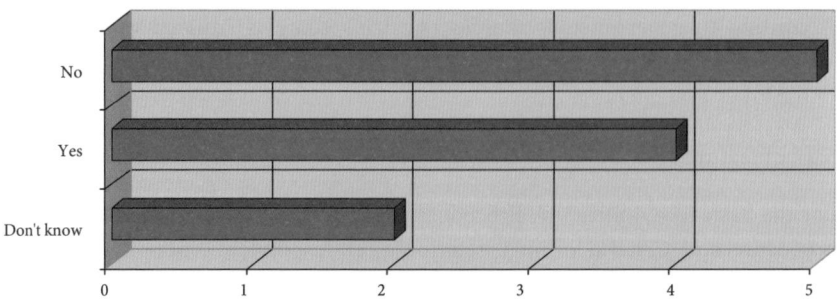

5. Existence of established procedure for ascertaining when there is a need for
translation or interpreting in criminal proceedings
(Government sources)

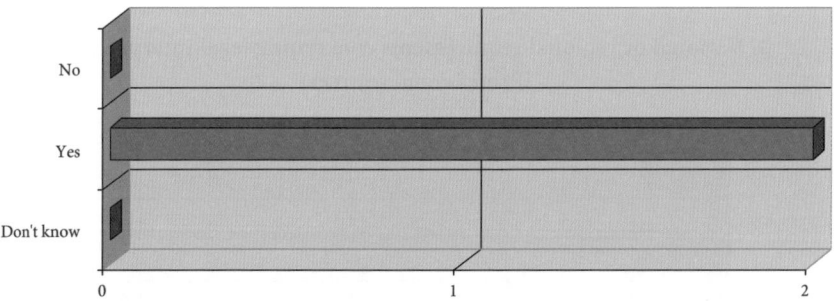

17. Is there any monitoring of the provision of legal interpreting or translation
in criminal proceedings?
(Professional sources)

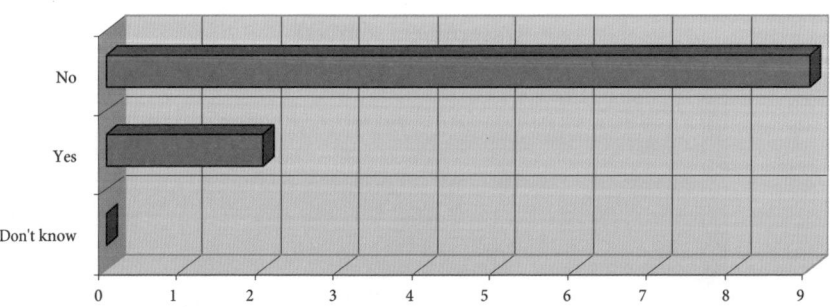

17. Is there any monitoring of the provision of legal interpreting or translation in criminal proceedings?
(Government sources)

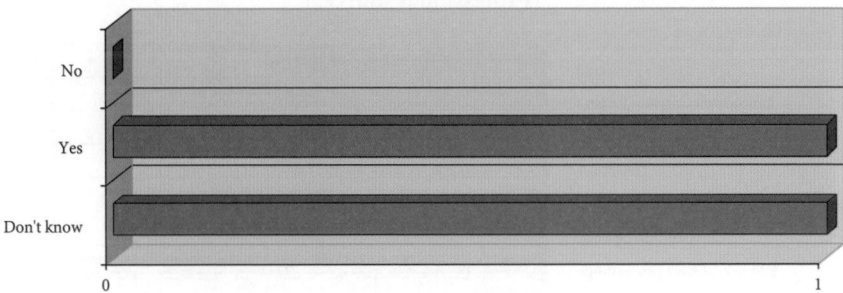

18. Are there national sanctions if the State fails to provide interpretation and translation when a person is entitled to it?
(Professional sources)

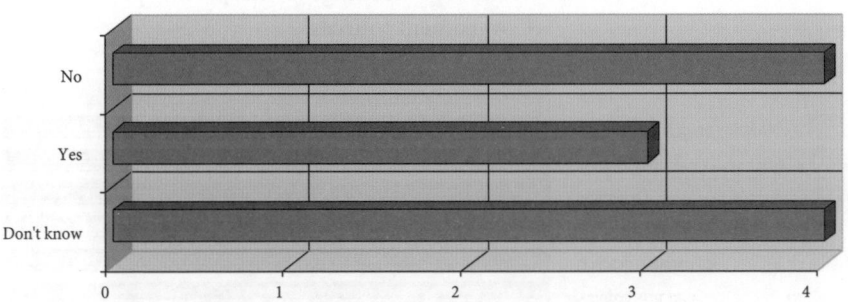

18. Are there national sanctions if the State fails to provide interpretation and translation when a person is entitled to it?
(Government sources)

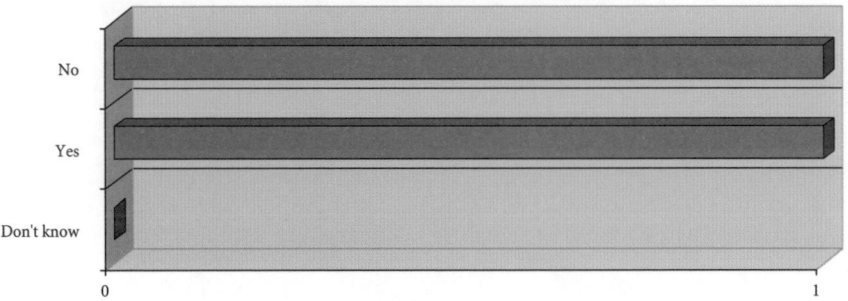

I1.2 Number of phases in the procedure

10. At what stages of the criminal proceedings is interpreting provided?
(Professional sources)

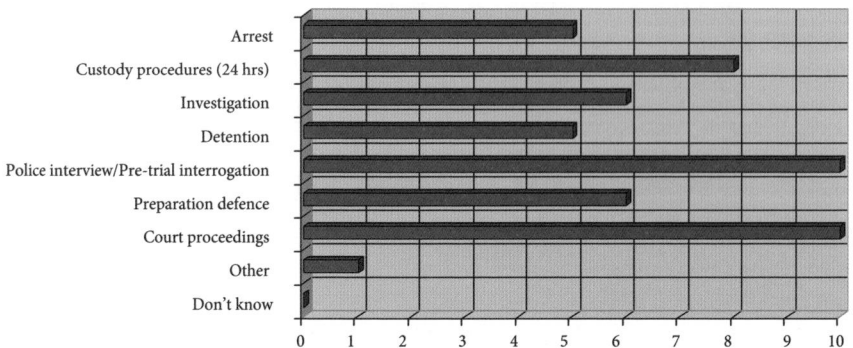

10. At what stages of the criminal proceedings is interpreting provided?
(Government sources)

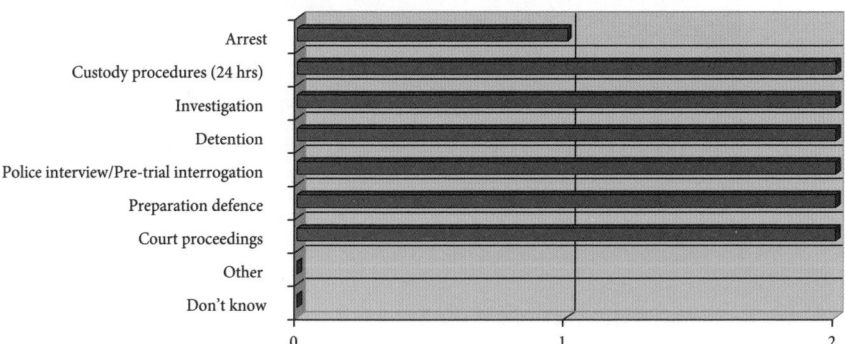

I1.3 Criteria for interpretation

12. Are there any criteria that establish the extent to which the proceedings should be interpreted?
(Professional sources)

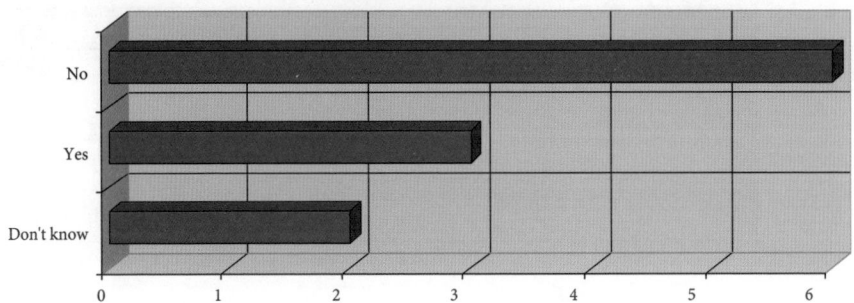

12. Are there any criteria that establish the extent to which the proceedings should be interpreted?
(Government sources)

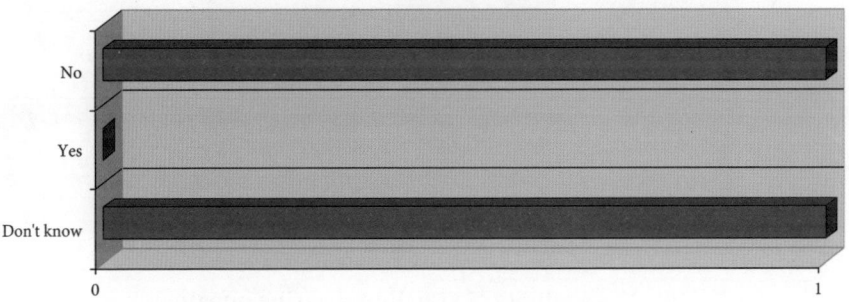

II.4 Vulnerable groups

19a. Vulnerability of foreign nationals
(Professional sources)

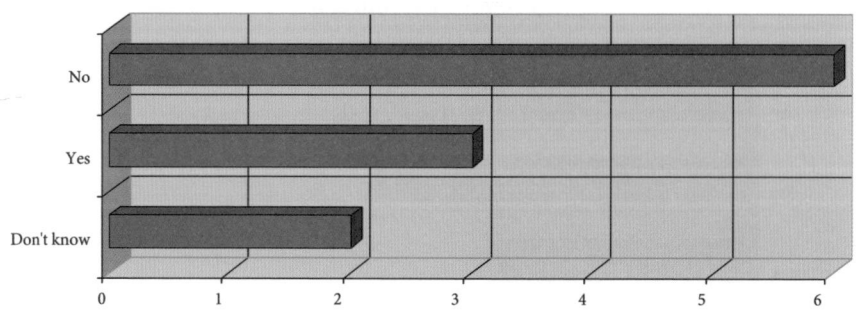

19a. Vulnerability of foreign nationals
(Government sources)

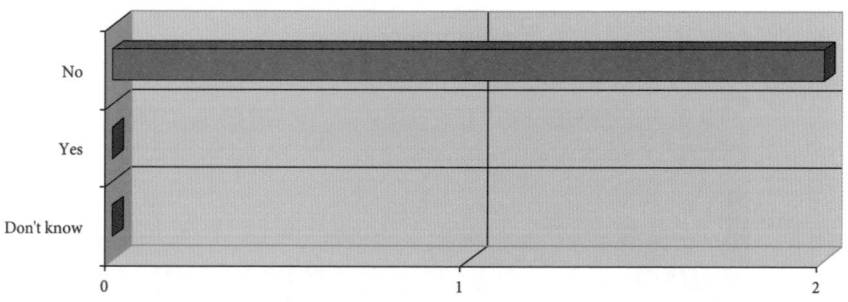

19b. Vulnerability of visually or hearing impaired
(Professional sources)

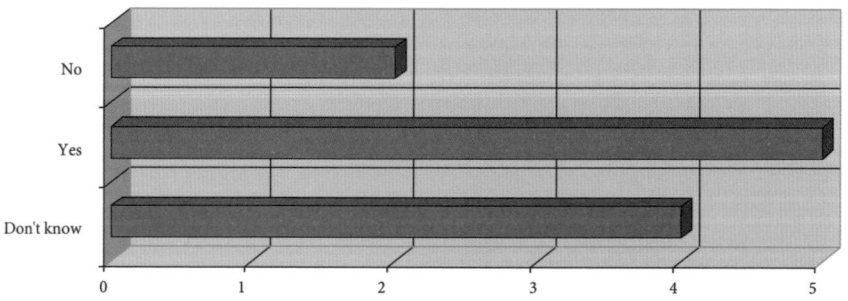

19b. Vulnerability of visually or hearing impaired
(Government sources)

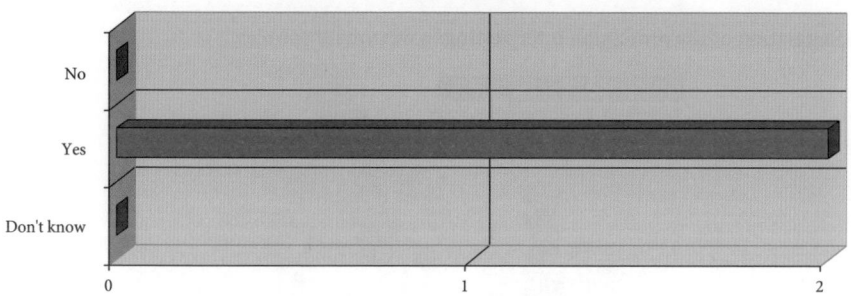

19c. Vulnerability of individuals with insufficient proficiency in the necessary language
(Professional sources)

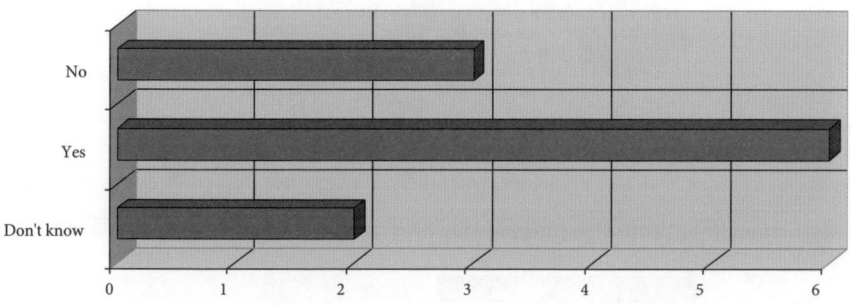

19c. Vulnerability of individuals with insufficient proficiency in the necessary language
(Government sources)

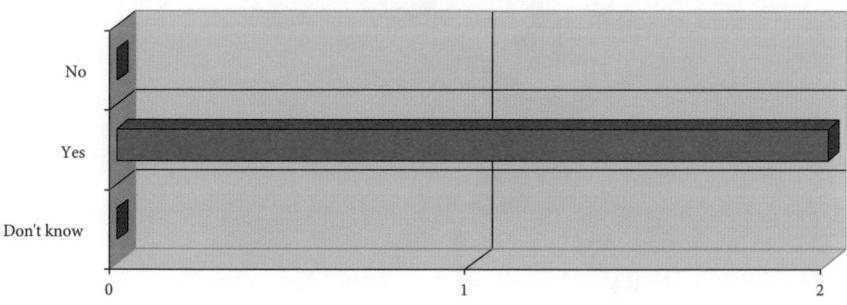

INDICATOR 2   REGULATION OF THE PROFESSION EU CONTEXTUAL INFORMATION

Regulation of the profession interpreting: government sources

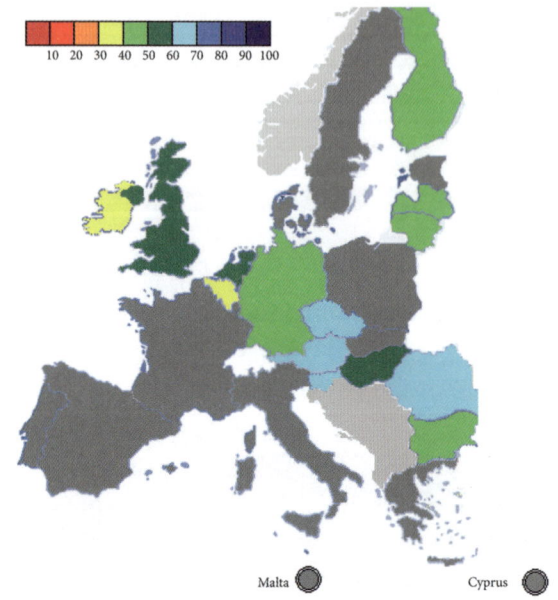

Regulation of the profession interpreting: professional sources

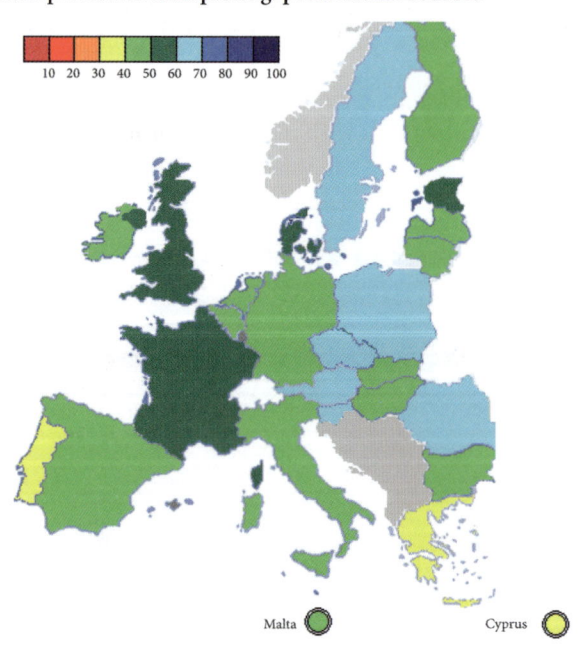

INDICATOR 2   REGULATION OF THE PROFESSION

Austria: Regulation of the profession (interpreting)
Government sources

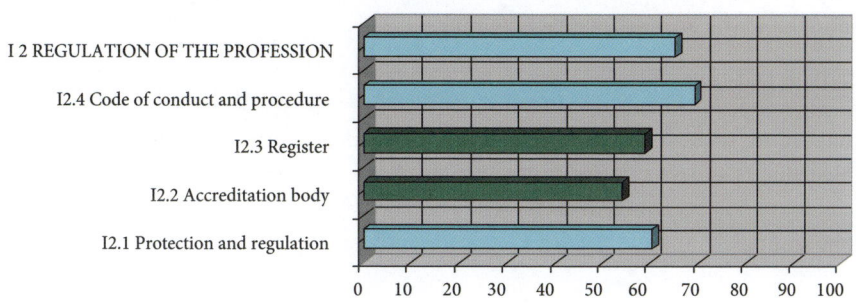

	I 2.1 Protection and regulation	I 2.2 Accreditation body	I 2.3 Register	I 2.4 Code of conduct and procedure	I 2 REGULATION OF THE PROFESSION
T Score	60,30	54,19	58,85	69,21	65,19

Austria: Regulation of the profession (interpreting)
Professional sources

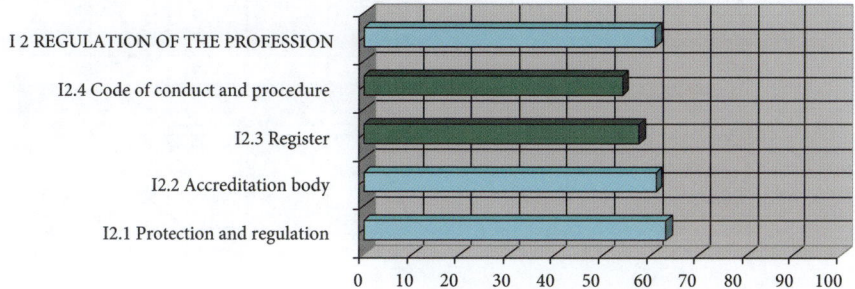

	I 2.1 Protection and regulation	I 2.2 Accreditation body	I 2.3 Register	I 2.4 Code of conduct and procedure	I 2 REGULATION OF THE PROFESSION
T Score	63,10	60,98	57,50	53,91	60,90

INDICATOR 2   REGULATION OF THE PROFESSION

General situation

According to both governmental and professional sources, Austria's score is situated in the lower above average range.

Salient features

According to both governmental and professional sources, the basic indicator 'Register' is situated in the upper average range, whereas the indicators 'Code of conduct and procedure' and 'Accreditation body' are placed in the same range by one source.

BASIC LEVEL INDICATOR 2 REGULATION OF THE PROFESSION
UNDERLYING QUESTION PROFILES

I2.1 Protection and regulation

21. Is the title of legal interpreter protected?
(Professional sources)

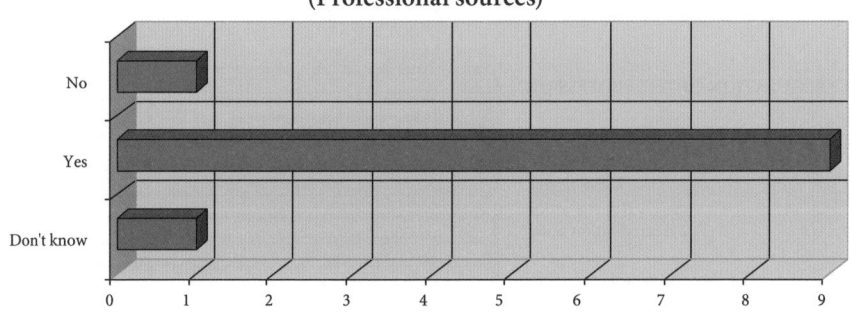

21. Is the title of legal interpreter protected?
(Government sources)

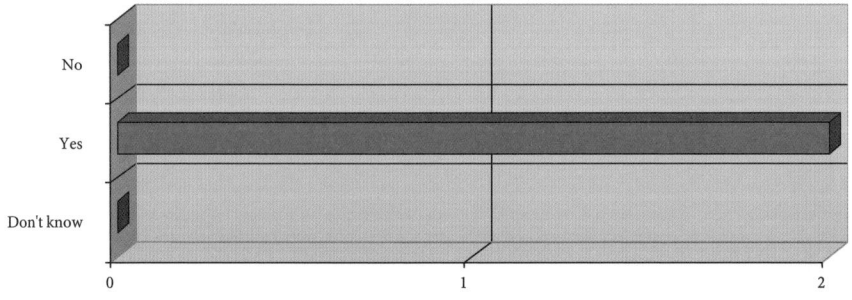

22. Is the profession of legal interpreter regulated?
(Professional sources)

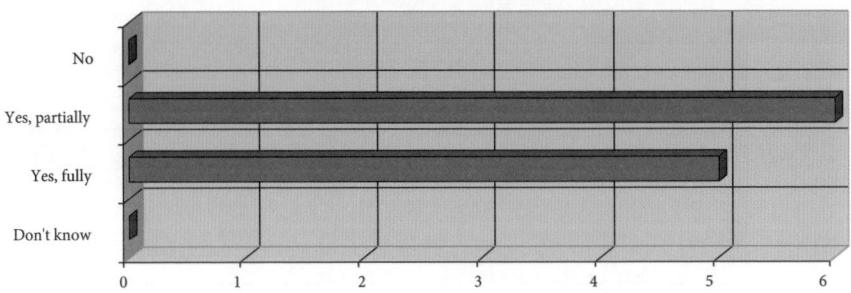

22. Is the profession of legal interpreter regulated?
(Government sources)

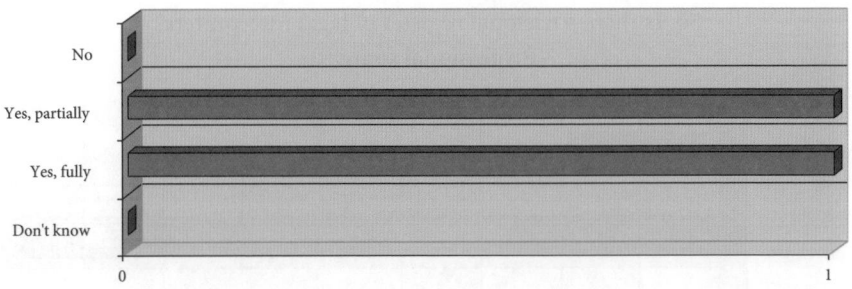

I2.2 Accreditation body

44. Is there an accrediting body for the accreditation of legal interpreters?
(Professional sources)

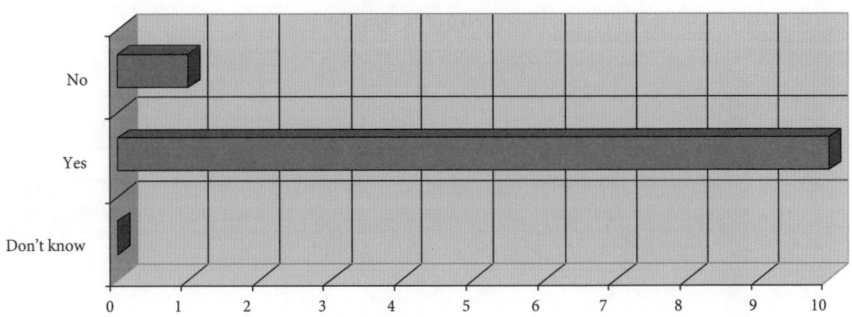

44. Is there an accrediting body for the accreditation of legal interpreters?
(Government sources)

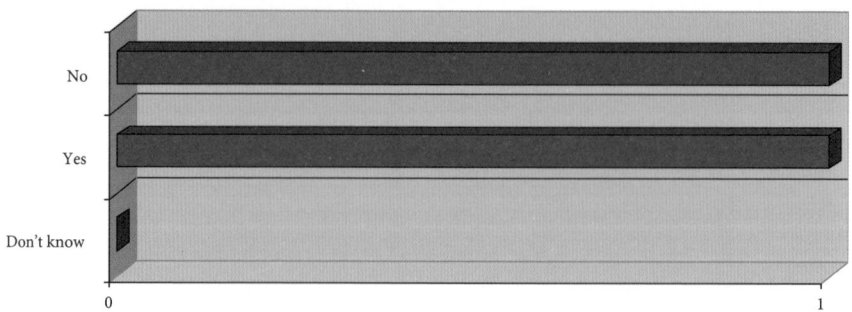

I2.3 Register

50. Is there a national register of legal interpreters?
(Professional sources)

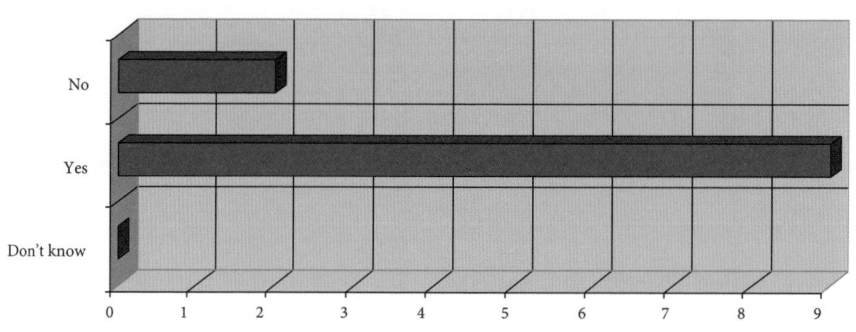

50. Is there a national register of legal interpreters?
(Government sources)

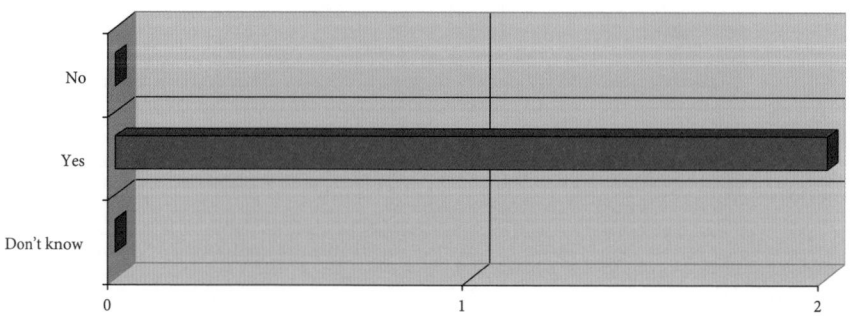

50. Is there a national register, what data is provided in the register?

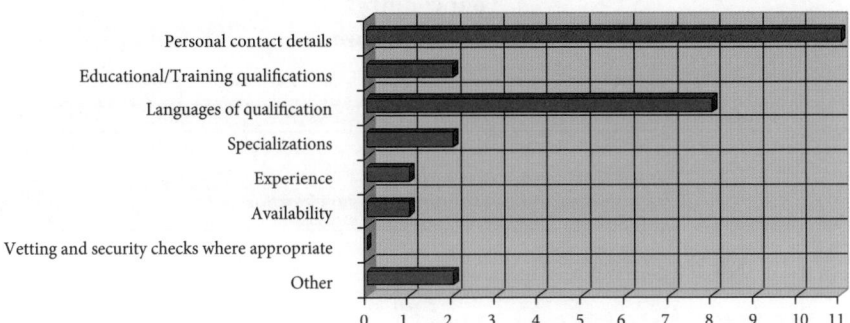

I2.4 Code of conduct and procedure

58. Is there a national or regional Code of Conduct for legal interpreters in your country?
(Professional sources)

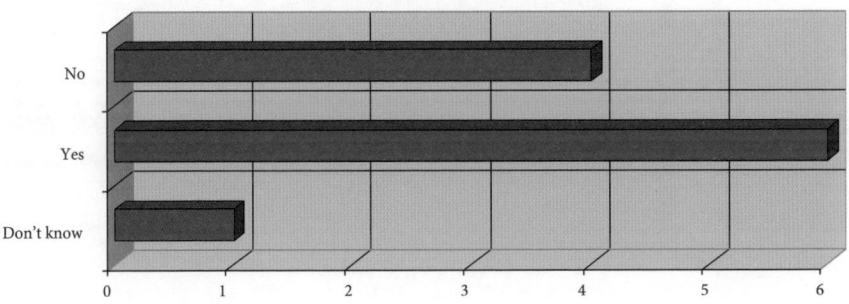

58. Is there a national or regional Code of Conduct for legal interpreters in your country?
(Government sources)

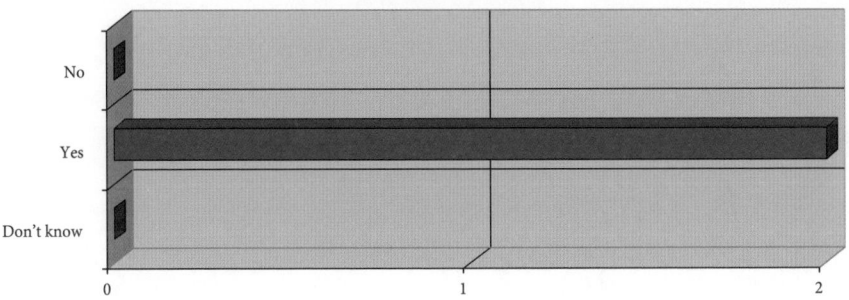

62. Is there a disciplinary procedures system in relation to legal interpreters in your country?
(Professional sources)

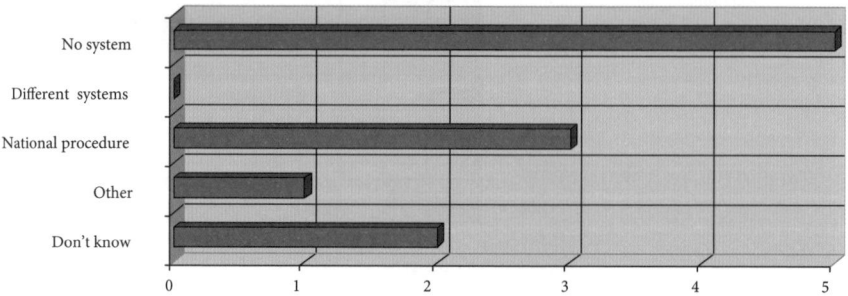

62. Is there a disciplinary procedures system in relation to legal interpreters in your country?
(Government sources)

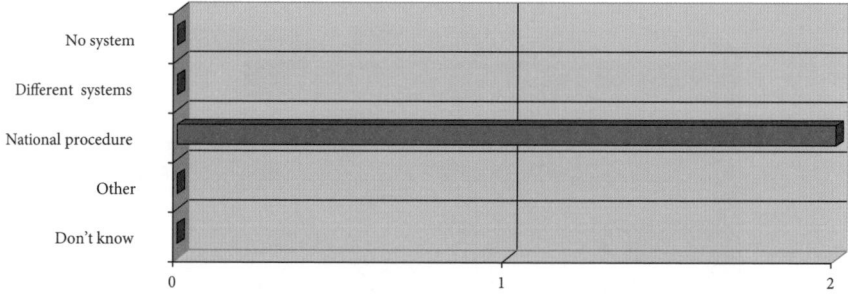

INDICATOR 3 QUALITY PROVISIONS EU CONTEXTUAL INFORMATION

Quality provisions interpreting: government sources

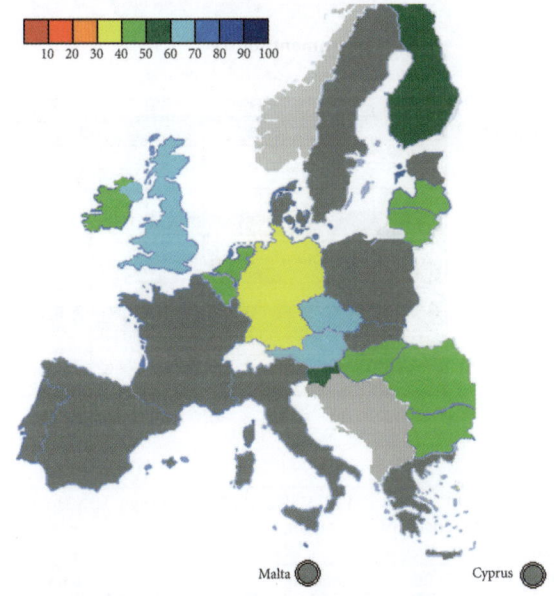

Quality provisions interpreting: professional sources

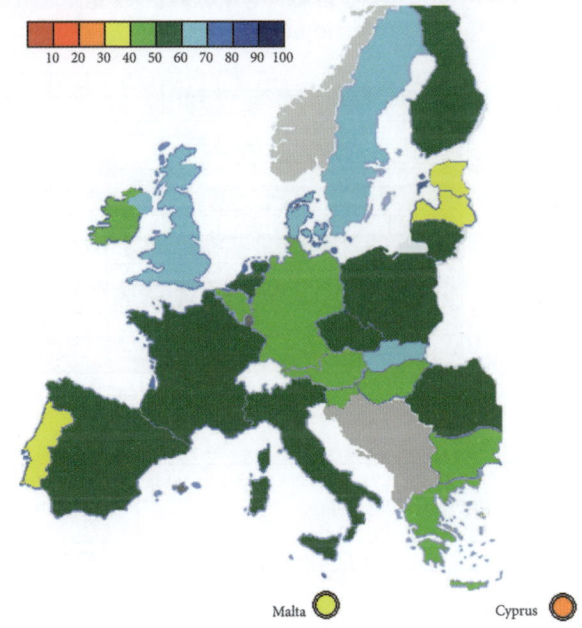

INDICATOR 3   QUALITY PROVISIONS

Austria: Quality provisions interpreting
Government sources

Government source

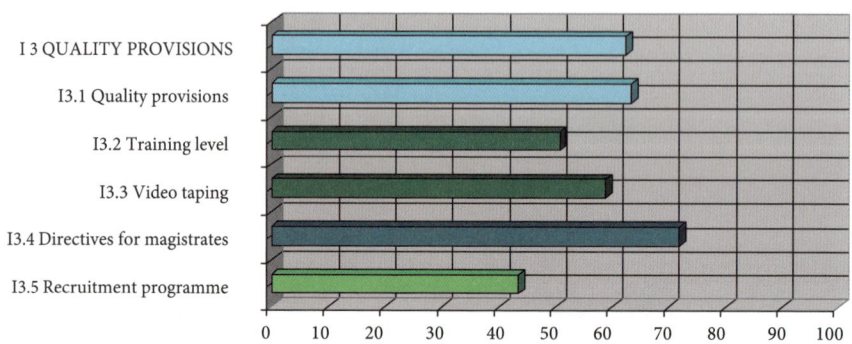

	I 3.5 Recruitment programme	I 3.4 Directives for magistrates	I 3.3 Video taping	I 3.2 Training level	I 3.1 Quality provisions	I 3 QUALITY PROVISIONS
T Score	43,44	72,00	58,85	50,71	63,33	62,39

Austria: Quality provisions interpreting
Professional sources

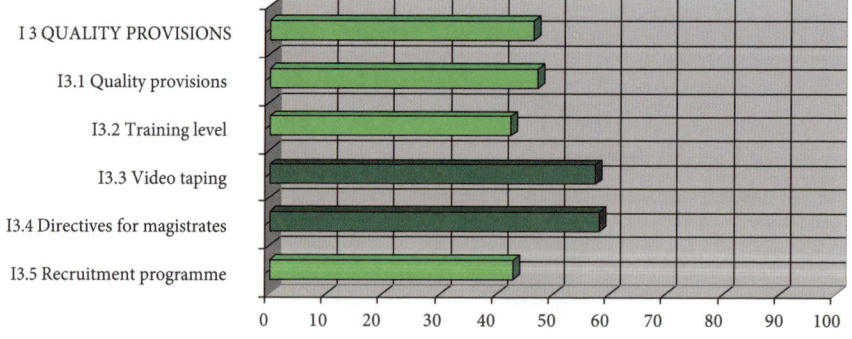

	I 3.5 Recruitment programme	I 3.4 Directives for magistrates	I 3.3 Video taping	I 3.2 Training level	I 3.1 Quality provisions	I 3 QUALITY PROVISIONS
T Score	43,08	58,18	57,50	42,59	47,27	46,54

INDICATOR 3   QUALITY PROVISIONS

General situation

According to governmental sources, Austria's score is situated in the lower above average range, whereas according to the professional sources the country scores in the lower average range.

Salient features

Both sources are in agreement on the basic level indicators 'Video taping' and 'Recruitment programme'. All other indicators are systematically scored higher by the government source. 'Directives for magistrates' is situated in the higher above average range by the government source.

BASIC LEVEL INDICATOR 3 QUALITY PROVISIONS UNDERLYING QUESTION PROFILES

I3.1 Quality provisions

27. Are there binding provisions regarding the quality of legal interpreting and translation in criminal proceedings?
Interpreters (Professional sources)

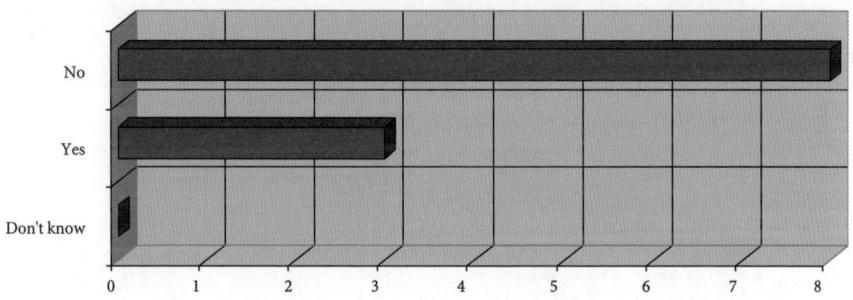

27. Are there binding provisions regarding the quality of legal interpreting and translation in criminal proceedings?
Interpreters (Government sources)

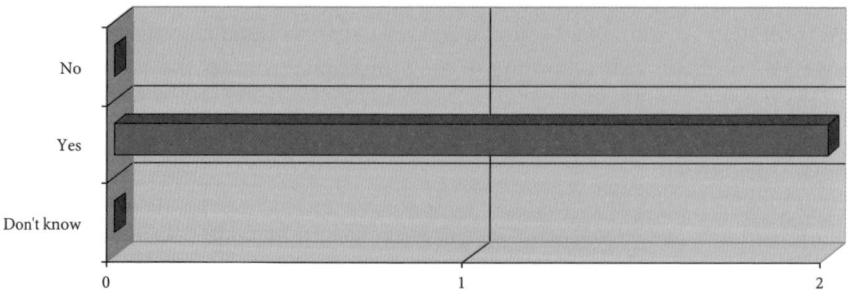

67. Is the quality of practice of legal interpreting or translation in criminal proceedings monitored?
Interpreters (Professional sources)

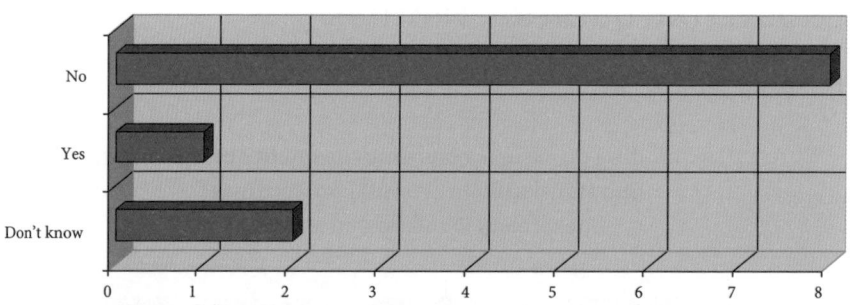

67. Is the quality of practice of legal interpreting or translation in criminal proceedings monitored?
Interpreters (Government sources)

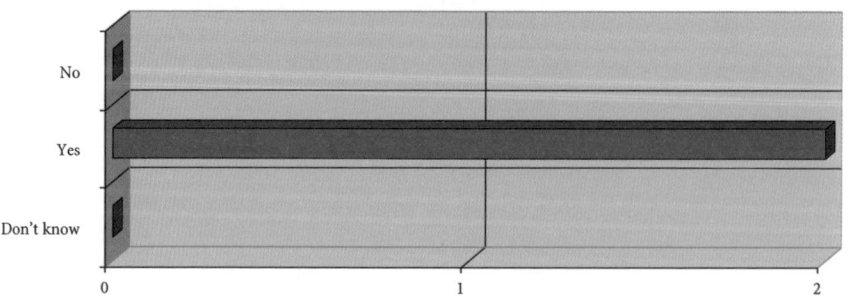

I3.2 Training level

40. What kind of training is available for training legal interpreters?
(Professional sources)

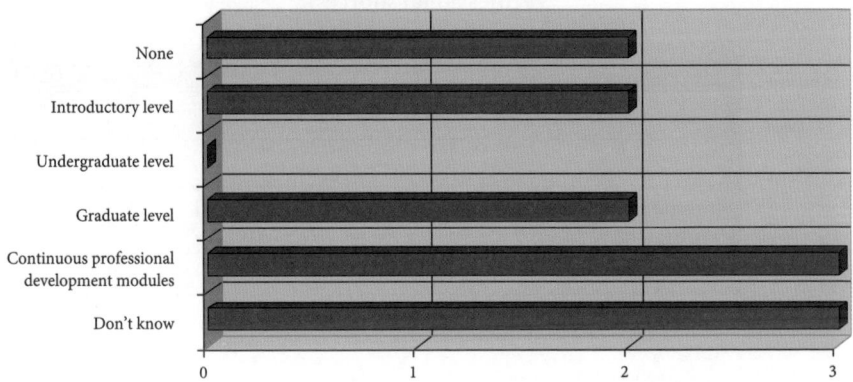

40. What kind of training is available for training legal interpreters?
(Government sources)

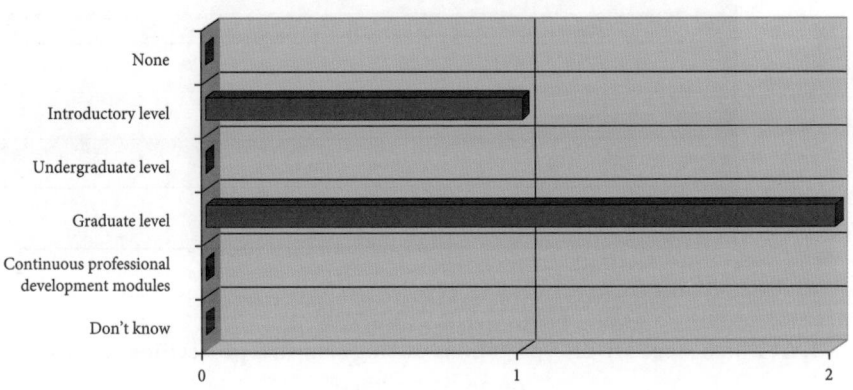

I3.3 Video taping

70. Are interpretations during criminal proceedings recorded on audio or video?
(Professional sources)

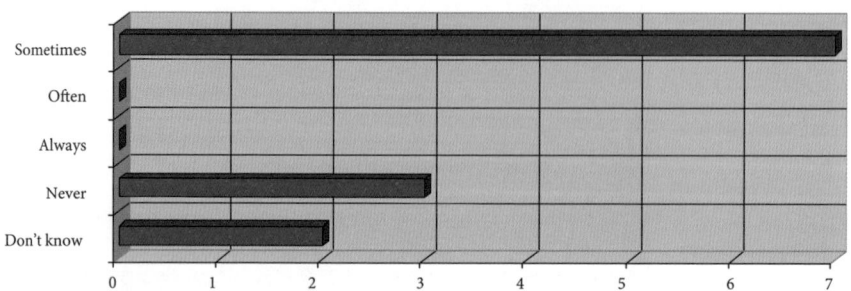

70. Are interpretations during criminal proceedings recorded on audio or video?
(Government sources)

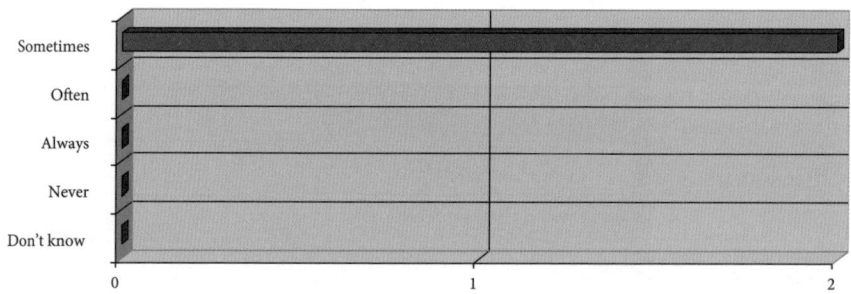

71. At which stage are interpretations during criminal proceedings recorded on audio or video?
(Professional sources)

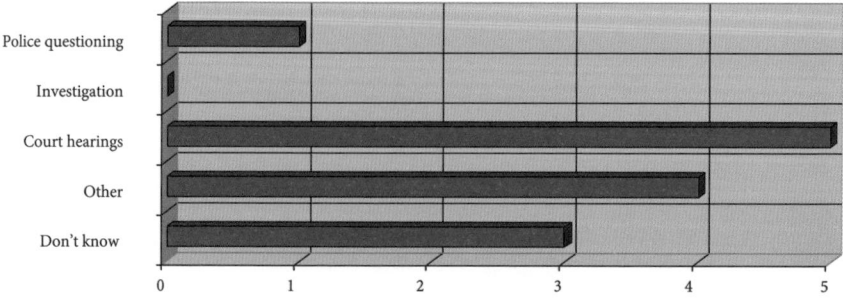

71. At which stage are interpretations during criminal proceedings recorded on audio or video?
(Government sources)

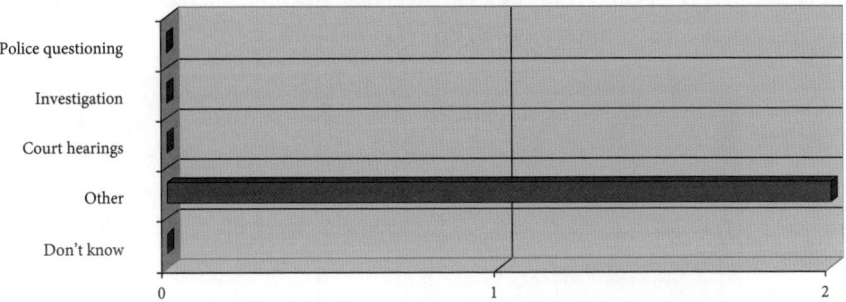

I3.4 Directives for magistrates

72. What good practice guidelines exist for members of the legal services on how to work with legal interpreters or translators?
(Professional sources)

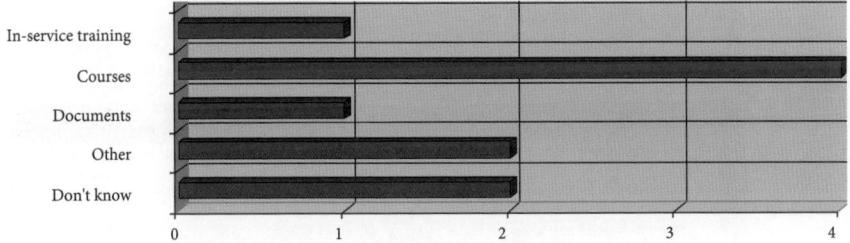

72. What good practice guidelines exist for members of the legal services on how to work with legal interpreters or translators?
(Government sources)

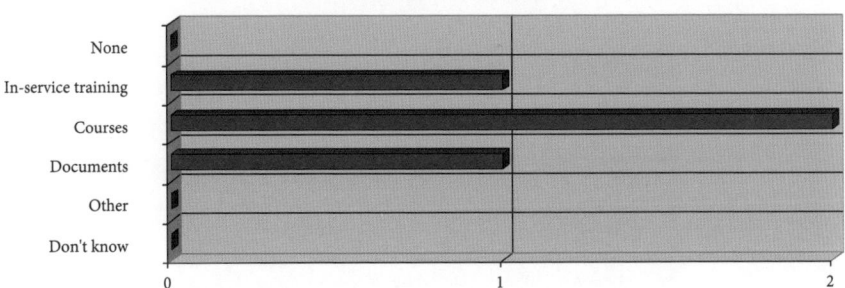

I3.5 Recruitment programme

73. Is there a national or regional programme to increase numbers and quality of legal interpreters and translators to meet demand and demographic changes? Interpreters (Professional sources)

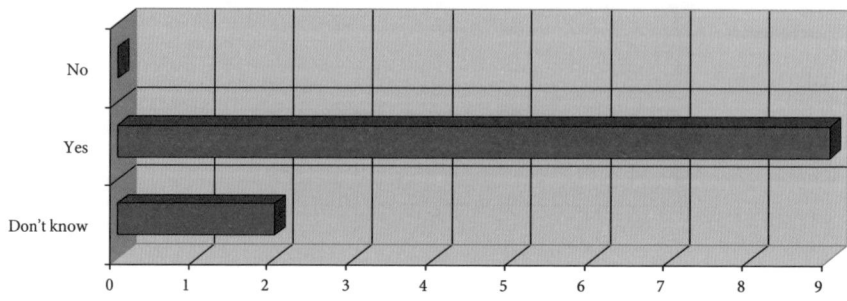

73. Is there a national or regional programme to increase numbers and quality of legal interpreters and translators to meet demand and demographic changes? Interpreters (Government sources)

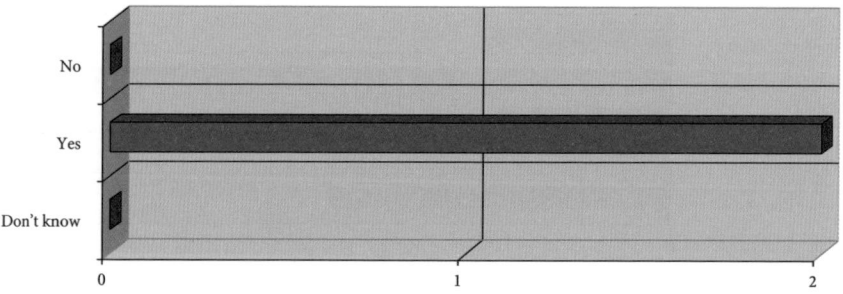

INDICATOR 4   QUANTITATIVE PROVISIONS EU
CONTEXTUAL INFORMATION

Quantitative provisions interpreting: government sources

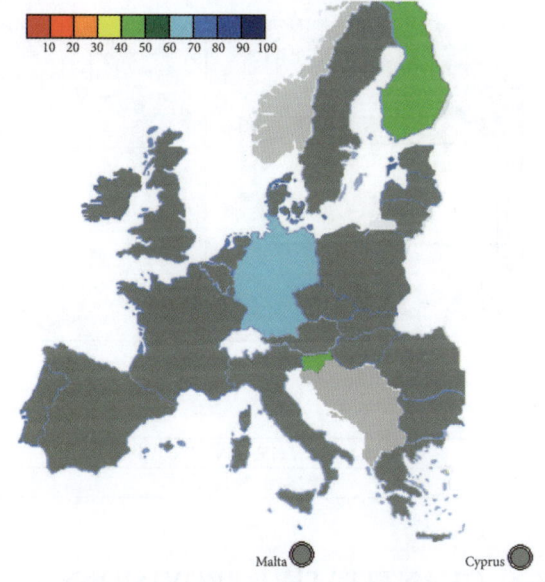

Quantitative provisions interpreting: professional sources

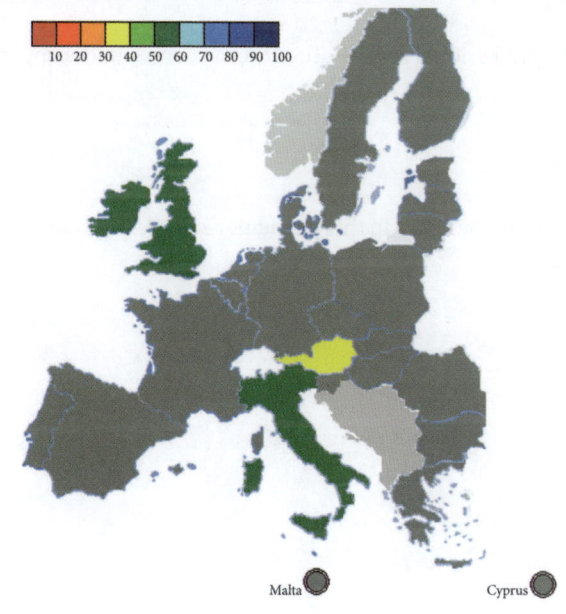

INDICATOR 4   QUANTITATIVE PROVISIONS

**Austria: Quantitative provisions interpreting
Professional sources**

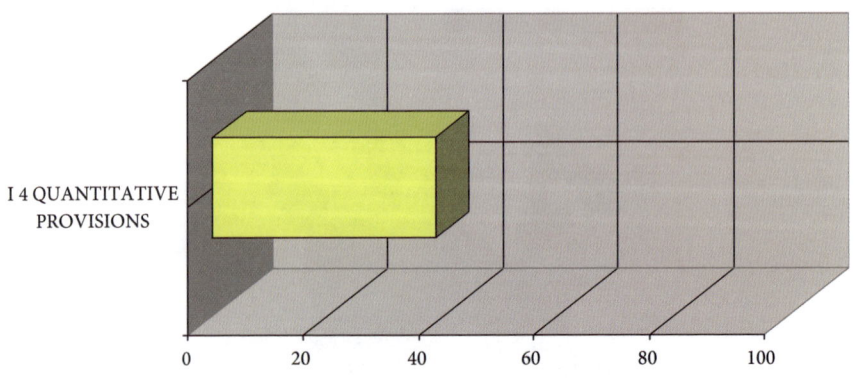

	I 4 QUANTITATIVE PROVISIONS
T Score	38,45

INDICATOR 4   QUANTITATIVE PROVISIONS

General situation

According to the professional sources, the country scores in the upper sub average range.

Salient features

As there are only four countries in this particular sample, the basis for comparison is rather narrow.

INDICATOR 4   QUANTITATIVE PROVISIONS
UNDERLYING QUESTION PROFILES

75. In how many cases is a legal interpreter currently required?

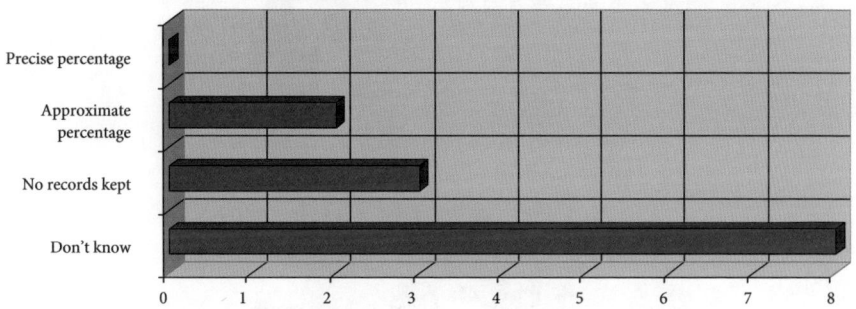

Approximate percentage	15%
Approximate percentage	10%

APEX INDICATOR EU CONTEXTUAL INFORMATION

Overall score interpreting: government sources

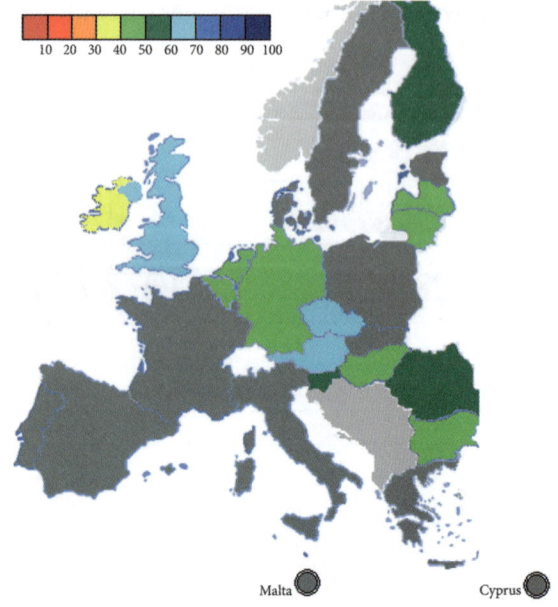

Overall score interpreting: professional sources

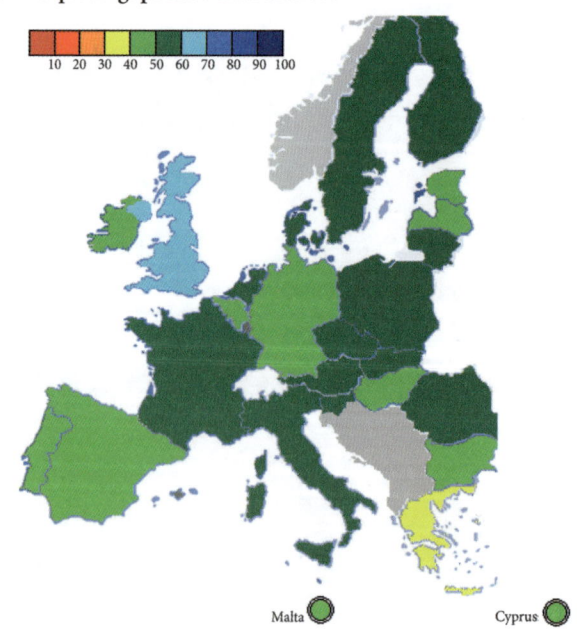

APEX AUSTRIA INDICATOR PROFILE

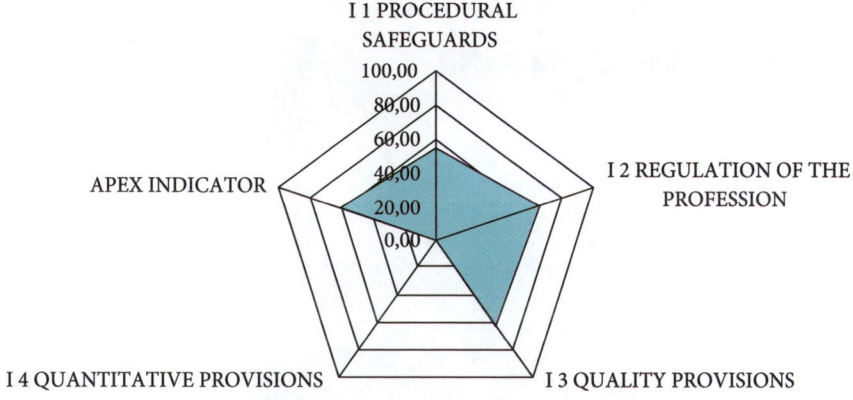

Austria: main indicators interpreting Government sources

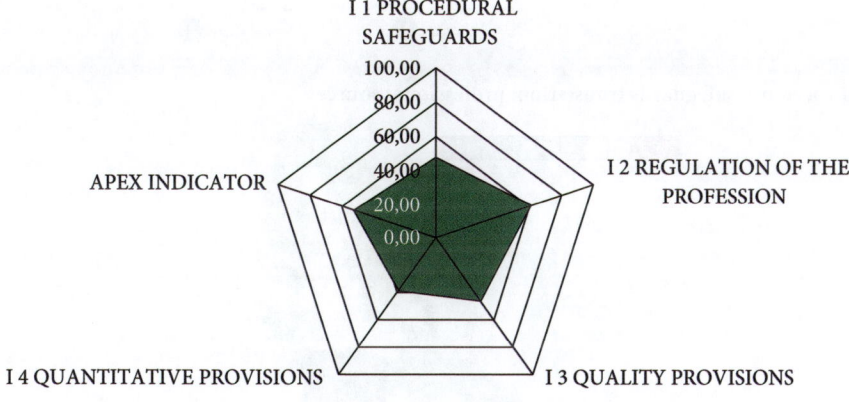

Austria: main indicators interpreting Professional sources

General situation

According to governmental sources, Austria's overall score is situated in the lower above average band, whereas the professional sources situate the country in the upper average range.

2. LEGAL TRANSLATION

INDICATOR 1 PROCEDURAL SAFEGUARDS EU CONTEXTUAL INFORMATION

Procedural safeguards translation: government sources

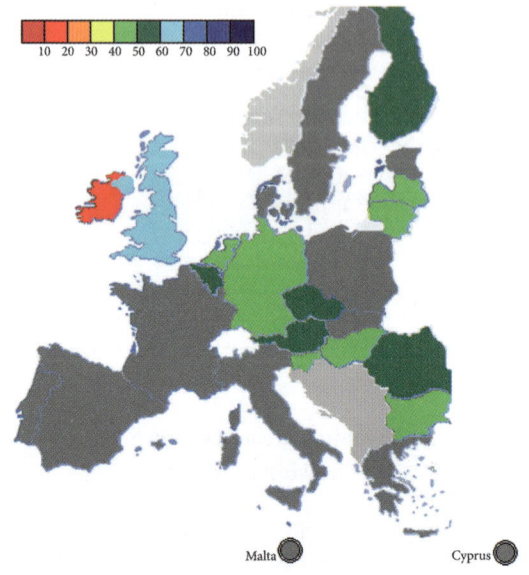

Procedural safeguards translation: professional sources

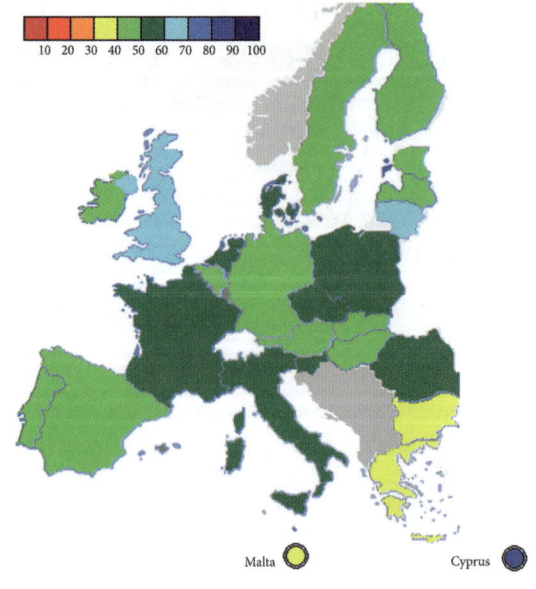

INDICATOR 1   PROCEDURAL SAFEGUARDS

Austria: Procedural safeguards translation
Government sources

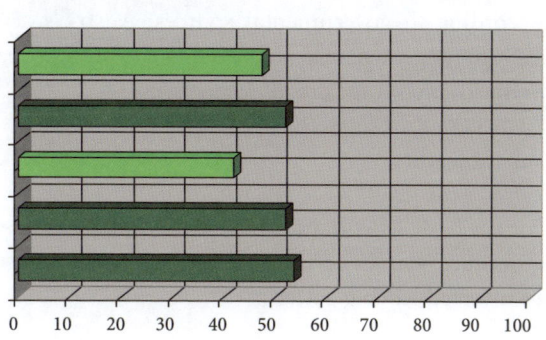

	I 1.4 Vulnerable groups	I 1.3 Criteria for translation	I 1.2 Number of phases in procedure	I 1.1 Procedural Guarantees	I 1 PROCEDURAL SAFEGUARDS
T Score	53,62	52,13	41,88	51,94	47,44

Austria: Procedural safeguards translation
Professional sources

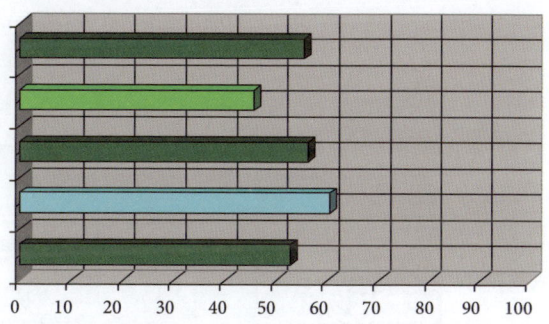

	I 1.4 Vulnerable groups	I 1.3 Criteria for translation	I 1.2 Number of phases in procedure	I 1.1 Procedural Guarantees	I 1 PROCEDURAL SAFEGUARDS
T Score	52,71	60,61	56,20	45,56	55,35

INDICATOR 1   PROCEDURAL SAFEGUARDS

General situation

According to governmental sources, Austria's score is situated in the upper average range, whereas according to the professional sources the country scores in the lower average range.

Salient features

For the basic level indicators 'Procedural guarantees', 'Number of phases in the procedure' and 'Criteria for interpretation', both respondent groups seem to have an inverted scoring pattern.

BASIC LEVEL INDICATOR 1 PROCEDURAL SAFEGUARDS UNDERLYING QUESTION PROFILES

I1.1 Procedural guarantees

4. National or regional requirements concerning legal translation
(Professional sources)

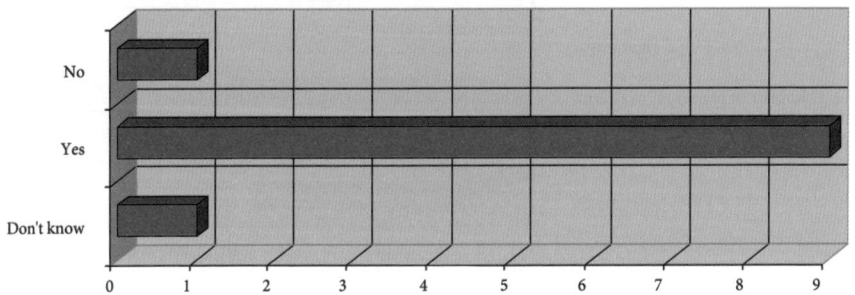

4. National or regional requirements concerning legal translation
(Government sources)

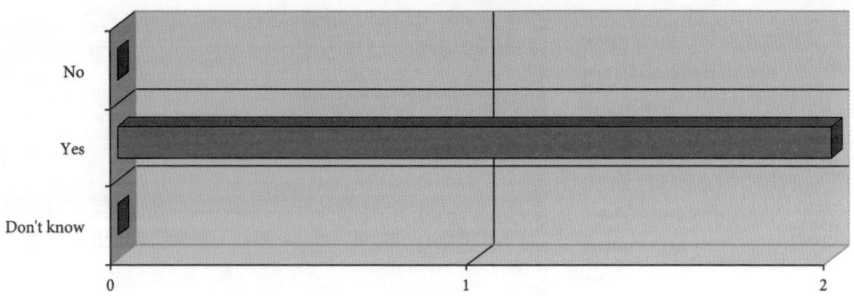

Please also refer to part 1. Legal Interpreting for the relevant corresponding graphs

I1.2 Number of phases in the procedure

11. At what stages of the criminal proceedings is translation provided?
(Professional sources)

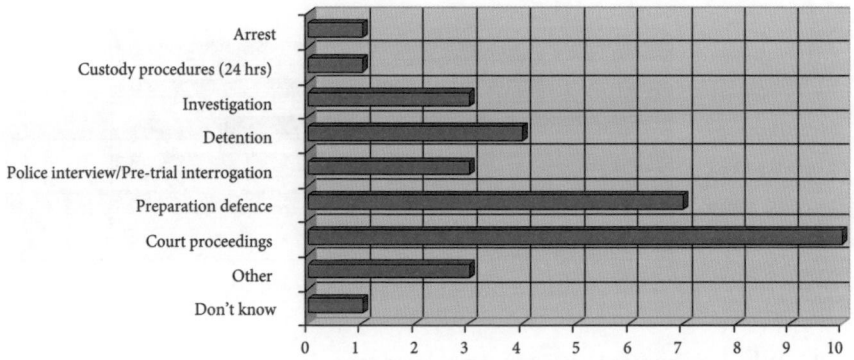

11. At what stages of the criminal proceedings is translation provided?
(Government sources)

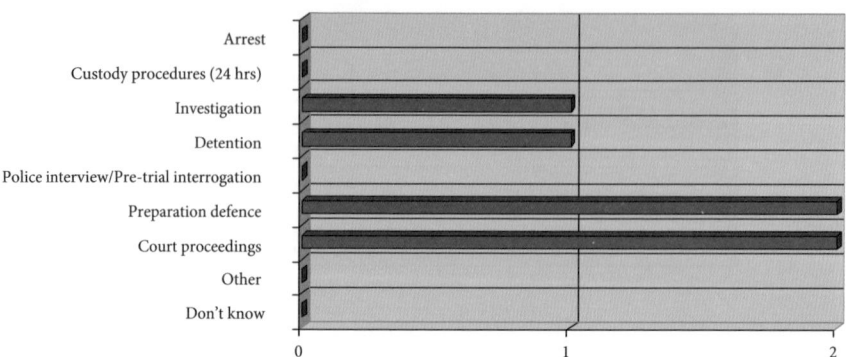

II.3 Criteria for translation

13. Which documents must be translated in order to ensure the minimum necessary for a fair trial?
(Professional sources)

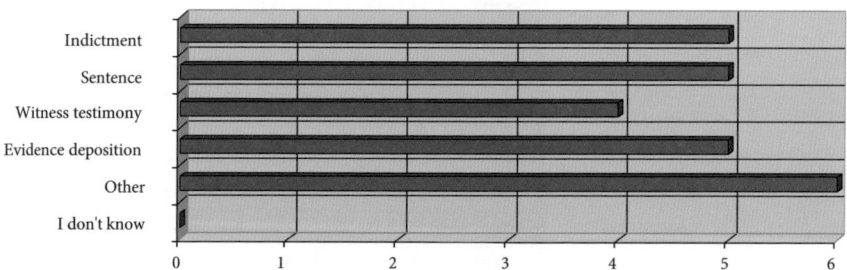

13. Which documents must be translated in order to ensure the minimum necessary for a fair trial?
(Government sources)

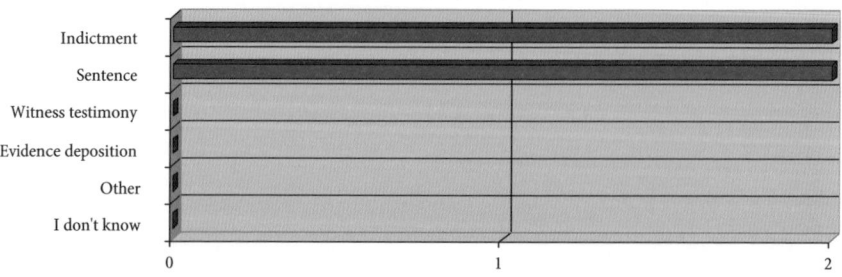

14. Are there limitations on translation in criminal proceedings?

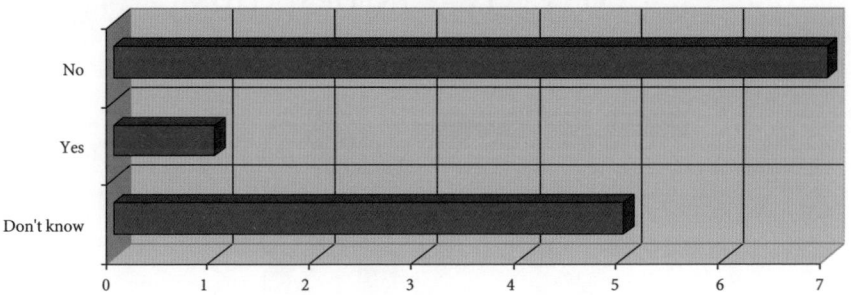

I1.4 Vulnerable groups

Please refer to part 1. Legal interpreting for the relevant corresponding graphs

INDICATOR 2 REGULATION OF THE PROFESSION EU CONTEXTUAL INFORMATION

Regulation of the profession translation: government sources

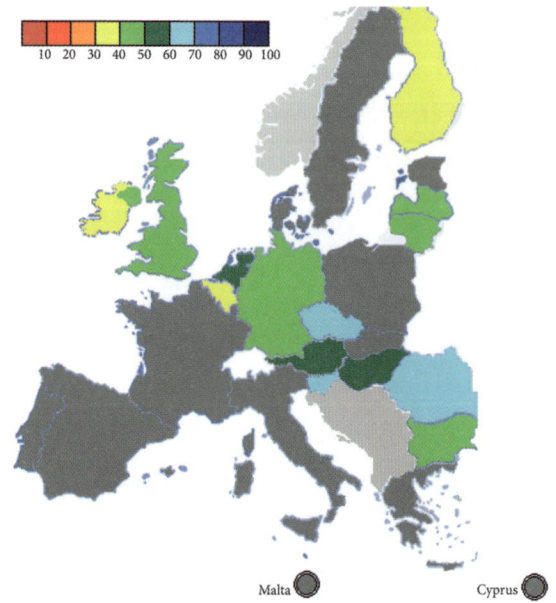

Regulation of the profession translation: professional sources

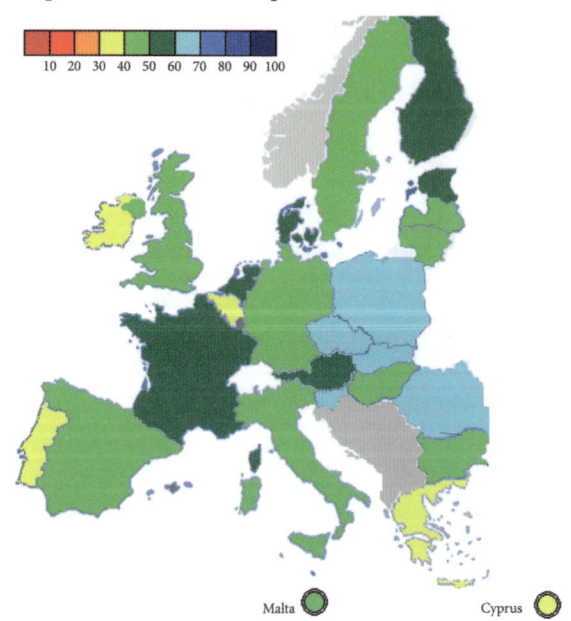

INDICATOR 2   REGULATION OF THE PROFESSION

Austria: Regulation of the profession (translation)
Government sources

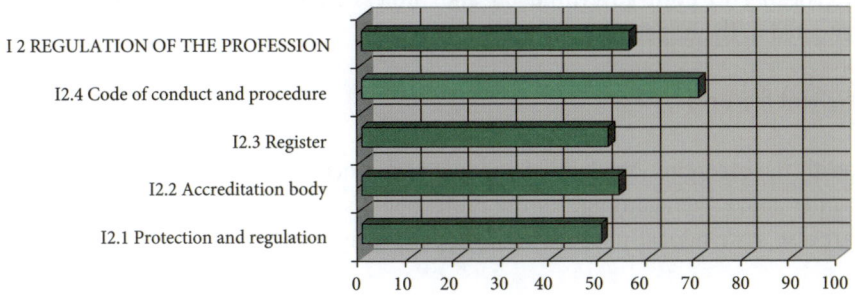

	I 2.1 Protection and regulation	I 2.2 Accreditation body	I 2.3 Register	I 2.4 Code of conduct and procedure	I 2 REGULATION OF THE PROFESSION
T Score	50	53,83	51,60	70,31	56,14

Austria: Regulation of the profession (translation)
Professional sources

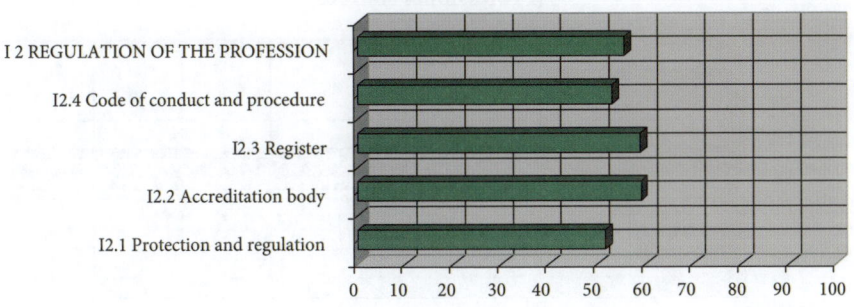

	I 2.1 Protection and regulation	I 2.2 Accreditation body	I 2.3 Register	I 2.4 Code of conduct and procedure	I 2 REGULATION OF THE PROFESSION
T Score	51,51	58,97	58,75	53,04	55,45

INDICATOR 2   REGULATION OF THE PROFESSION

General situation

According to both governmental and professional sources, Austria's score is situated in the upper average range.

Salient features

With the exception of 'Code of conduct and procedure', which is situated in the upper above average range by the professional sources, all basic level indicators are also systematically scored in the upper average range.

BASIC LEVEL INDICATOR 2 REGULATION OF THE PROFESSION
UNDERLYING QUESTION PROFILES

I2.1 Protection and regulation

23. Is the title of legal translator protected?
(Professional sources)

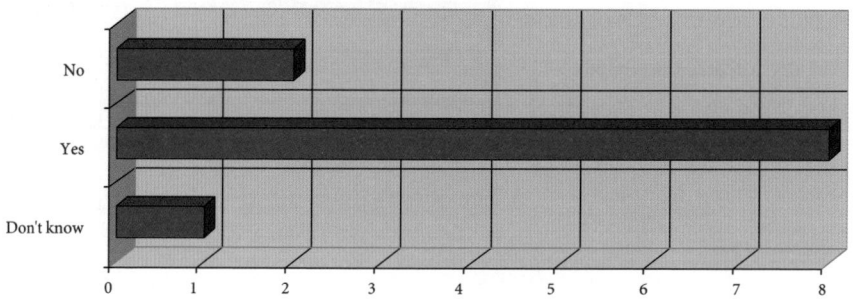

23. Is the title of legal translator protected?
(Government sources)

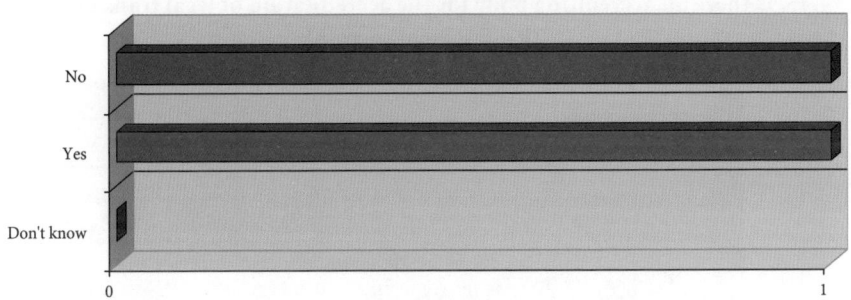

24. Is the profession of legal translator regulated?
(Professional sources)

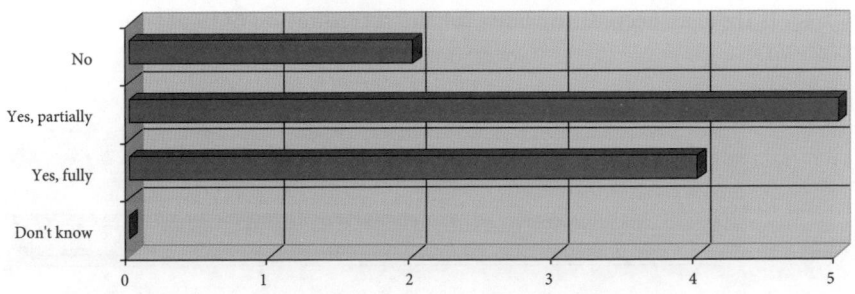

24. Is the profession of legal translator regulated?
(Government sources)

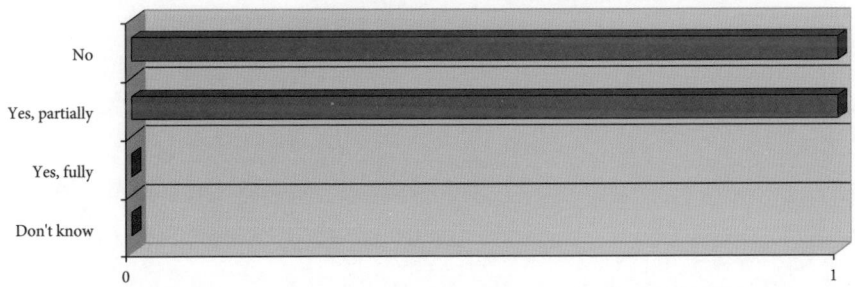

I2.2 Accreditation body

45. Is there an accrediting body for the accreditation of legal translators? (Professional sources)

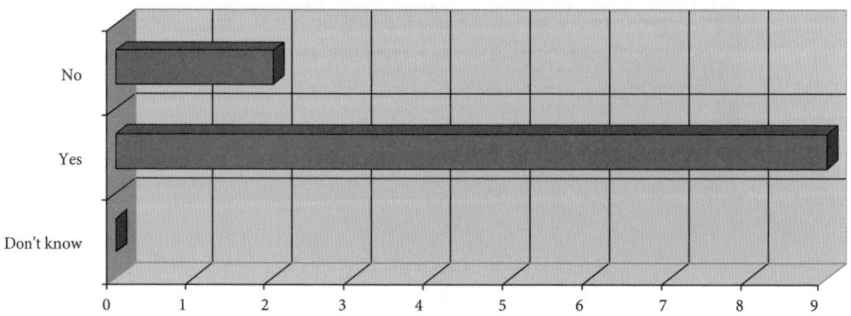

45. Is there an accrediting body for the accreditation of legal translators? (Government sources)

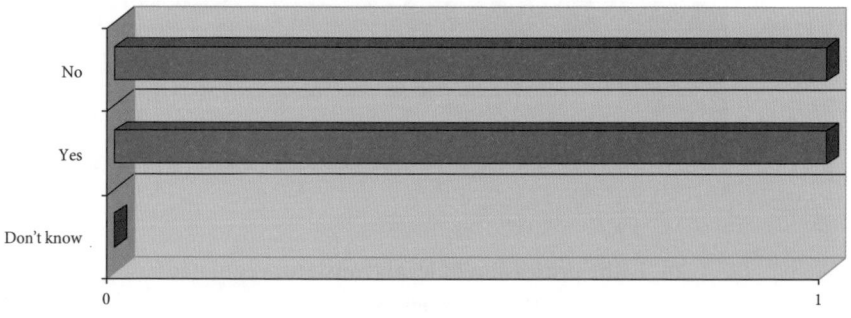

I2.3 Register

46. Is there a national register of legal translators?
(Professional sources)

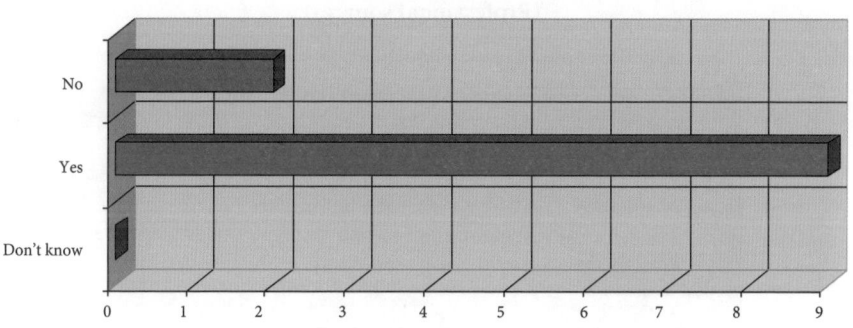

46. Is there a national register of legal translators?
(Government sources)

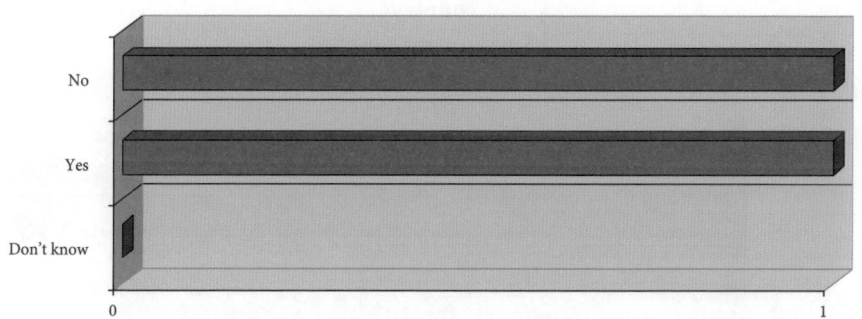

47. If there is a national register, what data is provided in the register?

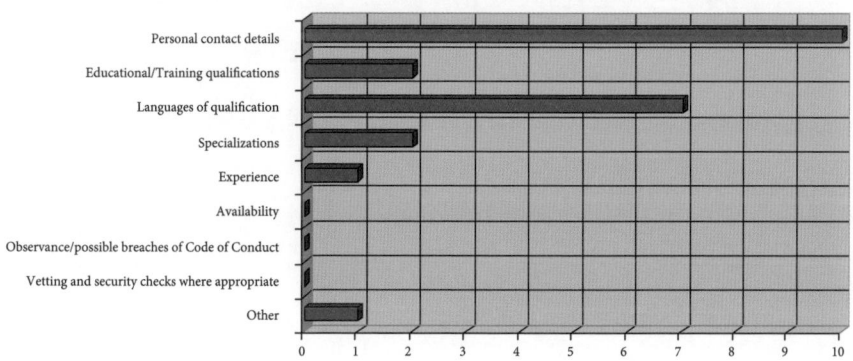

12.4 Code of conduct and procedure

59. Is there a national or regional Code of Conduct for legal translators in your country?
(Professional sources)

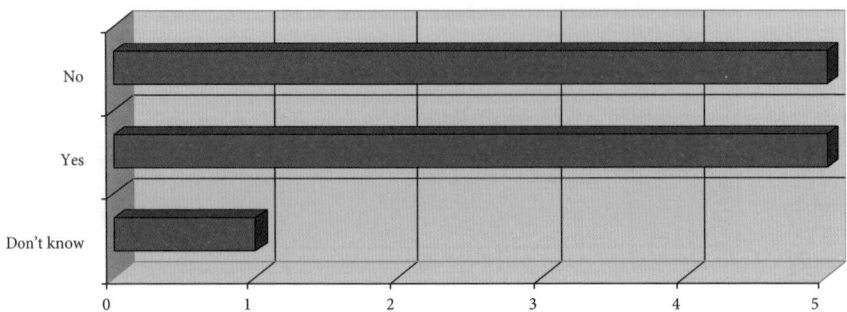

59. Is there a national or regional Code of Conduct for legal translators in your country?
(Government sources)

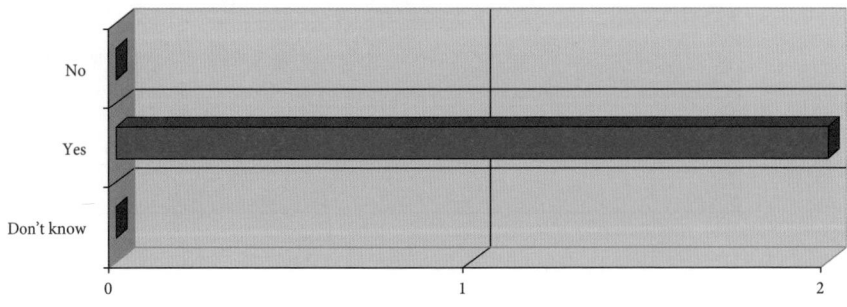

63. Is there a disciplinary procedures system in relation to legal translators in your country?
(Professional sources)

63. Is there a disciplinary procedures system in relation to legal translators in your country?
(Government sources)

INDICATOR 3   QUALITY PROVISIONS EU CONTEXTUAL INFORMATION

Quality provisions translation: government sources

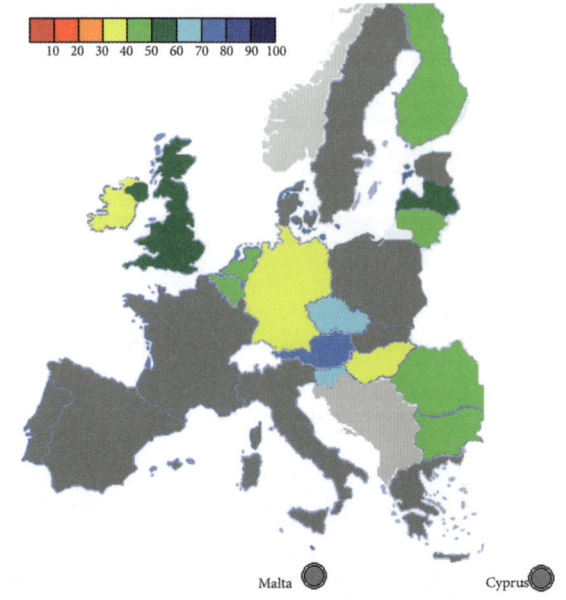

Quality provisions translation: professional sources

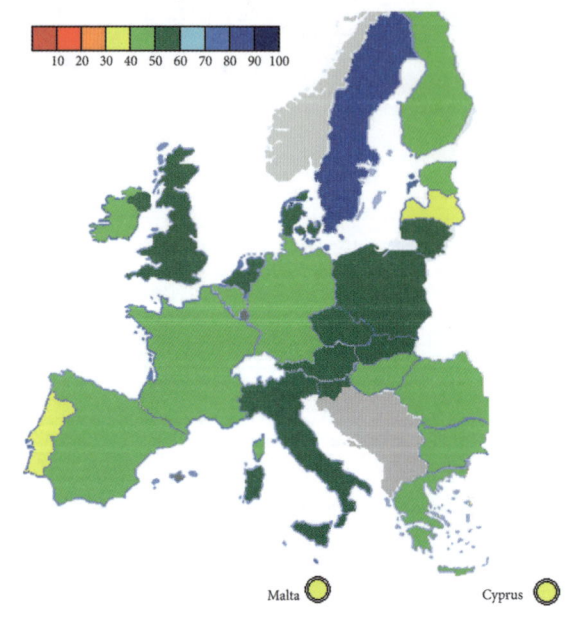

INDICATOR 3 QUALITY PROVISIONS

Austria: Quality provisions translation
Government sources

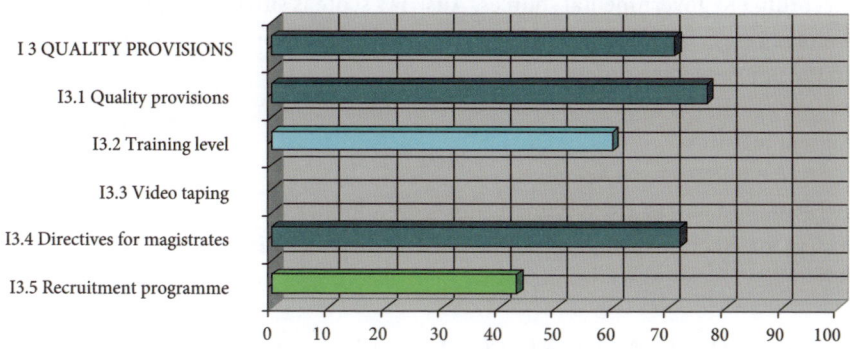

	I 3.5 Recruitment programme	I 3.4 Directives for magistrates	I 3.3 Video taping	I 3.2 Training level	I 3.1 Quality provisions	I 3 QUALITY PROVISIONS
T Score	42,93	72,00		60,00	76,58	71,06

Austria: Quality provisions translation
Professional sources

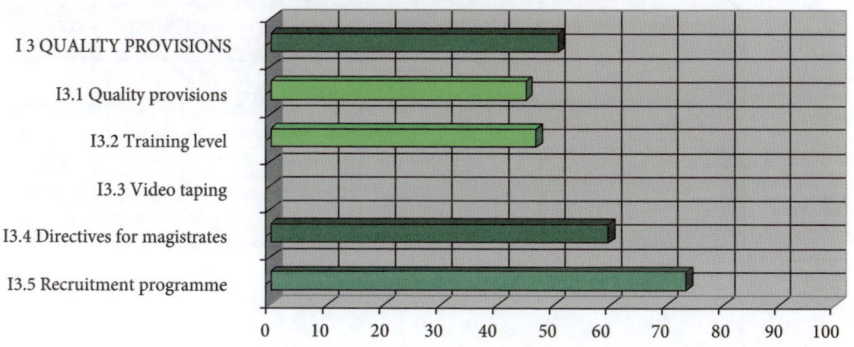

	I 3.5 Recruitment programme	I 3.4 Directives for magistrates	I 3.3 Video taping	I 3.2 Training level	I 3.1 Quality provisions	I 3 QUALITY PROVISIONS
T Score	73,48	59,71		46,86	45,00	50,71

INDICATOR 3   QUALITY PROVISIONS

General situation

According to governmental sources, Austria's score is situated in the upper above average range, whereas according to the professional sources the country scores in the upper average range.

Salient features

All basic indicators are systematically scored higher by the government source, except for 'Recruitment programme', where the pattern is inverted.

BASIC LEVEL INDICATOR 3 QUALITY PROVISIONS UNDERLYING QUESTION PROFILES

I3.1 Quality provisions

27. Are there binding provisions regarding the quality of legal interpreting and translation in criminal proceedings?
Translators (Professional sources)

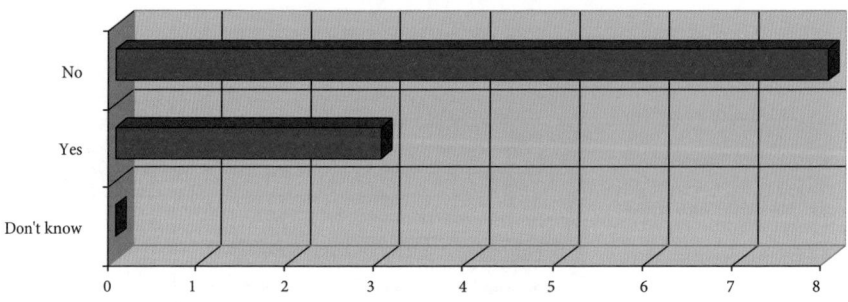

27. Are there binding provisions regarding the quality of legal interpreting and translation in criminal proceedings?
Translators (Government sources)

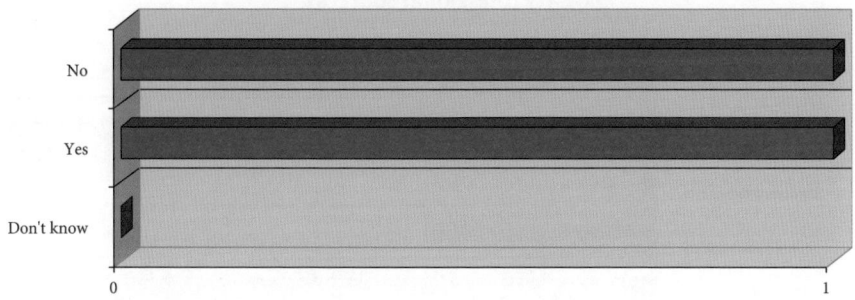

67. Is the quality of practice of legal interpreting or translation in criminal proceedings monitored?
Translators (Professional sources)

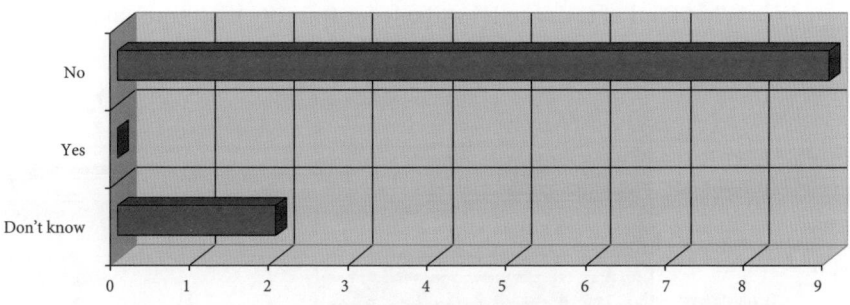

67. Is the quality of practice of legal interpreting or translation in criminal proceedings monitored?
Translators (Government sources)

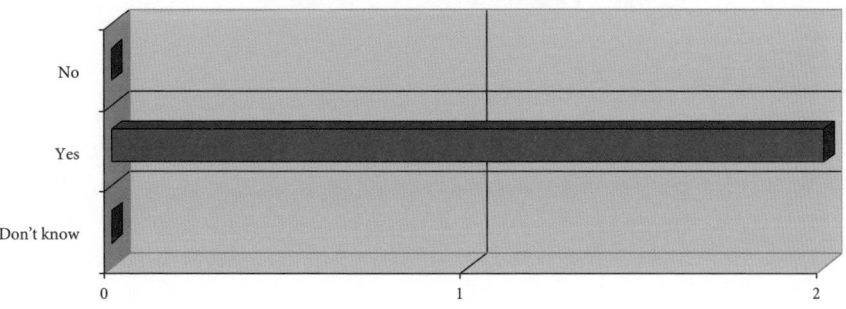

I3.2 Training level

**42. What kind of training is available for training legal translators?
(Professional sources)**

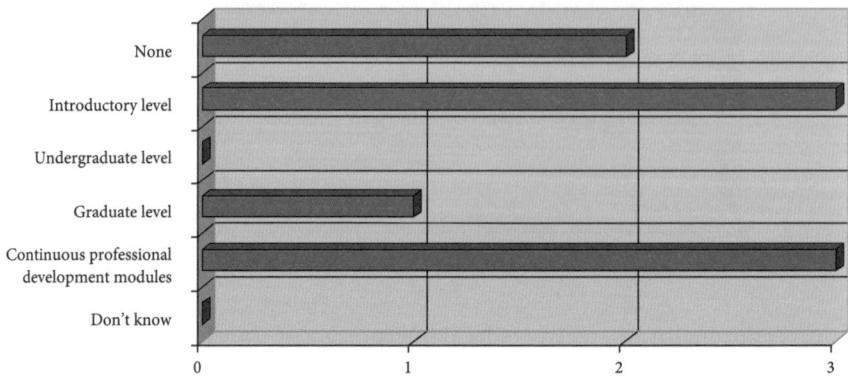

**42. What kind of training is available for training legal translators?
(Government sources)**

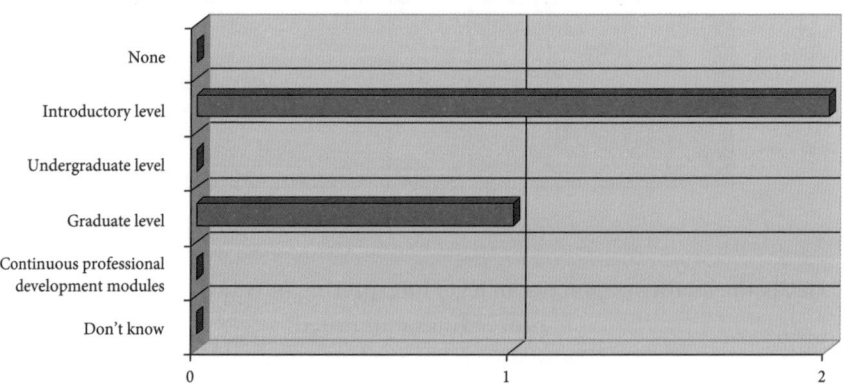

I3.4 Directives for magistrates

72. What good practice guidelines exist for members of the legal services on how to work with legal interpreters or translators?
(Professional sources)

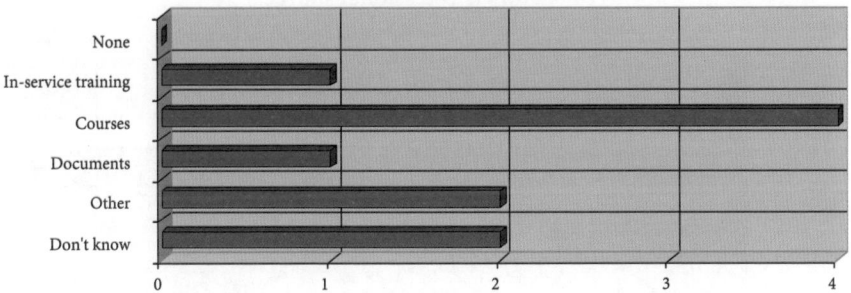

72. What good practice guidelines exist for members of the legal services on how to work with legal interpreters or translators?
(Government sources)

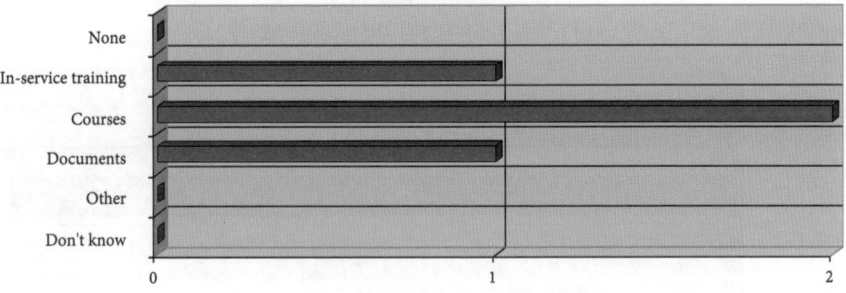

I3.5 Recruitment programme

73. Is there a national or regional programme to increase numbers and quality of legal interpreters and translators to meet demand and demographic changes?
Translators (Professional sources)

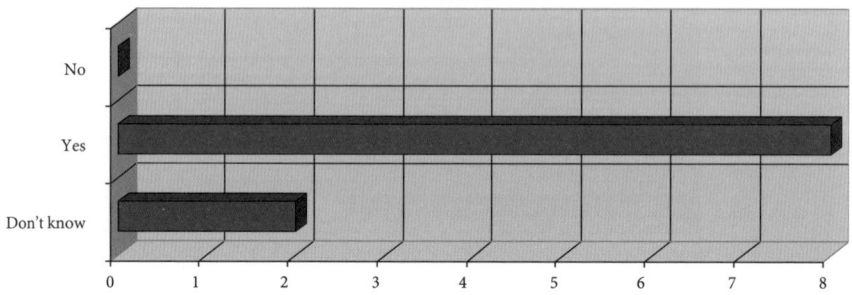

73. Is there a national or regional programme to increase numbers and quality of legal interpreters and translators to meet demand and demographic changes?
Translators (Government sources)

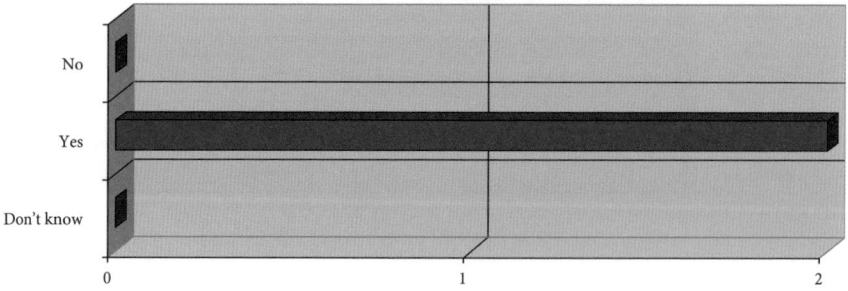

INDICATOR 4 QUANTITATIVE PROVISIONS EU CONTEXTUAL INFORMATION

Quantitative provisions translation: government sources

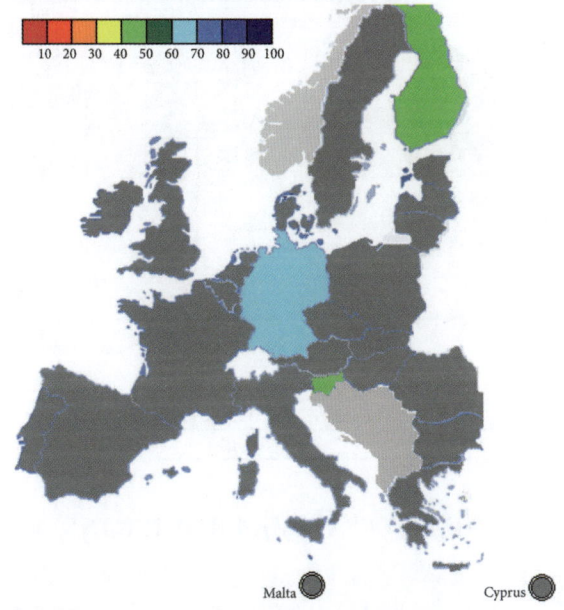

Quantitative provisions translation: professional sources

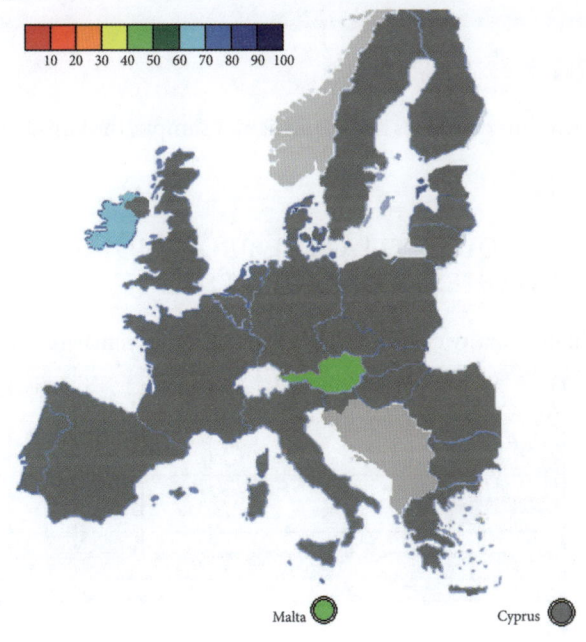

INDICATOR 4   QUANTITATIVE PROVISIONS

Austria: Quantitative provisions translation
Professional sources

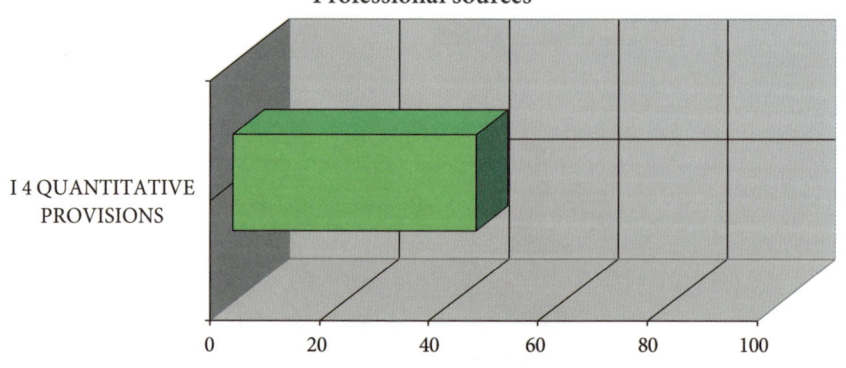

	I 4 QUANTITATIVE PROVISIONS
T Score	44,23

INDICATOR 4   QUANTITATIVE PROVISIONS

General situation

According to the professional sources, the country scores in the lower average range.

Salient features

As there are only four countries in this particular sample, the basis for comparison is rather narrow.

INDICATOR 4   QUANTITATIVE PROVISIONS
UNDERLYING QUESTION PROFILES

76. In how many cases is a legal translator currently required?

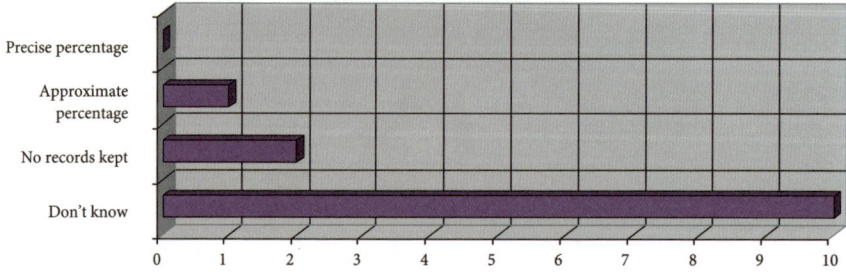

APEX INDICATOR EU CONTEXTUAL INFORMATION

Overall score translation: government sources

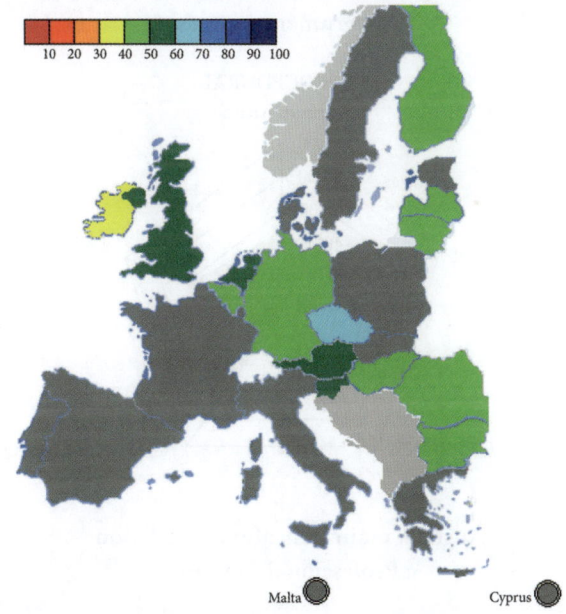

Overall score translation: professional sources

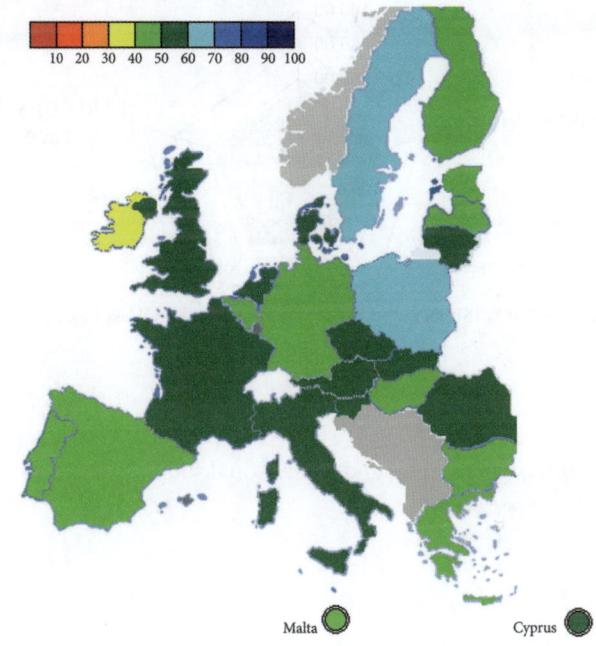

APEX AUSTRIA INDICATOR PROFILE

Austria: main indicators translation
Government sources

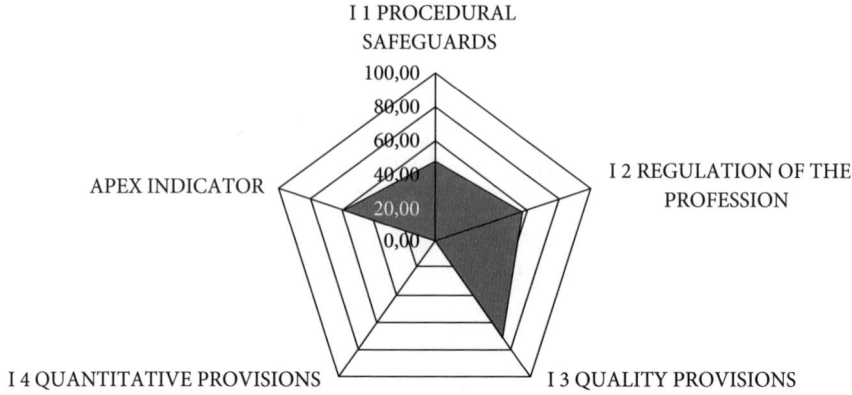

Austria: main indicators translation
Professional sources

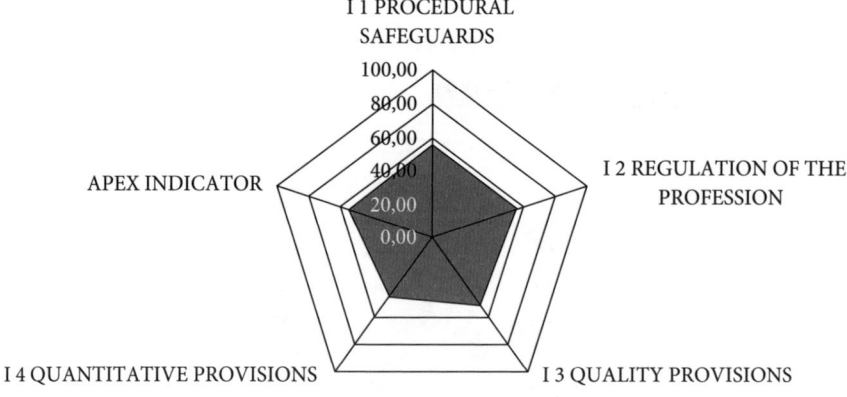

General situation

According to both governmental and professional sources, Austria's overall score is situated in the upper average range.

3.   FUTURE DEVELOPMENTS

INDICATOR 1: PROCEDURAL SAFEGUARDS

Better specific legislation

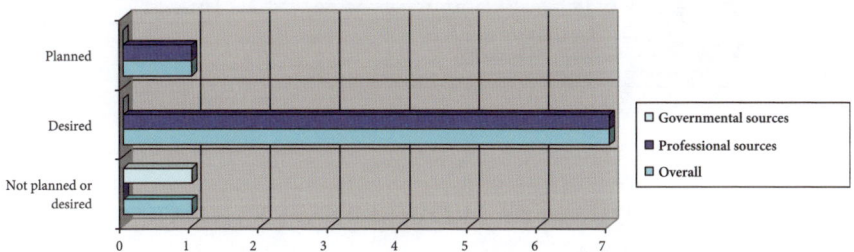

INDICATOR 2: REGULATION OF THE PROFESSION

The provision of a reliable and accessible register

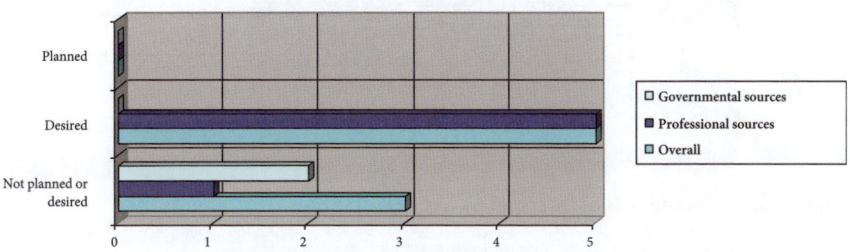

Better regulation of interpretation and translation Profession

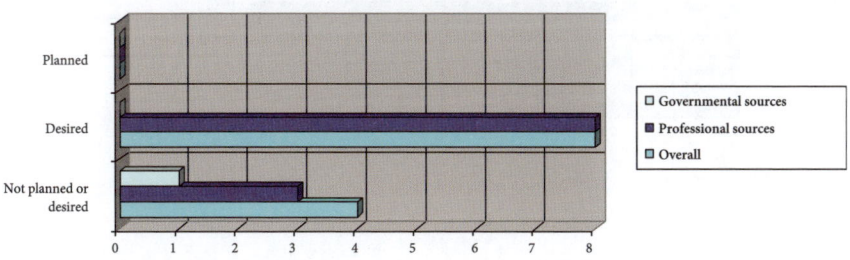

An enforceable Code of Conduct

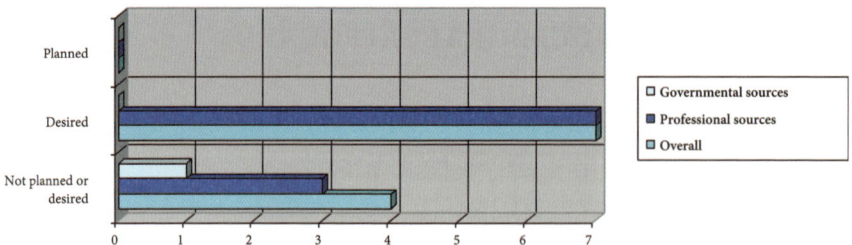

INDICATOR 3: QUALITY PROVISIONS: STANDARDS AND TRAINING

Better training of interpreters and translators

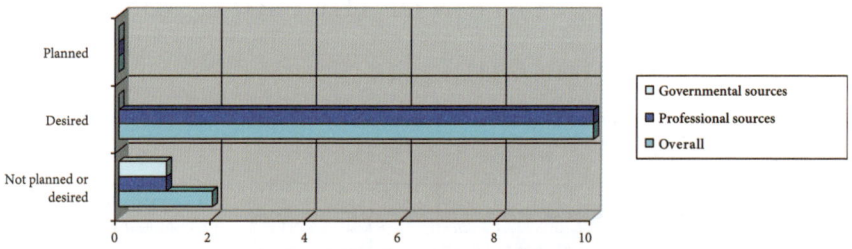

Higher quality standards of interpreters and translators

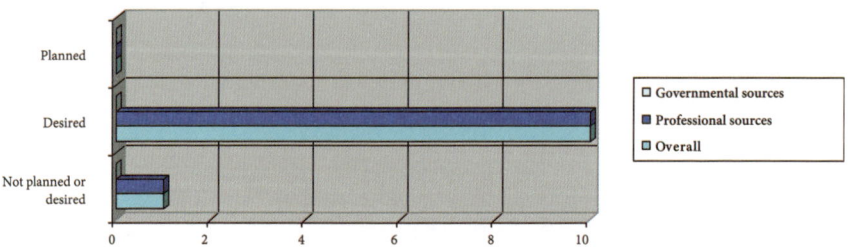

Independent testing of interpreters and translators

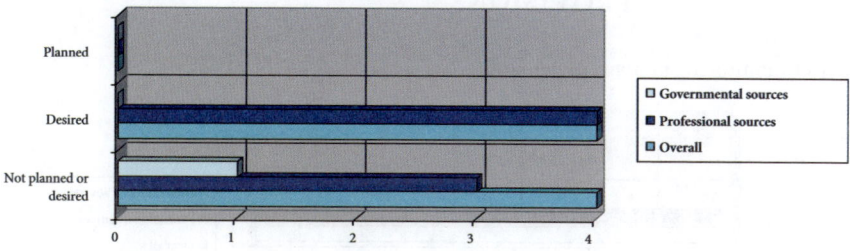

Continuous Professional Development

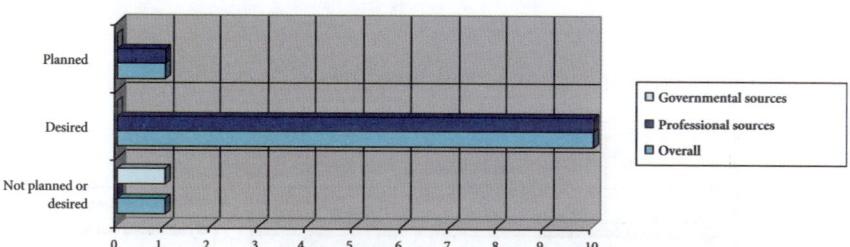

Peer testing and monitoring

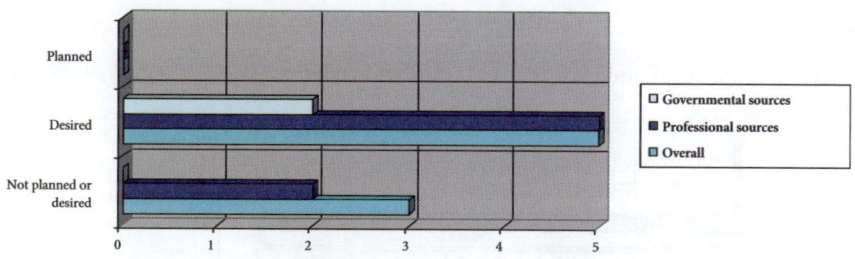

Occasional evaluations

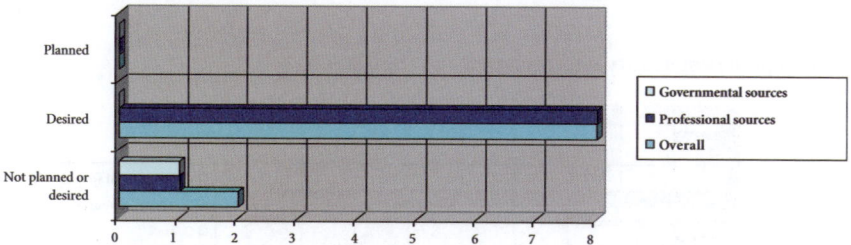

INDICATOR 3: QUALITY PROVISIONS: MANAGEMENT PROVISIONS

Better monitoring systems of demand

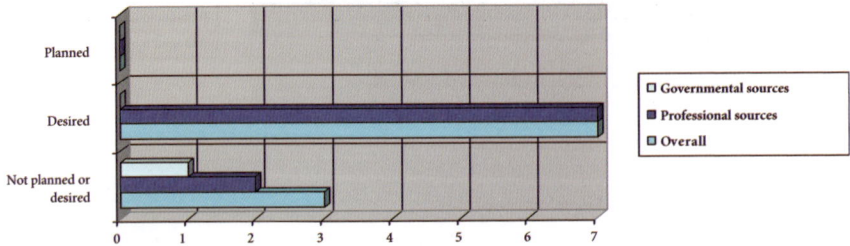

Better recruiting of interpreters and translators

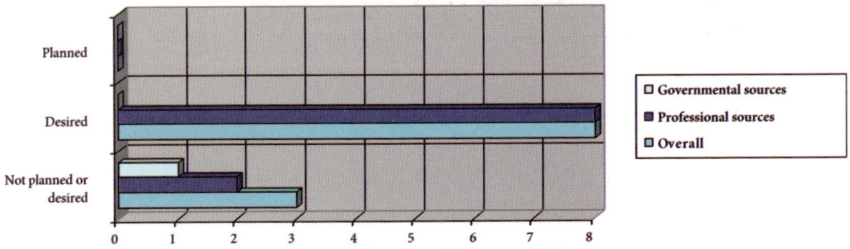

Better monitoring of interpretation and translation quality

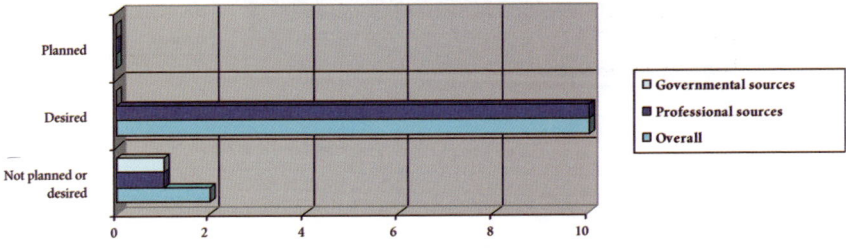

More suppliers of quality interpretation and translation

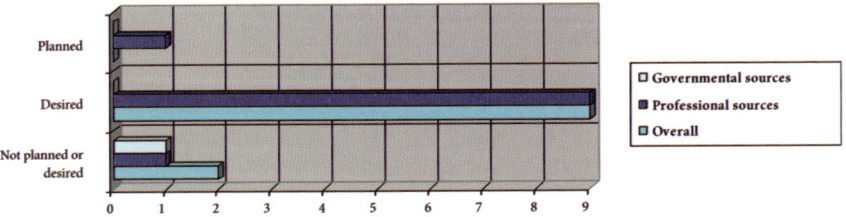

Training of legal services on working with interpreters and translators across languages and cultures

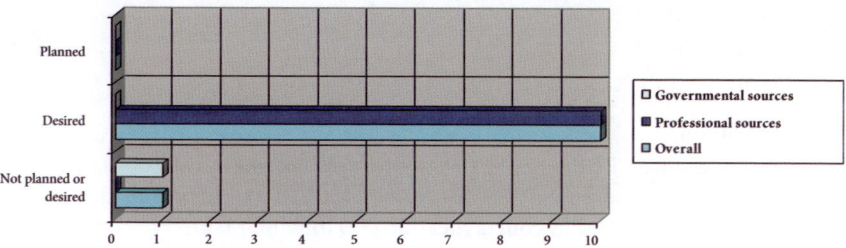

WORKING CONDITIONS FOR INTERPRETERS AND TRANSLATORS

Better remuneration of interpreters and translators

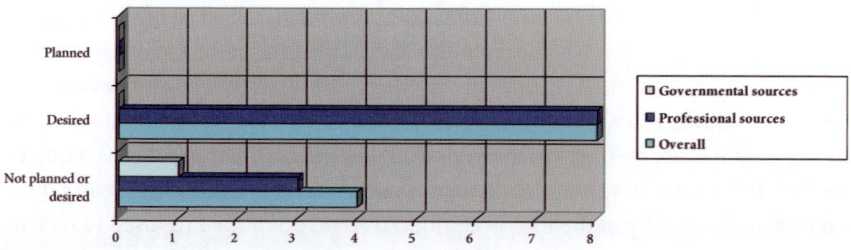

Better working conditions for interpreters and translators

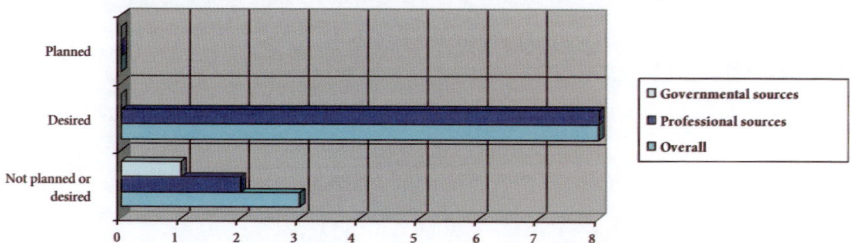

This part of the future developments section does not, as such, directly correspond with any of the basic or higher level indicators used in the study. However, because the provision of better working conditions and remuneration for legal interpreters and translators may prove an important factor in future quality management, these graphs are also shown.

4. ADDITIONAL COUNTRY INFORMATION

Austria

Population (× 1000)	8193
Area (km² × 1000)	83.9
GDP (€, billion)	267.6
Criminal cases dealt by the public prosecutor (per 100,000 inhabitants)	7697
Incoming criminal cases in courts (per 100,000 inhabitants)	1111

Source: Cepej

Right to interpretation and translation

Assistance of an interpreter and translator is provided, also for deaf and mute defendants. It is not mentioned whether this assistance is free of charge for the suspect and what kind of rules apply during the pre-trial investigation. It therefore remains unclear whether the provisions comply with Article 6 §2 of the Proposed FD stating that a person has the right to receive free interpretation of legal advice received throughout the criminal proceedings. The indictment and petition for sentences will be translated, other relevant documents are not mentioned in the answers, so it is not clear whether all relevant documents are translated as required in Article 7 of the Proposed FD. A list of sworn and certified interpreters must guarantee the quality of the interpretation, so Article 8 of the Proposed FD seems to be complied with. The interviews are not audio nor video recorded, as stipulated in Article 9 of the Proposed FD.

Source: *Procedural Rights in Criminal Proceedings: Existing Level of Safeguards in the European Union*
Taru Spronken and Marelle Attinger
Faculty of Law, Department of Criminal Law and Criminology
University of Maastricht

CHAPTER V
EU LINGUISTIC ASSISTANCE INDICATOR PROFILES

INTRODUCTION

In this chapter, comparative topographical maps are presented for the four higher level indicators i.e. 'procedural safeguards', 'regulation of the profession', 'quality provisions' and 'quantitative provisions', as well as for the 'apex indicator'. For a more robust ranking of Member States, both aspects of language support in criminal proceedings i.e. legal interpreting and legal translation were consolidated into one single 'linguistic assistance' category.

Every European indicator profile is made up out of two topographical maps and their corresponding data tables. The first map in the profile shows the EU Members States' scores according to the governmental sources, whereas the second shows the professional sources' evaluation.

In the corresponding data tables, the reader will find the overall ranking of Member States for a particular indicator and source.

To facilitate comparisons between Member States or between different indicators, the results have been converted to T-scores. By means of this data conversion technique, a country's score on any given performance indicator is essentially expressed in comparison with the EU average for that indicator. A score of 50 always corresponds with the EU average and every increment of 10 represents a distance of one standard deviation. This allows us to stratify the results in 10 point-bands that may be interpreted as shown in the following table:

Table: interpretation of T-scores

T – score	Category
91 to 100	High (high)
81 to 90	High (low)
71 to 80	Above average (High)
61 to 70	Above average (Low)
51 to 60	Average (High)
41 to 50	Average (Low)
31 to 40	Sub average (High)
21 to 30	Sub average (Low)
11 to 20	Low (High)
0 to 10	Low (low)

The colour coding is used to represent a Member State's score in the topographical maps and data tables.

INDICATOR 1 PROCEDURAL SAFEGUARDS –
GOVERNMENT SOURCES

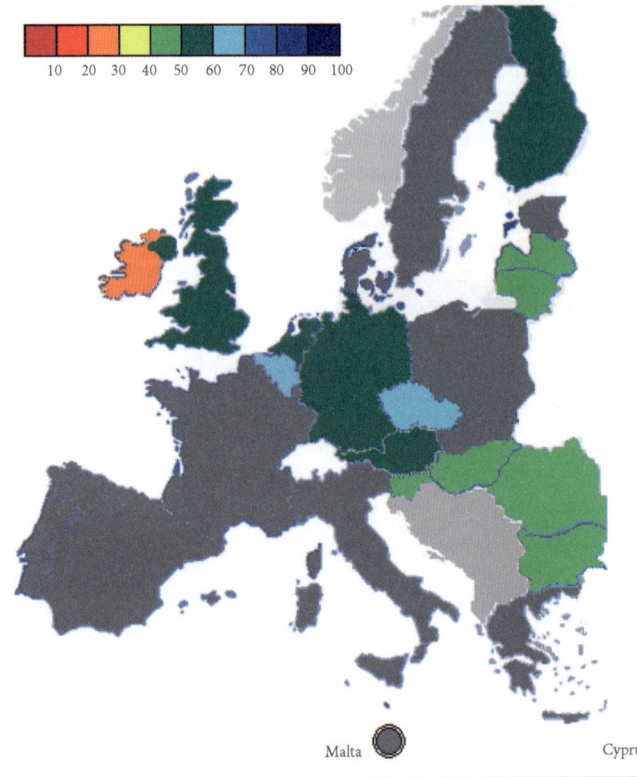

I. 1 PROCEDURAL SAFEGUARDS		
category	*country*	*T-score*
Above average (Low)	Belgium	60.66
	Czech Republic	60.66
Average (High)	Finland	59.22
	UK	58.27
	Netherlands	53.95
	Germany	52.52
	Austria	50.85
Average (Low)	Bulgaria	48.22
	Lithuania	47.90
	Slovenia	46.46
	Hungary	46.14
	Romania	45.67
	Latvia	45.03
Sub average (Low)	Ireland	24.45

INDICATOR 1 PROCEDURAL SAFEGUARDS – PROFESSIONIAL SOURCES

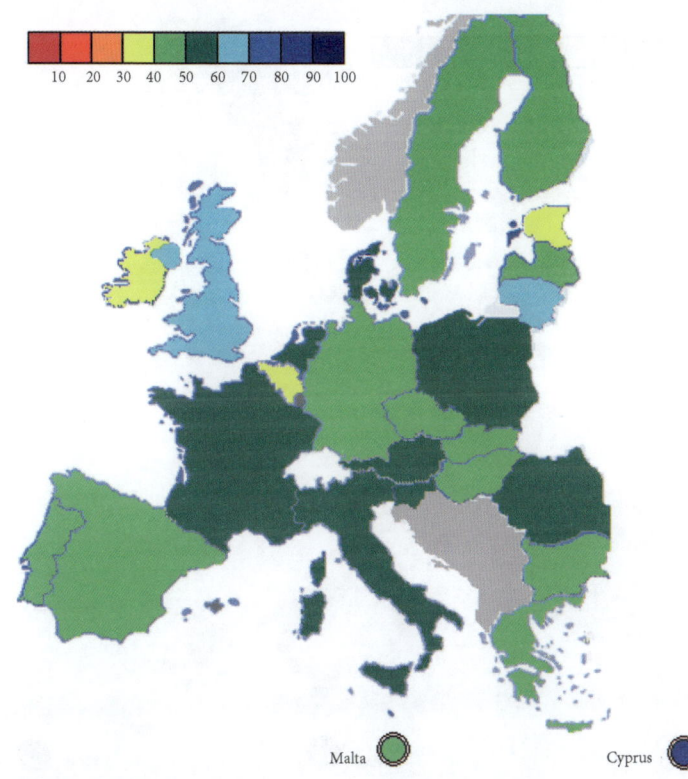

I. 1 PROCEDURAL SAFEGUARDS					
category	country	T-score	category	country	T-score
High (low)	Cyprus	83.55		Czech Republic	49.25
Above average (Low)	Lithuania	63.89		Germany	48.19
	UK	60.95		Hungary	46.86
Average (High)	Poland	55.25		Portugal	46.67
	Denmark	55.02		Spain	46.40
	Romania	53.33		Sweden	45.44
	Italy	52.78		Malta	44.58
	Slovenia	52.63		Greece	41.32
	Netherlands	52.59		Bulgaria	40.91
	Austria	51.38		Finland	40.50
	France	51.29	Sub average (High)	Ireland	39.36
Average (Low)	Latvia	49.71		Belgium	39.33
	Slovakia	49.71		Estonia	39.12

INDICATOR 2   REGULATION OF THE PROFESSION –
GOVERNMENT SOURCES

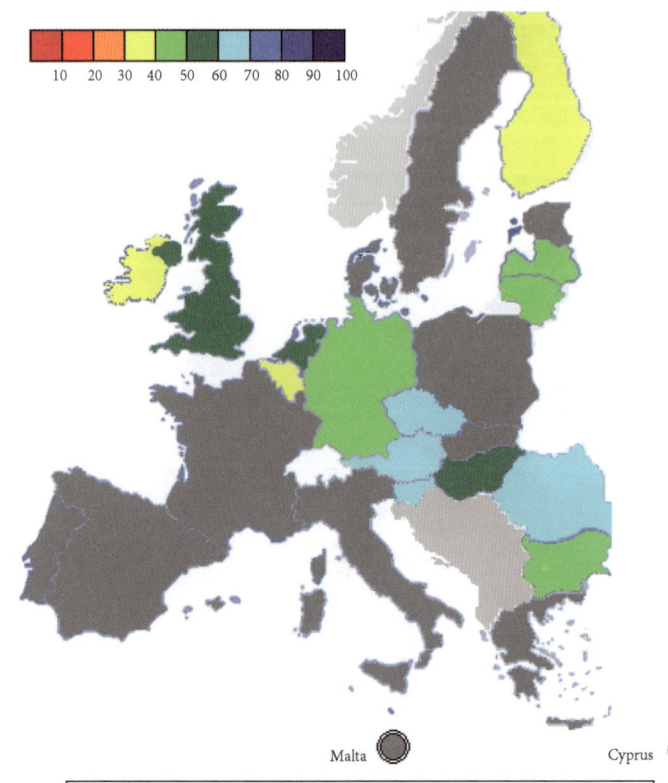

Malta   Cyprus

I. 2 REGULATION OF THE PROFESSION		
category	*country*	*T-score*
Above average (Low)	Slovenia	64.79
	Czech Republic	60.97
	Romania	60.97
	Austria	60.66
Average (High)	Hungary	53.34
	UK	52.02
	Netherlands	51.01
Average (Low)	Bulgaria	46.03
	Germany	41.04
	Latvia	41.04
	Lithuania	41.04
Sub average (High)	Finland	38.40
	Belgium	36.06
	Ireland	36.06

INDICATOR 2   REGULATION OF THE PROFESSION – PROFESSIONAL SOURCES

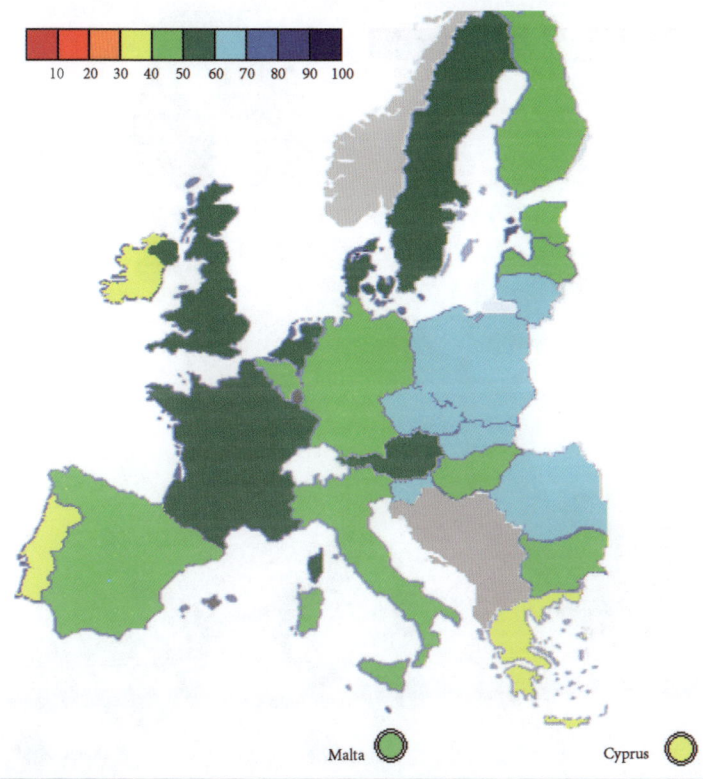

I. 2 REGULATION OF THE PROFESSION					
category	*country*	*T-score*	*category*	*country*	*T-score*
Above average (Low)	Poland	68.11		Finland	46.73
	Slovenia	67.55		Lithuania	46.26
	Slovakia	64.27		Germany	45.46
	Czech Republic	63.20		Malta	45.40
	Romania	62.09		Hungary	45.21
Average (High)	France	58.82		Bulgaria	43.00
	Austria	58.17		Belgium	42.64
	Sweden	55.04		Latvia	41.68
	UK	53.22		Spain	41.12
	Denmark	53.13	Sub average (High)	Ireland	39.69
	Estonia	51.18		Greece	39.18
	Netherlands	50.09		Portugal	36.45
Average (Low)	Italy	47.16		Cyprus	34.82

INDICATOR 3   QUALITY PROVISIONS –
GOVERNMENT SOURCES

I. 3 QUALITY PROVISIONS		
category	*country*	*T-score*
Above average (Low)	Austria	66.73
	Czech Republic	66.64
	UK	60.17
Average (High)	Slovenia	56.77
	Finland	52.75
	Latvia	50.51
Average (Low)	Lithuania	48.09
	Bulgaria	47.23
	Belgium	44.13
	Netherlands	42.57
	Romania	42.57
	Hungary	41.71
	Ireland	41.71
Sub average (High)	Germany	38.60

INDICATOR 3   QUALITY PROVISIONS –
PROFESSIONAL SOURCES

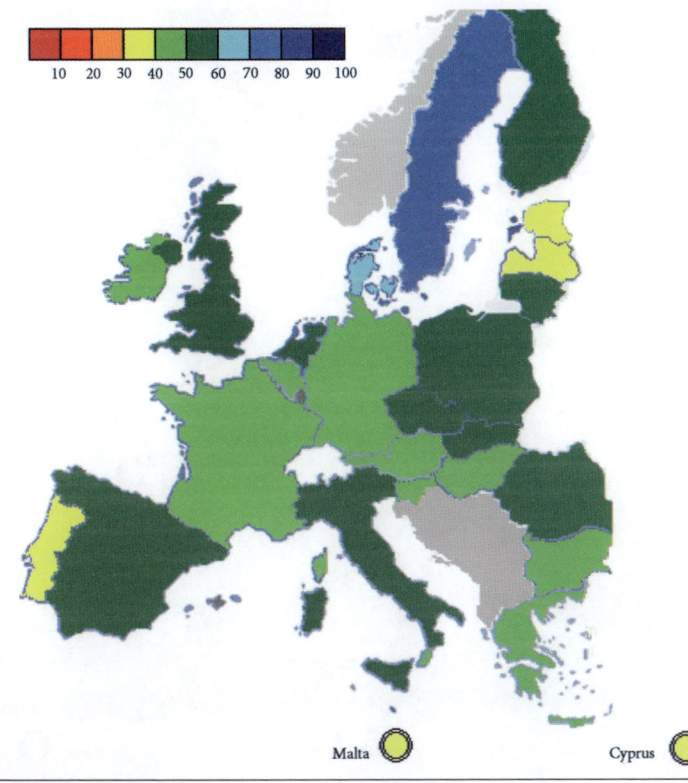

I. 3 QUALITY PROVISIONS					
category	*country*	*T-score*	*category*	*country*	*T-score*
Above average (High)	Sweden	77.64		Slovenia	49.32
Above average (Low)	Denmark	60.76		Austria	48.62
Average (High)	UK	59.44		Hungary	48.52
	Slovakia	59.37		Belgium	48.35
	Czech Republic	58.45		Germany	48.21
	Netherlands	54.57		Ireland	46.55
	Italy	54.44		Bulgaria	44.41
	Poland	54.43		Greece	42.34
	Lithuania	54.37	Sub average (High)	Malta	39.12
	Romania	53.08		Estonia	38.13
	Finland	51.66		Portugal	37.76
	Spain	50.72		Latvia	36.06
Average (Low)	France	49.99		Cyprus	33.62

INDICATOR 4   QUANTITATIVE PROVISIONS –
GOVERNMENT SOURCES

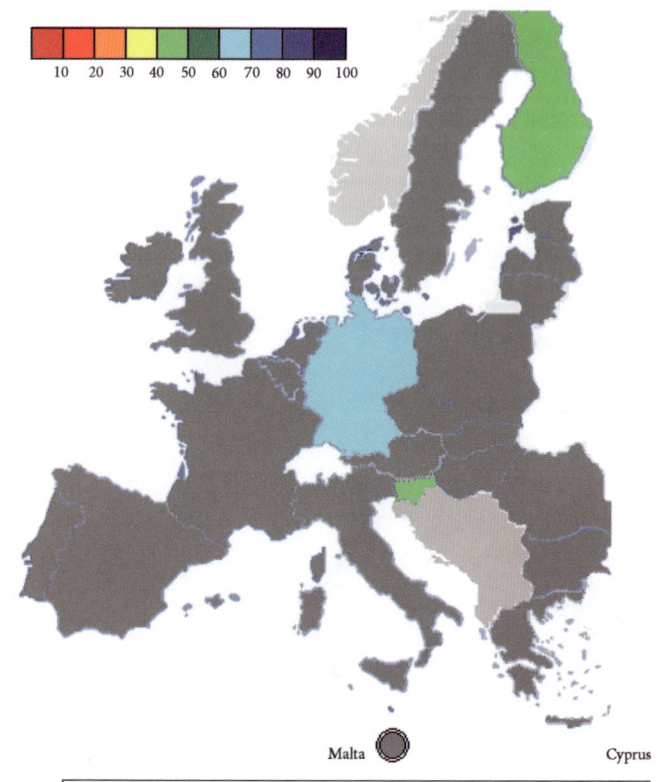

I. 4 QUANTITATIVE PROVISIONS		
category	*country*	*T-score*
Above average (Low)	Germany	61.21
Average (Low)	Finland	43.91
	Slovenia	43.91

INDICATOR 4   QUANTITATIVE PROVISIONS –
PROFESSIONAL SOURCES

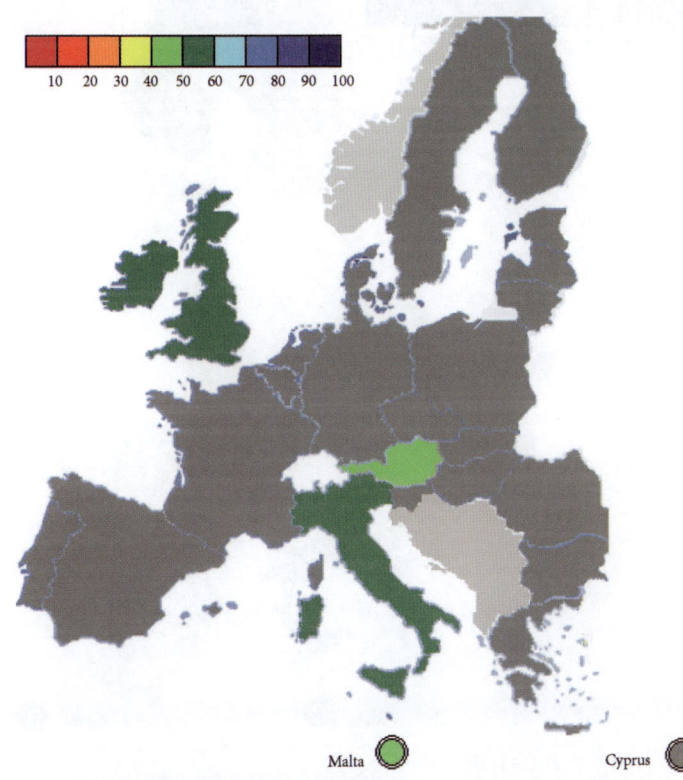

I 4 QUANTITATIVE PROVISIONS		
category	*country*	*T-score*
Average (High)	Ireland	58.67
	Italy	52.89
	UK	50.00
Average (Low)	Malta	47.12
	Austria	41.34

APEX INDICATOR – GOVERNMENT SOURCES

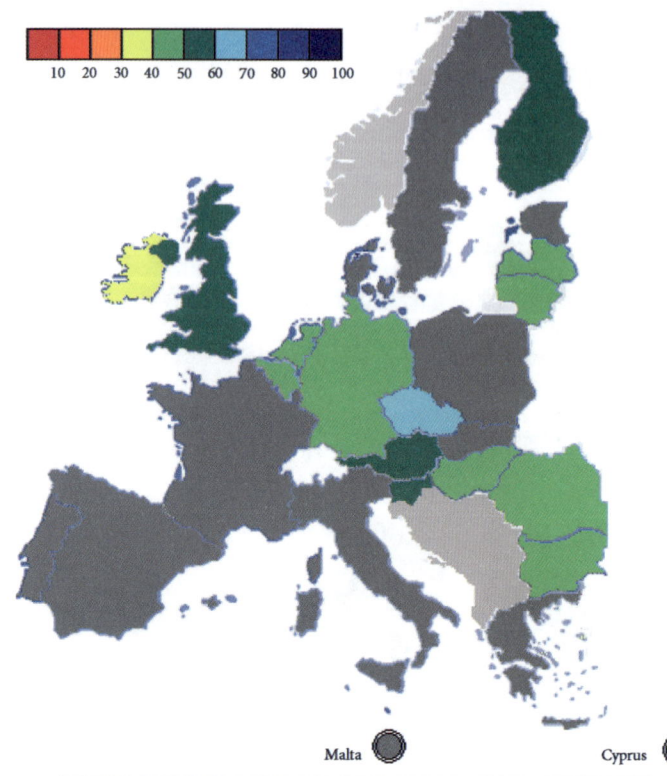

APEX INDICATOR		
category	*country*	*T-score*
Above average (Low)	Czech Republic	62.76
Average (High)	Austria	59.41
	UK	56.82
	Slovenia	56.01
	Finland	50.12
Average (Low)	Romania	49.74
	Netherlands	49.18
	Bulgaria	47.16
	Hungary	47.06
	Belgium	46.95
	Lithuania	45.68
	Latvia	45.53
	Germany	44.06
Sub average (High)	Ireland	34.07

APEX INDICATOR – PROFESSIONAL SOURCES

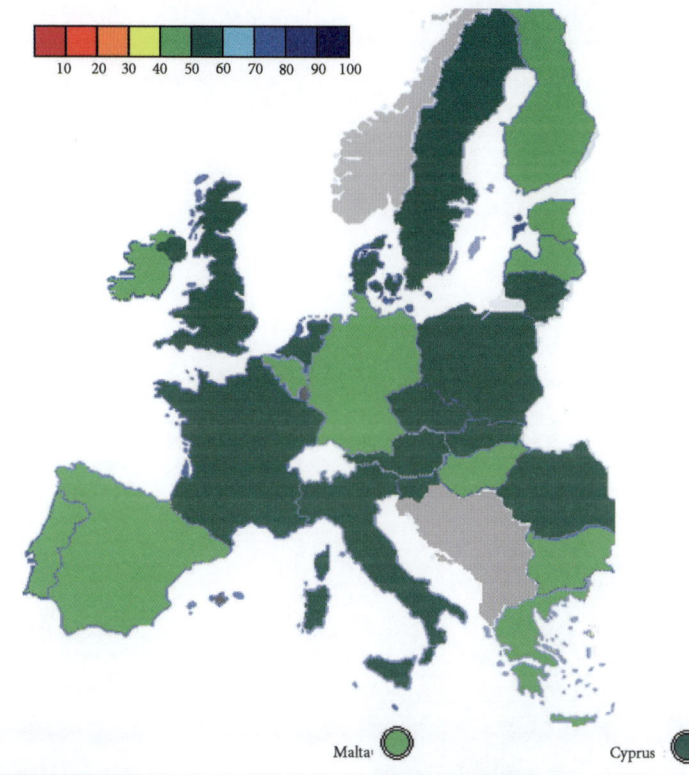

category	country	T-score	category	country	T-score
Average (High)	Sweden	59.37		Cyprus	50.66
	Poland	59.26	Average (Low)	Germany	47.28
	UK	57.87		Hungary	46.87
	Slovakia	57.78		Finland	46.30
	Czech Republic	56.97		Spain	46.08
	Slovenia	56.50		Belgium	43.44
	Denmark	56.30		Malta	43.03
	Romania	56.17		Estonia	42.81
	Lithuania	54.84		Bulgaria	42.77
	France	53.37		Latvia	42.48
	Austria	52.72		Ireland	41.87
	Netherlands	52.42		Greece	40.95
	Italy	51.46		Portugal	40.30

CHAPTER VI
EU GREEN PAPER INDICATOR PROFILES

INTRODUCTION

In this chapter, comparative topographical maps are presented, first of all, for the five basic level indicators that are specifically mentioned as key aspects in the Green Paper: 'Protection of vulnerable groups', 'Accrediting body', 'Register', 'Code of conduct and disciplinary procedures' and 'Training level'. In conclusion, also an overall 'Green paper indicator' is shown.

By way of a final bottom line, the professional and governmental sources' scores were averaged into a single 'Interdisciplinary sources' category.

In the corresponding data tables, the reader will find the overall ranking of Member States with regard to a particular indicator.

To facilitate the comparison between Member States or between different indicators, the results have been converted to T-scores. By means of this data conversion technique, a country's score on any given performance indicator is essentially expressed in comparison with the EU average for that indicator. A score of 50 always corresponds with the EU average and every increment of 10 represents a distance of one standard deviation. This allows us to stratify the results in 10 point-bands that may be interpreted as shown in the following table:

Table: interpretation of T-scores

T – score	Category
91 to 100	High (high)
81 to 90	High (low)
71 to 80	Above average (High)
61 to 70	Above average (Low)
51 to 60	Average (High)
41 to 50	Average (Low)
31 to 40	Sub average (High)
21 to 30	Sub average (Low)
11 to 20	Low (High)
0 to 10	Low (low)

The colour coding is used to represent a Member State's score in the topographical maps and data tables.

GP INDICATOR 1 VULNERABLE GROUPS – INTERDISCIPLINARY SOURCES

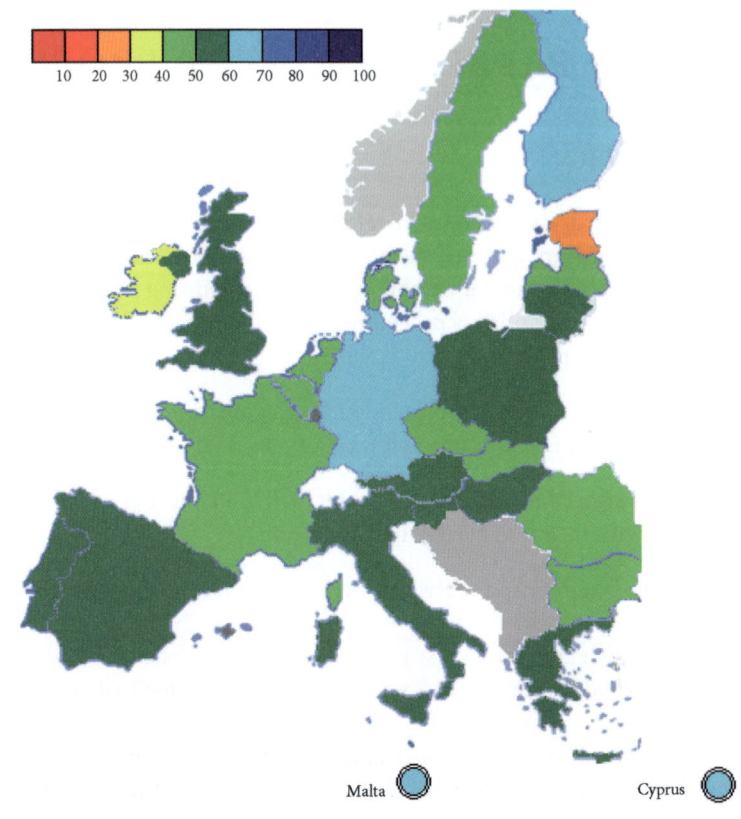

GPI 1 Vulnerable groups					
category	*country*	*T-score*	*category*	*country*	*T-score*
Above average (Low)	Cyprus	67.29		Poland	50.63
	Finland	61.27	**Average (Low)**	Denmark	48.54
	Malta	61.04		Bulgaria	47.37
	Germany	60.23		Sweden	46.46
Average (High)	Hungary	59.19		Czech Republic	44.83
	Italy	58.96		Belgium	42.75
	Spain	58.96		Slovakia	42.29
	UK	58.26		Latvia	42.17
	Austria	53.17		Netherlands	42.17
	Lithuania	53.17		Romania	42.17
	Slovenia	53.17		France	40.21
	Portugal	52.71	**Sub average (High)**	Ireland	38.00
	Greece	50.63	**Sub average (Low)**	Estonia	25.63

GP INDICATOR 2   ACCREDITATION BODY – INTERDISCIPLINARY SOURCES

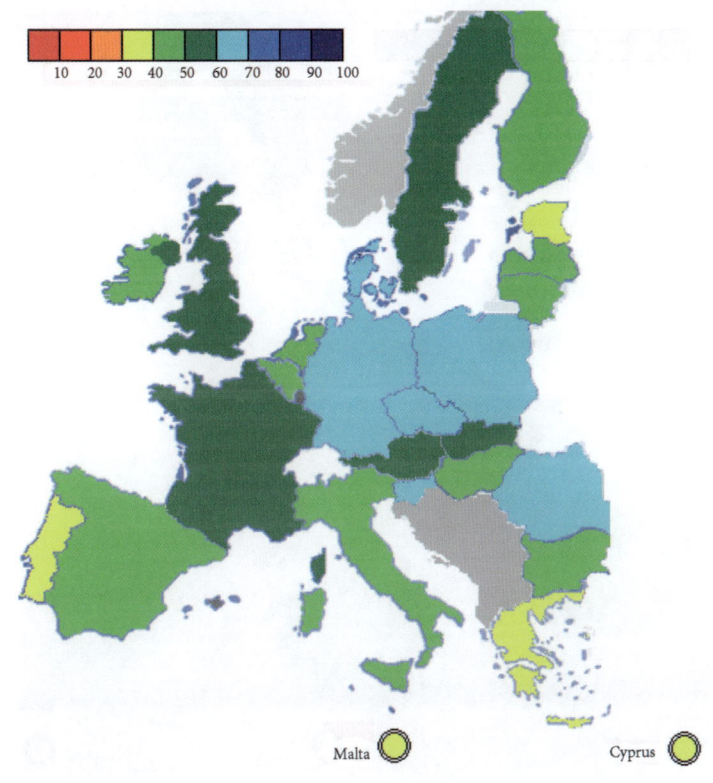

GPI 2 Accreditation body					
category	*country*	*T-score*	*category*	*country*	*T-score*
Above average (Low)	Czech Republic	64.45		Italy	44.97
	Romania	64.45		Finland	44.66
	Poland	63.76		Hungary	43.95
	Slovenia	61.54		Belgium	43.92
	Denmark	61.26		Spain	43.75
	Germany	60.09		Ireland	41.45
Average (High)	Sweden	59.91		Bulgaria	40.81
	Slovakia	58.76		Latvia	40.81
	Austria	56.99	**Sub average (High)**	Cyprus	38.74
	France	53.75		Estonia	38.74
	UK	53.08		Greece	38.74
Average (Low)	Netherlands	47.06		Malta	38.74
	Lithuania	45.78		Portugal	38.74

GP INDICATOR 3 REGISTER – INTERDISCIPLINARY SOURCES

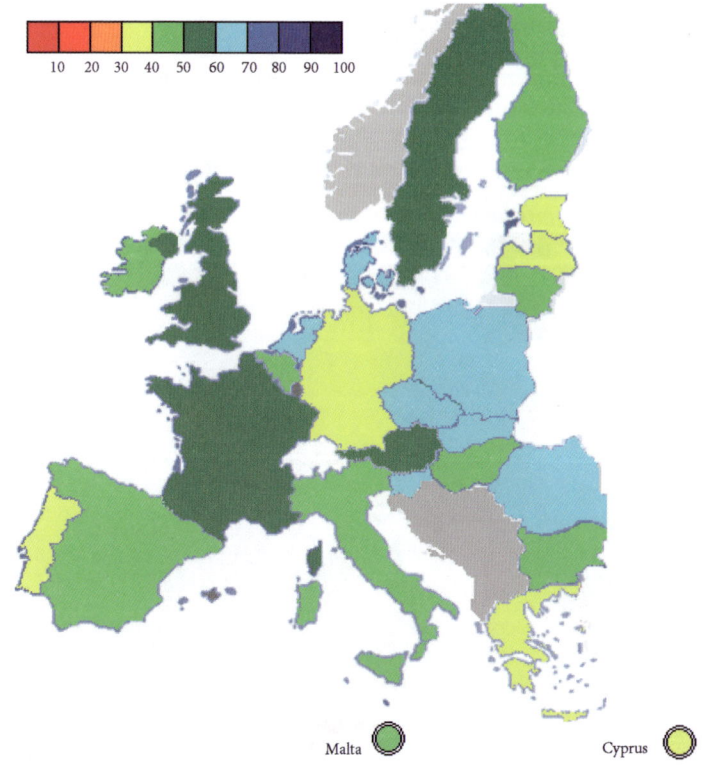

GPI 3 Register					
Category	*country*	*T-score*	*category*	*country*	*T-score*
Above average (Low)	Poland	62.90		Bulgaria	45.79
	Slovakia	62.90		Spain	45.06
	Czech Republic	61.56		Italy	43.81
	Netherlands	61.56		Finland	43.57
	Romania	61.56		Hungary	42.26
	Slovenia	61.56		Belgium	42.21
	Denmark	60.40		Ireland	42.21
Average (High)	France	58.13	**Sub average (High)**	Germany	39.82
	Austria	56.67		Latvia	39.82
	Sweden	55.40		Cyprus	39.03
	UK	51.62		Estonia	39.03
Average (Low)	Lithuania	49.63		Greece	39.03
	Malta	46.19		Portugal	39.03

GP INDICATOR 4 CODE OF CONDUCT AND DISCIPLINARY PROCEDURES – INTERDISCIPLINARY SOURCES

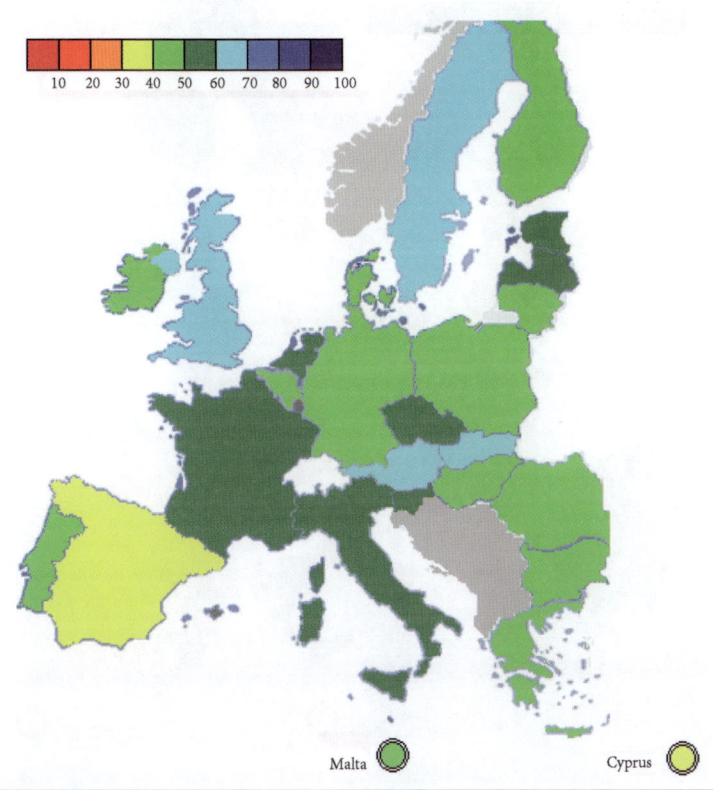

GPI 4 Code of conduct and disciplinary procedures					
category	*country*	*T-score*	*category*	*country*	*T-score*
Above average (Low)	Poland	67.61		Romania	47.62
	Sweden	66.52		Malta	45.87
	UK	64.04		Hungary	45.65
	Austria	61.62		Bulgaria	44.56
	Slovakia	61.09		Lithuania	44.36
Average (High)	France	58.91		Greece	43.70
	Czech Republic	58.69		Belgium	41.64
	Estonia	56.74		Denmark	41.52
	Slovenia	55.43		Portugal	41.52
	Italy	54.57		Germany	41.10
	Latvia	50.00		Ireland	40.55
	Netherlands	50.00	Sub average (High)	Spain	39.35
Average (Low)	Finland	48.33		Cyprus	35.00

GP INDICATOR 5 TRAINING LEVEL – INTERDISCIPLINARY SOURCES

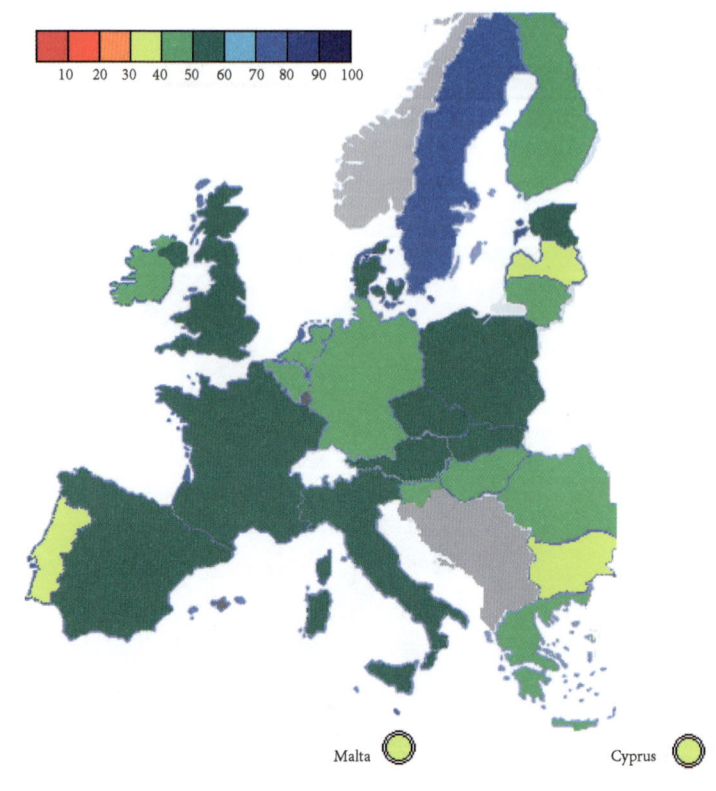

GPI 5 Training level					
Category	*country*	*T-score*	*category*	*country*	*T-score*
Above average (High)	Sweden	72.39		Lithuania	43.69
Average (High)	Czech Republic	58.84		Greece	42.88
	Denmark	56.94		Romania	42.85
	Slovakia	55.87		Belgium	42.62
	Poland	55.03		Finland	42.00
	UK	53.97		Hungary	40.65
	Spain	52.49		Ireland	40.20
	Austria	50.04	Sub average (High)	Bulgaria	39.88
Average (Low)	France	48.11		Latvia	39.40
	Netherlands	47.23		Malta	38.13
	Italy	47.03		Cyprus	35.60
	Slovenia	46.97		Estonia	35.60
	Germany	46.03		Portugal	35.60

GREEN PAPER OVERALL INDICATOR – INTERDISCIPLINARY SOURCES

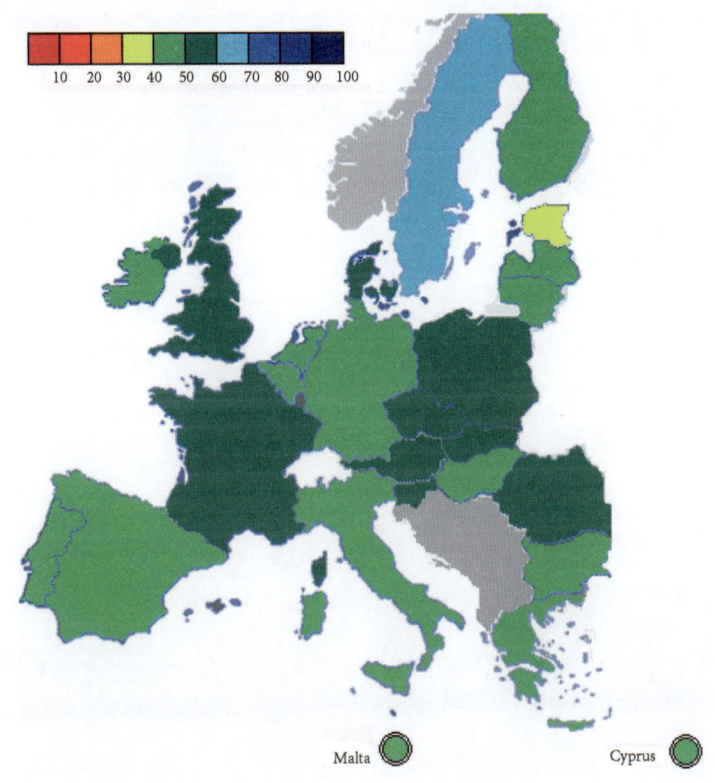

GREEN PAPER OVERALL INDICATOR					
category	*country*	*T-score*	*category*	*country*	*T-score*
Above average (Low)	Sweden	60.14		Finland	47.96
Average (High)	Poland	59.98		Spain	47.92
	Czech Republic	57.67		Lithuania	47.32
	UK	56.19		Hungary	46.34
	Slovakia	56.18		Malta	46.00
	Slovenia	55.73		Bulgaria	43.68
	Austria	55.70		Cyprus	43.13
	Denmark	53.73		Greece	42.99
	France	51.82		Belgium	42.63
	Romania	51.73		Latvia	42.44
Average (Low)	Italy	49.87		Portugal	41.52
	Netherlands	49.60		Ireland	40.48
	Germany	49.45	Sub average (High)	Estonia	39.15

CONCLUSIONS AND RECOMMENDATIONS

CORE CONCLUSION

The long-term goal of the Commission is to ensure that adequate legal interpreting and translation skills, and associated structures, are in place to meet legal and good practice requirements and enable:

- all Member States to have mutual trust in each other's systems in this regard
- all individuals, irrespective of language and culture, to have their procedural rights respected in each Member State.

The core conclusion of this survey on the provision of legal interpreting and translation in all Member States is twofold. Firstly, the survey shows that sufficient legal interpreting and translation skills and structures are *not yet* in place to meet these goals. Secondly, it shows a process of development to do so *is* in progress across the EU, albeit still variable in coherence, quality and quantity.

The purpose of this chapter is to bring together the main points arising from the survey process and data, which give instructive insights into how matters stand and how they may be taken forward. These are set out, together with comments and recommendations, under two main headings:

- General points
- Key indicators

The complete detail of the responses is set out in other parts of this report. In this chapter, selected responses are used for illustrative purposes.

GENERAL POINTS

The overall response rate was acceptable in that all Member States, except Luxembourg, replied to the questionnaire. There were only 14 responses from government sources, which was less than expected given the accompanying letters and reminders making clear that the questionnaire was part of the EU AGIS programme, and the rate of responses from professional groups varied widely.

There was a striking lack of consistency in the content of responses. Answers to factual questions from government sources and from other professionals were often contradictory. Even within categories of respondents, there were significant discrepancies.

In all countries, across all the categories, there was a lack of adequate information about such matters as the existing state of affairs concerning the employment, deployment and quality of legal interpreters and translators in criminal cases.

There was some evidence that the concept, whereby reliable legal interpreters and translators are required by law and good practice, was not always fully appreciated. Responses did not, however, show indications of large-scale non-compliance or other abuses.

COMMENTS

Notwithstanding the proper recognition of the factors described above, the project group considers that the survey provides the best possible assessment of the situation under current circumstances, through gathering such information as exists and consulting a range of respondents among the stakeholders in each Member State.

The primary reason for the discrepancies in the answers, between and within categories, is likely to be due to the absence of full and accurate recording of relevant data. Government sources, in particular, are understandably likely to be reluctant to submit answers without being in a position to be very sure of their facts, and to be able to access them easily and quickly.

In some cases, the cause of discrepancies may have been in the detail within the broader question. For example, it may have been that training courses existed for legal interpreters and translators but not in every language and every practitioner may not have attended them. Therefore, two respondents could have answered differently but correctly. Regional differences, within a country, may also have contributed to discrepancies.

It is self-evident that efficient, cost-effective and co-ordinated planning of incremental solutions to meet requirements cannot be carried out unless it is based upon adequate, nationally consistent information on demand and supply of legal interpreters and translators. That includes information on indigenous linguistic diversity in countries such as Spain.

It should not be a difficult or over-costly task to collect this information, especially through the use of computerised data collection tools, and to organise regular collation, analysis and dissemination.

This current lack of relevant data may, in some part, arise from what the project group considers to be a matter of crucial concern. That is the apparent lack of appreciation, in some Member States, of the legal and good practice requirements in respect of legal interpreting and translation and how that is an essential pre-requisite to underpin significant areas of EU legislation they have agreed to. The question may therefore justifiably be asked as to whether data was not available because Member States:

- had insufficient interest in the subject area
- could not identify what data was needed in order to collect it
- did not wish to collect the data because they did not feel themselves to be in a position to respond to it in financial and organisational practical terms
- did not see it as a priority in the face of other competing demands and commitments.

RECOMMENDATIONS

1   The competent authorities, in each Member State, should have their attention drawn again to the relevant legal and good practice requirements in relation to legal interpreting and translation. They should also be encouraged to cascade down that information to legal service practitioners and ascertain whether there is a need for in-service training or readjustment of priorities or a revision of budgets.

2   Relevant data should be collected, collated, analysed and disseminated as a basis for nationally co-ordinated and informed future planning for meeting requirements in relation to legal interpreting and translation, and to monitor progress.

The type of data to be collected is suggested at Appendix IV.
It is for Member States to decide how they should carry out this task but it is likely that it would be collected regionally, through nationally consistent core questions, although local regions may wish to add factors which reflect their

particular concerns. A common EU approach to data collection would be advantageous.

In the criminal justice process, a range of agencies may be involved in any one matter. Accurate communication is needed in each to preserve the integrity of the whole. Therefore, information data in respect of the demand and supply of legal interpreters and translators should include what is needed throughout, for example, in investigative and judicial proceedings and in preparing a defence.

All relevant agencies should be included in the data. For instance, the post-sentencing phase has not been specifically mentioned in the questionnaire but, in the interests of justice, sentencing options should not be limited on the grounds of language barriers and prisons and community based sentences should be supported by language assistance where appropriate. Such assistance is also needed by the probation (or equivalent) and other services for such activities as preparing reports for the courts. This applies not only for procedures within Member States but also for matters relating, for example, to bail and supervision orders under mutual recognition agreements.

It seems probable that the criminal justice services will be best placed to collect data about demand and the language professions should concern themselves with information about supply. Clearly communication between the various disciplines is necessary to achieve the gradual eventual synergy between supply and demand.

KEY INDICATORS

The project group has focussed its analysis of the responses on three key indicators, which represent the core essentials. They are:

- procedural safeguards
- regulation of the interpreting and translation professions
- quality assurance.

Almost all Member States have degrees of compliance with all three indicators but, equally, improvement is necessary in all Member States.

1. PROCEDURAL SAFEGUARDS

These are included in European law, including the European Convention for the Protection of Human Rights and Fundamental Freedoms and its case law. In many Member States there is corresponding domestic legislation. The procedures necessary to implement and safeguard those requirements include the points in the legal process at which legal interpreters or translators must be engaged, the criteria (e.g. defendant's degree of language competence) for engaging them and the measures to be taken to protect vulnerable groups.

On average, the scores on this aspect, from government sources and professionals broadly coincided. The exception was Belgium, where the professionals were less positive than the government sources.

In Cyprus, professionals consider their safeguards are of a high standard but it is difficult to know what, if any, interpretation to place on the absence of any response on this aspect from their government sources.

In Ireland, a country for whom significant immigration is a relatively new experience, both groups state that procedural safeguards are poor and this is confirmed by the low average score on this aspect in comparison to other countries.

Comments

The project group considers establishment and dissemination of procedures important because they ensure and safeguard consistent implementation of the principle. Such procedures allow the various practitioners to approach specific matters properly and with a degree of confidence, especially where it is a matter they may not often come across. They also provide a structure whereby non-compliance with the procedures can be challenged and dealt with.

Procedural safeguards in the context under discussion include those needed for the appropriate engagement of legal interpreters and translators, when and how.

Good practice guidelines promote the practical implementation on a day to day basis.

Recommendations

Member States should:

1 ensure better compliance with ECHR fundamental rights and with procedural safeguards as proposed in the Green Paper or the Framework Decision
2 share good practice to push standards up effectively in practice and to enhance the rights of the citizens.

This good practice guidance should include:

- a clear commitment to aim to engage qualified, registered legal interpreters and translators where they are required
- criteria, which can also be understood by a non-language specialist, to assess an individual's competence in reading, writing, speaking and comprehending a language, together with their true understanding of the formal and informal terminology, and of the legal procedures and processes likely to be involved. It should be indicated that legal interpreters or translators must be engaged where there is any doubt.
- once it has been established that legal interpreting and translation are necessary for reliable communication, points should be identified in the legal process where they must be engaged in order for a defendant sufficiently to prepare a defence and for defendants and witnesses to participate in the proceedings with an understanding mind. Forward planning and management of the series of communication needs in any one case is helpful, and may include such details as placing interpreting and translation records on individual files
- consideration should be given as to when and where separate interpreters are required to preserve the separation of function e.g. between the investigative and judicial
- systems should be established to meet the fees of interpreters and translators, by the courts or through legal aid. Thought should also be given to the fact that, where individuals are paying their own defence costs, any payment of such fees would be additional to the costs borne by someone who possessed the necessary language skills and may be even more inappropriate where individuals need language assistance because they are deaf.

2. REGULATION OF THE INTERPRETING AND TRANSLATION PROFESSIONS

This refers to national systems for formal professional structures, such as those required for the regulation and protection of other professions in the criminal justice system e.g. lawyers. These include systems for the selection, training, assessment and accreditation and registration of legal interpreters and translators and the requirement to observe a code of conduct and guides to good practice, subject to the disciplinary procedures of their own profession. (See Appendix III).

While elements exist in Member States, it is worth noting that Slovenia, The Czech Republic, Romania and Austria show a slightly above average score from both government sources and professionals. Belgium and Ireland score below average.

Comments

The pre-requisites for regulating a profession include: access to appropriate training, nationally recognised assessments, a central registration system, effective and acceptable working conditions and rewards which are adequate to attract and retain individuals with the skills required.

It should be noted that criminal justice systems compete with other employers for interpreters and translators with the level of skills and professionalism required. Interpreters and translators often work in the criminal justice system as part of a portfolio career, along with free-lance work in other areas such as commerce. This approach is practical and allows for logistical flexibility, given the unpredictable demand for their services by the criminal justice system. Where and when language assistance may be needed, in which languages and for how long, are difficult to foresee. Legal interpreters and translators also work in a free-lance capacity because they need to be impartial and independent, and be seen to be by the legal services and the public.

Historically, interpreters and translators may voluntarily have joined a professional language body, with varying requirements as to qualification and behaviour, but there may have been no requirement yet to do so. Training and assessments, specific for the legal context, vary within and between Member States, as do registration systems where they exist.

The encouraging outcomes, however, demonstrate that the systems are beginning to emerge, albeit in varying ways and at varying stages in each Member State. Bringing together these interdependent elements into a coherent structure, in order to produce similar standards in each Member State is one of the main planks of development. Equivalencies in standards and practice does not necessarily mean the same. The target of similar standards and good practice can be sought through the national conventions and systems of each Member State.

While it may be thought that the implementation of such standards is the responsibility of individual Member States, under the principle of subsidiarity, the benefits of equivalent standards are unarguable. Equivalencies would enable the development of an extensive, EU wide reliable resource in a multiplicity of languages, mutual support in training and assessment and the practical benefits of legal interpreters and translators able to work and improve their skills, where applicable, in both or all their languages.

National registers of equivalent standard and common codes of conduct could allow mutual access, provided there were also equivalent similar professional frameworks for employment and good practice.

Consideration should be given as to whether equivalent national registers would be preferable to a common EU professional register, whose very size and complexity could be challenging to administer.

Recommendations

Individual Member States should be encouraged to:

1   establish national professional independent registers for legal interpreters and translators with – to encourage EU consistency – similar

- entrance criteria
- incremental levels of membership, within defined time-scales, and continuous professional development to encourage up-skilling
- codes of conduct
- disciplinary procedures
- guides to good practice.

2   establish training courses for legal interpreters and translators at graduate and undergraduate level, which would allow for exchanges of students between Member States for applicable modules where the language combinations are appropriate.

It should be noted that national Education Ministries should be firmly encouraged to invest, where necessary, in training of this nature. New arrivals, in particular, are unlikely to be financially equipped to pay fully for professional level course and examination fees. It follows that those ministries should consider putting in place what is needed in schools to formalise and enhance skills in a wide range of languages, in order to lay a solid foundation for higher education courses. The languages involved for legal interpreting and translation are likely to include those which will also meet many of their own national needs for a broad range of languages for trade, industry and social interaction in a global economy.

3   establish nationally recognised professional assessments for legal interpreters and translators at graduate and post-graduate levels (see e.g. *www.cilt.org.uk/ standards* and as recommended by *Aequitas* EU Grotius project 96/GR/131).

4   establish nationally agreed terms and conditions of work for legal interpreters and translators

5   establish in-service training and directions for legal service staff on working with interpreters and translators

6   consider carefully what is needed for each Member State to match their developments and progress with other Member States, so that skills and cost resources can be maximised.

3.   QUALITY ASSURANCE

Only a minority of Member States appear to have an acceptable level of quality assurance strategies. There appears to be little video-taping and audio taping seems to be the exception, not the rule. In many countries there is no verbatim record of the proceedings of any type.

The Czech Republic and the UK perform comparatively well, according to both government and professional responses, whereas Germany and Ireland performed below average. The Swedish responses from professional groups show that this Member State performs extremely well in this respect, although there is no supporting government response to back that up. Estonia appears to have the furthest to go but, again, there was no response from government sources.

Comments

The systems by which professional skills and services that carry significant responsibilities are delivered should have checks and balances embedded in them in order to protect and preserve quality at each stage and the integrity of the whole. This includes the necessity to identify quickly any deficiencies in quality and to take remedial action. For example, deficiencies in communication during the collection of evidence should be spotted before the case comes to court. Quality assurance strategies are particularly needed when recipients of the service are not in a position to judge quality accurately for themselves. This self-evidently applies to interpreting and translation when the parties involved do not speak or read both languages fluently.

In the criminal justice context, concrete strategies for quality assurance in this area include: tape or video recording of interpreted exchanges for objective assessment by an independent qualified third party where appropriate; monitoring of translated texts; objective assessment of interpreting and translation skills; the existence of (and compliance with) directives to the judiciary and other members of the legal services on how to work with legal interpreters and translators.

As a practical example, the absence of a record of interpreted communication at the investigative and judicial stages makes it almost impossible to monitor the accuracy of interpreting. Furthermore, should an appeal be brought, there would be no evidence as to what the speaker of the other-language said or how it was interpreted. Random checking of translations and routine checking of essential ones, by qualified third parties would provide similar quality assurance.

Experience has shown that in Member States where that is developing, it is advantageous to offer in-service training for the judiciary, police forces and others to promote and assure the quality of how they work with interpreters and translators and across cultures. This is accompanied by directives, which also act as an aide mémoire. Investigative interviews, cross examinations in court, taking instructions from a distressed or confused client and establishing levels of cognitive development are examples of what are, even in a shared culture and language, complex interactions. Skills and understanding need to be extended to enable those tasks to be carried out across a language and culture, and for judges and magistrates to be in a position to monitor that it is, or has been done satisfactorily.

This includes the necessity of ensuring that other-language-speakers sufficiently understand their rights and the procedures and processes involved in their particular matter. Experienced people working in the legal services appreciate that such information has to be given, as it does under normal circumstances, not once but in repeated layers. This promotes the return of other-language-speakers to the level of those fluent in the language of the country, who can contribute to quality assurance in their own right.

Quality assurance strategies are almost the last element to be fully formalised in a development process. As development unfolds it reveals risks and their associated costs, which had previously been hidden or submerged. For example, tape-recording is likely to reveal the huge risk involved in engaging unqualified interpreters in preparing evidential matters. So, while quality assurance strategies carry with them an inevitable initial cost, these are likely to be outweighed in the long-term by avoiding risks, including the costs of appeals to higher domestic and EU courts.

Costs include what is needed to select, train and organise those who carry out quality assurance strategies. These tasks range from those that become part of a routine, such as the process of tape-recording police interviews which are part of the responsibility of the police forces, and the individual instances whereby experienced interpreters or translators are required to check the work of colleagues. Both types of task require thought, preparation and good practice guidelines to establish consistency of standards and approach.

Until such time as mutual trust can be firmly established in the reliability of each others' systems of legal interpreting and translation, it would be only prudent to require objective information about that reliability from the other Member State(s) involved when working together on such matters as those covered by mutual recognition agreements. Where that satisfactory information is not forthcoming, or in doubt, it follows that evidence, for example, may be excluded from the case.

Recommendations

Member States should be encouraged to identify similar quality assurance strategies relating to legal interpreting and translation in order to protect their criminal justice systems, to promote mutual trust between Member States and trust on the part of those living in or visiting their countries.

The following should be considered:

- tape- recording of police interviews and court hearings
- video-recording of police interviews and hearings, where appropriate and particularly where deaf people are involved
- selecting and training experienced interpreters and translators, who may be called upon to act as independent assessors when required, and agreeing an approach and good practice guide
- selecting and training senior members of the legal services, who may train and assess their colleagues' skills in working with interpreters and translators and across cultures
- an appreciation by the judiciary and by legal practitioners on what constitutes sufficient quality interpreting and translation and the facilities to appeal where it is considered this has not been provided.

FINAL POINTS

Criminal justice systems form the essential framework for just and fair societies, where the innocent may be protected and the guilty brought to justice irrespective of their language and culture.

The increase in movement of people between countries has found most Member States ill-prepared to deal with the inevitable resulting language barriers. As part of that, there is a paucity of relevant statistics on such basic facts as how many people will need the services of legal interpreters and translators, in which languages and where. Nonetheless, through eliciting information from a variety of sources this questionnaire has managed to grasp a worthwhile map of what provisions exist.

It is encouraging to note the stages of development in each country, the different elements that have been created and the enthusiasm to get things done in the face of multiple frustrations.

It is the view of the project group that the point has been reached where foundations have been laid. Worthwhile progress could be made if co-ordinated management strategies were put in place to reach long-term goals through incremental stages, within a sensible time-scale.

APPENDIX I

QUESTIONNAIRE

IDENTIFICATION
RESPONDENT

1. Country:

2. In what capacity are you familiar with legal **interpreting and/or translation**
    in criminal proceedings? As a member of:

    01 ☐ A professional association of interpreters or translators
    02 ☐ The police force
    03 ☐ The Prosecution
    04 ☐ The Judiciary
    05 ☐ Defence counsel
    06 ☐ Civil servant in a Government Department
    07 ☐ Interpreting or Translation Training Institute
    08 ☐ Victim or witness support organization
    09 ☐ NGO. Please specify:
    10 ☐ As an interpreter or translator
    11 ☐ Translation or Interpreting Service Provider
    96 ☐ Other: Please specify

Part I: **Provisions for legal translators and interpreters in criminal proceedings**

3. Are there national or regional requirements concerning legal **interpreting**
    in criminal proceedings in your country?

    1 ☐ No
    2 ☐ Yes
    7 ☐ Don't know

(selection: if V3 is 'yes')

3b. Which one(s)?
     (more answers possible)

     1   ☐   Legislation
     2   ☐   Government policy
     3   ☐   Agency or service provider regulations
     4   ☐   Ad hoc regulations
     6   ☐   Other: Please specify

     ┌───┐
     │   │
     │   │
     │   │
     └───┘

4.   Are there national or regional requirements concerning legal **translation** in criminal proceedings in your country?

     1   ☐   No
     2   ☐   Yes
     7   ☐   Don't know

(selection: if V4 is 'yes')

4b. Which one(s)?
     (more answers possible)

     1   ☐   Legislation
     2   ☐   Government policy
     3   ☐   Agency or service provider regulations
     4   ☐   Ad hoc regulations
     6   ☐   Other: Please specify

     ┌───┐
     │   │
     │   │
     │   │
     └───┘

5.   In your country, is there any established procedure for ascertaining when there is a need for **translation or interpreting** in criminal proceedings or police investigations?

     1   ☐   No
     2   ☐   Yes

7   ☐   Don't know

6.   Who decides whether an **interpreter or translator** is needed? (more answers possible)

1   ☐   Defence
2   ☐   Prosecution
3   ☐   Court
4   ☐   Police
5   ☐   Suspect or witness
6   ☐   Other: Please specify

7   ☐   Don't know

7.   Who determines in what language **interpreting or translation** is needed? (more answers possible)

01   ☐   Defence
02   ☐   Prosecution
03   ☐   Court
04   ☐   Police
05   ☐   Suspect or witness
06   ☐   Interpreter or translator
96   ☐   Other: Please specify

97   ☐   Don't know

8.   Who engages the **interpreter or translator**? (more answers possible)

1   ☐   Lawyer
2   ☐   Police
3   ☐   Court
6   ☐   Other: Please specify

7   ☐   Don't know

9. How is the **interpreter or translator** located and contacted? (more answers possible)

   01 ☐ Via a national register
   02 ☐ Via a regional or local list
   03 ☐ Via an agency
   04 ☐ Staff interpreter or translator
   05 ☐ Directly
   06 ☐ Via websites
   07 ☐ Via databases
   08 ☐ Via the Yellow Pages
   96 ☐ Other: Please specify

   97 ☐ Don't know

10. At what stages of the criminal proceedings is **interpreting** provided? (more answers possible)

    01 ☐ Arrest
    02 ☐ Custody procedures (24 hrs)
    03 ☐ Investigation
    04 ☐ Detention
    05 ☐ Police interview/Pre-trial interrogation
    06 ☐ Preparation of a defence
    07 ☐ Court proceedings
    96 ☐ Other: Please specify

    97 ☐ Don't know

11. At what stages of the criminal proceedings is **translation** provided? (more answers possible)

    01 ☐ Arrest
    02 ☐ Custody procedures (24 hrs)
    03 ☐ Investigation
    04 ☐ Detention
    05 ☐ Police interview/Pre-trial interrogation

06 ☐ Preparation of a defence
07 ☐ Court proceedings
96 ☐ Other: Please specify

```
┌─────────────────────────────────────────────┐
│                                             │
│                                             │
│                                             │
│                                             │
└─────────────────────────────────────────────┘
```

97 ☐ Don't know

12. Are there any criteria that establish the extent to which the proceedings should be **interpreted**?

1 ☐ No
2 ☐ Yes
7 ☐ Don't know

(selection: if V12 is yes)

12b. Which criteria?
(more answers possible)

1 ☐ Nature of the communication
2 ☐ Time restrictions
3 ☐ Costs
6 ☐ Other: Please specify

```
┌─────────────────────────────────────────────┐
│                                             │
│                                             │
│                                             │
└─────────────────────────────────────────────┘
```

13. Which documents must be **translated** in order to ensure the minimum necessary for a fair trial? *(more answers possible)*

1 ☐ Indictment
2 ☐ Sentence
3 ☐ Witness testimony
4 ☐ Evidence deposition
6 ☐ Other: Please specify

```
┌─────────────────────────────────────────────┐
│                                             │
│                                             │
│                                             │
└─────────────────────────────────────────────┘
```

7 ☐ Don't know

14. Are there limitations on **translation** in criminal proceedings?

    1   ☐   No
    2   ☐   Yes
    7   ☐   Don't know

(selection: if V14 is Yes)

14b. Which limitations?
    (more answers possible)

    1   ☐   Size (nr of pages)
    2   ☐   Nature of the documents
    3   ☐   Costs
    6   ☐   Other: Please specify

15. Are there criteria to determine when it is necessary for the defendant or the prosecution or court to have a separate **translator or interpreter**?

    1   ☐   No
    2   ☐   Yes
    7   ☐   Don't know

(selection: if V15 is 'yes')

16. What criteria?

17. Is there any monitoring of the provision of legal **interpreting or translation** in criminal proceedings?

    1   ☐   No
    2   ☐   Yes
    7   ☐   Don't know

(selection: if V17 is 'yes')

17b. **What kind of monitoring?**
(more answers possible)

01 ☐ Through a controlling body
02 ☐ By lawyers in individual cases
03 ☐ By court officials in individual cases
04 ☐ Via a complaints procedure
05 ☐ Via budget management by the responsible authority
06 ☐ Not in an organized way
96 ☐ Other: Please specify

```
┌─────────────────────────────────────────────┐
│                                              │
│                                              │
│                                              │
│                                              │
└─────────────────────────────────────────────┘
```

18. Are there national sanctions if the State fails to provide **interpretation and translation** when a person is entitled to it?

1 ☐ No
2 ☐ Yes
7 ☐ Don't know

(selection: if V18 is 'yes')

18b. **Which national sanctions?**
(more answers possible)

1 ☐ Retrial procedure
2 ☐ Appeal procedure
3 ☐ Reduction in budget allocation
6 ☐ Other: Please specify

```
┌─────────────────────────────────────────────┐
│                                              │
│                                              │
│                                              │
│                                              │
└─────────────────────────────────────────────┘
```

19. Are suspects from the following categories classified as particularly vulnerable in criminal proceedings?

19a. Foreign nationals

1 □ No
2 □ Yes
7 □ Don't know

(selection: if V19a is 'yes)

19a2. What protection is provided for them in criminal proceedings?

```
┌─────────────────────────────────────────────────────────┐
│                                                         │
│                                                         │
│                                                         │
│                                                         │
└─────────────────────────────────────────────────────────┘
```

19b. The visually or hearing impaired

1 □ No
2 □ Yes
7 □ Don't know

(selection: if V19b is 'yes)

19b2. What protection is provided for them in criminal proceedings?

```
┌─────────────────────────────────────────────────────────┐
│                                                         │
│                                                         │
│                                                         │
│                                                         │
└─────────────────────────────────────────────────────────┘
```

19c. individuals with insufficient proficiency in the necessary language

1 □ No
2 □ Yes
7 □ Don't know

(selection: if V19c is 'yes)

19c2. What protection is provided for them in criminal proceedings?

```
┌─────────────────────────────────────────────────────┐
│                                                     │
│                                                     │
│                                                     │
│                                                     │
└─────────────────────────────────────────────────────┘
```

Part II: Quality of legal interpreting and translation

21. Is the title of legal **interpreter** protected?

1 ☐ No
2 ☐ Yes
7 ☐ Don't know

22. Is the profession of legal **interpreter** regulated?

1 ☐ No
2 ☐ Yes, partially
3 ☐ Yes, fully
7 ☐ Don't know

23. Is the title of legal **translator** protected?

1 ☐ No
2 ☐ Yes
7 ☐ Don't know

24. Is the profession of legal **translator** regulated?

1 ☐ No
2 ☐ Yes, partially
3 ☐ Yes, fully
7 ☐ Don't know

25. Is membership of a professional organization compulsory in order to work in criminal proceedings? (more answers possible)

   for interpreters

   1 ☐ No
   2 ☐ Yes
   7 ☐ Don't know

   for translators

   1 ☐ No
   2 ☐ Yes
   7 ☐ Don't know

26. Are there provisions or recommended guidelines concerning payment/ allowance of legal **interpreters and translators?**

   1 ☐ No
   2 ☐ Yes
   7 ☐ Don't know

27. Are there binding provisions regarding the quality of legal **interpreting and translation** in criminal proceedings? (more answers possible)

   for interpreters

   1 ☐ No
   2 ☐ Yes
   7 ☐ Don't know

   for translators

   1 ☐ No
   2 ☐ Yes
   7 ☐ Don't know

   (selection: if V27 is 'yes, for interpreters' or 'yes, for translators'.

28. Where are these provisions on nationally consistent quality established? (more answers possible)

1 ☐ In legislation
2 ☐ Government policy
3 ☐ Policies of responsible authorities
4 ☐ Membership criteria of professional bodies
6 ☐ Other: Please specify

```
[                                    ]
```

7 ☐ Don't know

29. Which competences or qualities are required to meet these provisions? (more answers possible)

01 ☐ Knowledge of source language
02 ☐ Knowledge of target language
03 ☐ Knowledge of culture of source language
04 ☐ Knowledge of culture of target language
05 ☐ Knowledge of legal system/terminology of source language
06 ☐ Knowledge of legal system/terminology of target language
07 ☐ Integrity, e.g. no criminal record, character investigation, compliance with a Code of Conduct, etc.
08 ☐ Interpreting skills, e.g. memory skills, listening skills, analytical skills, transfer skills, body language, etc.
09 ☐ Translation skills, e.g. comprehension skills, writing skills, register matching, etc.
10 ☐ Interpreting aptitudes, e.g. concentration, empathy, stress management, punctuality, professional behaviour, etc.
11 ☐ Translation aptitudes, e.g. meticulousness, flexibility, inquisitiveness, responsibility, perseverance, etc.
96 ☐ Other: Please specify

```
[                                    ]
```

97 ☐ Don't know

30. In your opinion do legal **interpreters and translators** master these skills?

 1 ☐ Never
 2 ☐ Sometimes
 3 ☐ Most of the time
 4 ☐ Always
 7 ☐ Don't know

31. Who establishes these competences? (more answers possible)

 1 ☐ Government
 2 ☐ Contracting authority
 3 ☐ Professional organization
 4 ☐ Training institutes
 5 ☐ Agencies
 6 ☐ Other: Please specify

 7 ☐ Don't know

32. Who tests the legal **interpreters or translators** to verify whether they meet the standards to work in criminal proceedings? (more answers possible)

 01 ☐ Government
 02 ☐ Controlling authority of register
 03 ☐ Nationally recognised examinations body
 04 ☐ Contracting authority
 05 ☐ Professional organization
 06 ☐ Training institutes
 07 ☐ Agencies
 08 ☐ No one
 96 ☐ Other: Please specify

 97 ☐ Don't know

33. Which documents are required to demonstrate that legal **interpreters or translators** possess the necessary competences?
    (more answers possible)

    1 ☐ None (niet in combinatie met andere antwoorden)
    2 ☐ Degree in Interpreting or Translation
    3 ☐ Certified Training Courses
    4 ☐ Standard test per competence
    5 ☐ Standard specifications for experience
    6 ☐ Other: Please specify

    _____

    7 ☐ Don't know (niet in combinatie met andere antwoorden)

34. What happens when no qualified legal **interpreter or translator** is available?
    (more answers possible)

    1 ☐ There is no translation or interpretation
    2 ☐ Communication is established via a third language
    3 ☐ A less qualified or unqualified legal interpreter or translator is used
    6 ☐ Other: Please specify

    _____

    7 ☐ Don't know

35. Are **interpreters** allowed to communicate with the police or court officials or to the defence in order to prepare for the assignment?

    1 ☐ No
    2 ☐ Yes, always
    3 ☐ Yes, in some cases
    7 ☐ Don't know

36. Do **interpreters** have access to trial documents in order to prepare for the proceedings?

    1 ☐ No
    2 ☐ Yes, always

3 ☐ Yes, in some cases
7 ☐ Don't know

37. Are proceedings predominantly **interpreted**

Simultaneously from an interpreting booth

1 ☐ No
2 ☐ Yes
7 ☐ Don't know

Consecutively when the other-language-speaker is being addressed directly and otherwise simultaneously by chuchotage/whispering

1 ☐ No
2 ☐ Yes
7 ☐ Don't know

Otherwise? Please specify:

38. When **interpreting**, are the proceedings usually or predominantly interpreted

In full:

1 ☐ No
2 ☐ Yes
7 ☐ Don't know

In summary:

1 ☐ No
2 ☐ Yes
7 ☐ Don't know

39. What national or regional quality improvement strategies regarding legal **interpreting or translation** are implemented?

    1   ☐ None
    2   ☐ Continuous professional development
    3   ☐ Peer monitoring
    4   ☐ Occasional evaluations
    6   ☐ Other: Please specify

    7   ☐ Don't know

40. What kind of training is available for training legal **translators**? (more answers possible)

    1   ☐ None
    2   ☐ Introductory level
    3   ☐ Undergraduate level
    4   ☐ Graduate level
    5   ☐ Continuous professional development modules (e.g. fraud, child abuse, etc.)
    7   ☐ Don't know

(selection: if V40 is not 'none' or 'don't know)

41. Who provides this training? (more answers possible)

    1   ☐ Translation and Interpreting Institutes
    2   ☐ Universities
    3   ☐ Accredited Course Organizers
    4   ☐ Ad hoc organizations
    6   ☐ Other: Please specify

    7   ☐ Don't know

42. What kind of training is available for training legal **interpreters**? (more answers possible)

    1   ☐   None
    2   ☐   Introductory level
    3   ☐   Undergraduate level
    4   ☐   Graduate level
    5   ☐   Continuous professional development modules (e.g. fraud, child abuse, etc.)
    7   ☐   Don't know

(selection: if V42 is not 'none' or 'don't know)

43. Who provides this training? (more answers possible)

    1   ☐   Translation and Interpreting Institutes
    2   ☐   Accredited Course Organizers
    3   ☐   Ad hoc organizations
    6   ☐   Other: Please specify

    7   ☐   Don't know

44. Is there an accrediting body for the accreditation of legal **interpreters**?

    1   ☐   No
    2   ☐   Yes
    7   ☐   Don't know

45. Is there an accrediting body for the accreditation of legal **translators**?

    1   ☐   No
    2   ☐   Yes
    7   ☐   Don't know

46. Is there a national register of legal **translators**?

    1   ☐   No
    2   ☐   Yes
    7   ☐   Don't know

(selection: if V46 is 'yes')

47   What data is provided in the register? (more answers possible)

01   ☐   Personal contact details
02   ☐   Educational/Training qualifications
03   ☐   Languages of qualification
04   ☐   Specializations
05   ☐   Experience
06   ☐   Availability
07   ☐   Observance and possible breaches of Code of Conduct
08   ☐   Vetting and security checks where appropriate
96   ☐   Other: Please specify

```



```

(selection: if V46 is 'yes')

48.   Is there a system of renewable registration?

1   ☐   No
2   ☐   Yes
7   ☐   Don't know

(selection: if V48 is 'yes')

49.   For how long:

```



```

50.   Is there a national register of legal **interpreters**?

1   ☐   No
2   ☐   Yes
7   ☐   Don't know

(selection: if V50 is 'yes')

51. What data is provided in the register? (more answers possible)

01 ☐ Personal contact details
02 ☐ Educational/Training qualifications
03 ☐ Languages of qualification
04 ☐ Specializations
05 ☐ Experience
06 ☐ Availability
07 ☐ Vetting and security checks where appropriate
96 ☐ Other: Please specify

(selection: if V50 is 'yes')

52. Is there a system of renewable registration?

1 ☐ No
2 ☐ Yes
7 ☐ Don't know

(selection: if V52 is 'yes')

53. For how long:

54. Do you have a national register?

1 ☐ No
2 ☐ Yes
7 ☐ Don't know

(selection: if V54 is 'yes')

54b. Who has access to it?
(more answers possible)

1 ☐ Police
2 ☐ Judiciary
3 ☐ Prosecution
4 ☐ Lawyers
6 ☐ Other: Please specify

```



```

7 ☐ Don't know

55. Would you consider it useful to have a single EU register of legal **interpreters and translators** in stead of the current national or regional registers?

1 ☐ No
2 ☐ Yes
7 ☐ Don't know

56 Should responsible authorities in EU Member States have access to a register of equivalent standards of other Member States under agreed protocols?

1 ☐ No
2 ☐ Yes
7 ☐ Don't know

57. If an EU register or mutual access to national registers were available, who should have access to it? (more answers possible)

1 ☐ Police
2 ☐ Lawyers
3 ☐ Judiciary
4 ☐ Prosecution
6 ☐ Other: Please specify

```



```

58. Is there a national or regional Code of Conduct for legal **interpreters** in your country?

    1   ☐   No
    2   ☐   Yes
    7   ☐   Don't know

59. Is there a national or regional Code of Conduct for legal **translators** in your country?

    1   ☐   No
    2   ☐   Yes
    7   ☐   Don't know

(selection: if V59 is 'yes')

60. By whom is the Code of Conduct drawn up? (more answers possible)

    1   ☐   Government
    2   ☐   Responsible Special Authority
    3   ☐   Translation or Interpreting Professional Organization
    6   ☐   Other: Please specify

61. How is the ethical conduct of the legal **interpreter or translator** regulated in the criminal proceedings? (more answers possible)

    1   ☐   Taking an oath
    2   ☐   Listed in a Register
    3   ☐   Recognition of professional qualifications
    4   ☐   Monitoring
    6   ☐   Other: Please specify

    7   ☐   Don't know

62. Is there a disciplinary procedures system in relation to legal **interpreters** in your country?

   1 ☐ There is no disciplinary procedures system
   2 ☐ There are different disciplinary procedures systems
   2 ☐ There is a national procedure
   6 ☐ Other: Please specify

   7 ☐ Don't know

63. Is there a disciplinary procedures system in relation to legal **translators** in your country?

   1 ☐ There is no disciplinary procedures system
   2 ☐ There are different disciplinary procedures systems
   3 ☐ There is a national procedure
   6 ☐ Other: Please specify

   7 ☐ Don't know

64. After proper investigation and according to the level of seriousness, which disciplinary measures can be taken against legal **interpreters or translators**? (more answers possible)

   01 ☐ Caution
   02 ☐ Temporary suspension
   03 ☐ Obligation to follow Continuous Professional Development or retraining
   04 ☐ Removal from the membership list of professional organization
   05 ☐ Reduction in payment
   05 ☐ Removal from the register
   07 ☐ Criminal procedure
   08 ☐ Civil procedure
   09 ☐ None

96 ☐ Other: Please specify

97 ☐ Don't know

65. Are complaints ever filed against legal **interpreters or translators?**

1 ☐ Never
2 ☐ Sometimes
3 ☐ Always in the case of an infringement of the code of conduct
7 ☐ Don't know

66. Are sanctions applied in the case of proven professional malpractice of legal **interpreters or translators?**

1 ☐ Never
2 ☐ Sometimes
3 ☐ Always
7 ☐ Don't know

67. Is the quality of practice of legal **interpreting or translation** in criminal proceedings monitored?

for interpreters

1 ☐ No
2 ☐ Yes
7 ☐ Don't know

for translators

1 ☐ No
2 ☐ Yes
7 ☐ Don't know

68. How is the quality of legal **interpreting** in criminal proceedings monitored? (more answers possible)

01 ☐ Not
02 ☐ Not in an organized way

03 ☐ Through a controlling body
04 ☐ By lawyers in individual cases
05 ☐ By court officials in individual cases
06 ☐ Via a complaints procedure
07 ☐ Via budget management by the responsible authority
97 ☐ Don't know

69. How is the quality of practice of legal **translation** in criminal proceedings monitored? (more answers possible)

01 ☐ Not
02 ☐ Not in an organized way
03 ☐ Through a controlling body
04 ☐ By lawyers in individual cases
05 ☐ By court officials in individual cases
06 ☐ Via a complaints procedure
07 ☐ Via budget management by the responsible authority
97 ☐ Don't know

70. Are **interpretations** during criminal proceedings recorded on audio or video?

1 ☐ Sometimes
2 ☐ Often
3 ☐ Always
4 ☐ Never
7 ☐ Don't know

71. At which stage are **interpretations** during criminal proceedings recorded on audio or video? (more answers possible)

1 ☐ Police questioning
2 ☐ Investigation
3 ☐ Court hearings
6 ☐ Other: Please specify

7 ☐ Don't know

72. What good practice guidelines exist for members of the legal services such as lawyers, judges, the police etc. on how to work with legal **interpreters or translators?**

    1 ☐ None
    2 ☐ In-service training
    3 ☐ Courses
    4 ☐ Documents
    6 ☐ Other: Please specify

    ┌───┐
    │   │
    │   │
    │   │
    └───┘

    7 ☐ Don't know

73. Is there a national or regional programme to increase numbers and quality of legal **interpreters and translators** to meet demand and demographic changes?

    Interpreters:

    1 ☐ No
    2 ☐ Yes
    7 ☐ Don't know

    Translators:

    1 ☐ No
    2 ☐ Yes
    7 ☐ Don't know

Part III: Factual information

74. How many criminal proceedings are there currently in your country?

    1 ☐ Precise number:
    2 ☐ Approximate number:
    3 ☐ No records kept
    7 ☐ Don't know

75. In how many cases is a legal **interpreter** currently required?

   1 ☐ Precise percentage:
   2 ☐ Approximate percentage:
   3 ☐ No records kept
   7 ☐ Don't know

76. In how many cases is a legal **translator** currently required?

   1 ☐ Precise percentage:
   2 ☐ Approximate percentage:
   3 ☐ No records kept
   7 ☐ Don't know

77. How many legal **interpreters** are currently available for criminal cases?

   1 ☐ Precise number:
   2 ☐ Approximate number:
   3 ☐ No records kept
   7 ☐ Don't know

78. In how many languages?

   1 ☐ Precise number:
   2 ☐ Approximate number:
   3 ☐ No records kept
   7 ☐ Don't know

79. How many languages that are currently in demand are not covered by the current provisions?

   1 ☐ 0–10
   2 ☐ 11–20
   3 ☐ 21–50
   4 ☐ More than 50
   5 ☐ No records kept
   7 ☐ Don't know

80. Are **Sign Language interpreters** currently available?

   1 ☐ No
   2 ☐ Yes
   7 ☐ Don't know

81. How many legal **translators** are currently available for criminal cases?

 1 □ Precise number:
 2 □ Approximate number:
 3 □ No records kept
 7 □ Don't know

82. In how many languages?

 1 □ Precise number:
 2 □ Approximate number:
 3 □ No records kept
 7 □ Don't know

83. How many languages not covered by the present provisions?

 1 □ 0–10
 2 □ 11–20
 3 □ 21–50
 4 □ More than 50
 5 □ No records kept
 7 □ Don't know

84. What is the annual budget spent on Criminal Justice?

2003	_____ €	-2 □ Don't know
2004	_____ €	-2 □ Don't know
2005	_____ €	-2 □ Don't know
2006	_____ €	-2 □ Don't know

85. What is the annual budget spent on legal **interpreting**?

2003	_____ €	-1 □ No records kept	-2 □ Don't know
2004	_____ €	-1 □ No records kept	-2 □ Don't know
2005	_____ €	-1 □ No records kept	-2 □ Don't know
2006	_____ €	-1 □ No records kept	-2 □ Don't know

86. What is the annual budget spent on legal **translation**?

| 2003 | _____ € | -1 □ No records kept | -2 □ Don't know |
| 2004 | _____ € | -1 □ No records kept | -2 □ Don't know |

2005 _____ €   -1 ☐ No records kept   -2 ☐ Don't know
2006 _____ €   -1 ☐ No records kept   -2 ☐ Don't know

87. Who pays for legal **interpreters** in criminal proceedings? (more answers possible)

01 ☐ Ministry of Justice
02 ☐ Other Ministry
03 ☐ Police
04 ☐ Judiciary
05 ☐ Suspect or defendant
06 ☐ Via a complaints procedure
06 ☐ Other: Please specify

97 ☐ Don't know

88. Who pays for legal **translators** in criminal proceedings? (more answers possible)

01 ☐ Ministry of Justice
02 ☐ Other Ministry
03 ☐ Police
04 ☐ Judiciary
05 ☐ Suspect or defendant
06 ☐ Via a complaints procedure
07 ☐ Other: Please specify

97 ☐ Don't know

89. Are there standard rates of fees for legal **interpreting**?

1 ☐ No
2 ☐ Yes
7 ☐ Don't know

90. Are there different rates per: (more answers possible)

	yes	no	don't know
Language or language rarity	1 ☐	2 ☐	7 ☐
Subject matter	1 ☐	2 ☐	7 ☐
Person/Organization engaging the interpreter	1 ☐	2 ☐	7 ☐
Time of day	1 ☐	2 ☐	7 ☐
Kind of activity 'e.g. simultaneous)	1 ☐	2 ☐	7 ☐
Other: Please specify	1 ☐	2 ☐	7 ☐

```
┌─────────────────────────────────────────────┐
│                                             │
│                                             │
│                                             │
└─────────────────────────────────────────────┘
```

91. Are there standard rates of fees for legal **translation**?

1   ☐   No
2   ☐   Yes
7   ☐   Don't know

92. Are there different rates per: (more answers possible)

	yes	no	don't know
Language or language rarity	1 ☐	2 ☐	7 ☐
Person/Organization engaging the translation	1 ☐	2 ☐	7 ☐
Kind of activity (e.g. translation of surveillance tapes)	1 ☐	2 ☐	7 ☐
Deadline	1 ☐	2 ☐	7 ☐
Other: Please specify	1 ☐	2 ☐	7 ☐

```
┌─────────────────────────────────────────────┐
│                                             │
│                                             │
│                                             │
└─────────────────────────────────────────────┘
```

93. Are any records kept about legal **interpreters** used in criminal proceedings?

1   ☐   No
2   ☐   Yes
7   ☐   Don't know

93b. Which information is recorded about legal interpreters used in criminal proceedings?

    1   ☐   Numbers
    2   ☐   Languages
    3   ☐   Geographic location
    4   ☐   Which legal service (e.g. police, lower courts, higher courts) keeps the records
    6   ☐   Other: Please specify

94. Are any records kept about legal **translators** used in criminal proceedings?

    1   ☐   No
    2   ☐   Yes
    7   ☐   Don't know

94b. Which information is recorded about legal translators used in criminal proceedings?

    1   ☐   Numbers
    2   ☐   Languages
    3   ☐   Geographic location
    4   ☐   Which legal service (e.g. police, lower courts, higher courts) keeps the records
    6   ☐   Other: Please specify

95. If records are kept, which legal service keeps the records?

    1   ☐   Police
    2   ☐   Judiciary
    3   ☐   No records are kept
    6   ☐   Other: Please specify

    7   ☐   Don't know

Part IV: Future developments

96. What type of changes and development are planned or desired in the foreseeable future?
(more answers possible)

	Planned	Desired	Not planned or desired
Better specific legislation	1 ☐	2 ☐	7 ☐
The provision of a reliable and accessible register	1 ☐	2 ☐	7 ☐
Better training of interpreters and translators	1 ☐	2 ☐	7 ☐
Higher quality standards of interpreters and translators	1 ☐	2 ☐	7 ☐
Independent testing of interpreters and translators	1 ☐	2 ☐	7 ☐
Better monitoring systems of demand	1 ☐	2 ☐	7 ☐
Better recruiting of interpreters and translators	1 ☐	2 ☐	7 ☐
Better monitoring of interpretation and translation quality	1 ☐	2 ☐	7 ☐
Better remuneration of interpreters and translators	1 ☐	2 ☐	7 ☐
Better working conditions for interpreters and Translators	1 ☐	2 ☐	7 ☐
More suppliers of quality interpretation and translation	1 ☐	2 ☐	7 ☐
Better regulation of interpretation and translation Profession	1 ☐	2 ☐	7 ☐
Continuous Professional Development	1 ☐	2 ☐	7 ☐
Peer testing and monitoring	1 ☐	2 ☐	7 ☐
Occasional evaluations	1 ☐	2 ☐	7 ☐
An enforceable Code of Conduct	1 ☐	2 ☐	7 ☐
Training of legal services on working with	1 ☐	2 ☐	7 ☐
interpreters and translators across languages and cultures	1 ☐	2 ☐	7 ☐
Other: Please specify			
_____	1 ☐	2 ☐	7 ☐
_____	1 ☐	2 ☐	7 ☐
_____	1 ☐	2 ☐	7 ☐

97. Do you have any further remarks or suggestions?

    1   ☐ No
    2   ☐ Yes, Please specify

Please indicate whether you wish to receive the summary report of this survey.

    1   ☐ No
    2   ☐ Yes

Please provide an email address and/or personal data if you so wish:

Thank you very much for your cooperation.

AGIS 2006

With financial support from the AGIS programme
European Commission – Directorate General Justice, Freedom and Security

APPENDIX II

ADDITIONAL CEPEJ AND SPRONKEN-ATTINGER DATA ON THE MEMBER STATES

Austria

Population (× 1000)	8193
Area (km² × 1000)	83.9
GDP (€, billion)	267.6
Criminal cases dealt by the public prosecutor (per 100,000 inhabitants)	7697
Incoming criminal cases in courts (per 100,000 inhabitants)	1111

Right to interpretation and translation
Assistance of an interpreter and translator is provided, also for deaf and mute defendants. It is not mentioned whether this assistance is free of charge for the suspect and what kind of rules apply during the pre-trial investigation. It therefore remains unclear whether the provisions comply with Art. 6 §2 of the Proposed FD stating that a person has the right to receive free interpretation of legal advice received throughout the criminal proceedings. The indictment and petition for sentences will be translated, other relevant documents are not mentioned in the answers, so it is not clear whether all relevant documents are translated as required in Article 7 of the Proposed FD. A list of sworn and certified interpreters must guarantee the quality of the interpretation, so Art. 8 of the Proposed FD seems to be complied with. The interviews are not audio nor video recorded, as stipulated in Article 9 of the Proposed FD.

Belgium

Population (× 1000)	10379
Area (km² × 1000)	30.5
GDP (€, billion)	325
Criminal cases dealt by the public prosecutor (per 100,000 inhabitants)	7863
Incoming criminal cases in courts (per 100,000 inhabitants)	311

Right to interpretation and translation
Free assistance of an interpreter and a translator is provided for all persons who do not understand the language of the court and for persons with hearing impairments. There is no emergency scheme for linguistic assistance. Relevant documents are only translated for free into Dutch, French and German.

The interviews are not audio or video recorded, nor is there a system to verify the accuracy of the interpretation and translation. Furthermore, interpreters and translators do not have to meet certain qualifications. This implies that the quality of the interpreters and translators cannot be guaranteed and that the proposed provisions in Art. 6 §2, Art. 8 and Art. 9 of the Proposed FD are not met.

Bulgaria

Population (× 1000)	7385
Area (km^2 × 1000)	110.9
GDP (€, billion)	71.5
Criminal cases dealt by the public prosecutor (per 100,000 inhabitants)	?
Incoming criminal cases in courts (per 100,000 inhabitants)	870

No further information on the right to interpretation and translation

Cyprus

Population (× 1000)	784
Area (km^2 × 1000)	9.2
GDP (€, billion)	0
Criminal cases dealt by the public prosecutor (per 100,000 inhabitants)	?
Incoming criminal cases in courts (per 100,000 inhabitants)	11884

Right to interpretation and translation
An interpreter will assist the suspect during trial and also translates relevant documents orally. The latter does not comply with the proposed provisions prescribing free interpretation of legal advice and free translation of relevant documents in Art. 6 §2 and Art. 7 of the Proposed FD.

Other proposed provisions are (partly) met. Suspects with language difficulties or hearing impairments will be assisted by a specialised interpreter. Emergency linguistic assistance on a 24-hour basis is provided by qualified police interpreters. It is not clear whether these interpreters are independent or employed by the police. Court interpreters have to be approved by the court, depending on their fulfillment of the relevant legal requirements. The interviews are only recorded in writing and not audio or video recorded as proposed in Art. 9 of the FD. A verification system is provided by law and the court may test the ability of the interpreter.

Czech Republic

Population (× 1000)	10235
Area (km² × 1000)	78.9
GDP (€, billion)	199.4
Criminal cases dealt by the public prosecutor (per 100,000 inhabitants)	1093
Incoming criminal cases in courts (per 100,000 inhabitants)	773

Right to interpretation and translation
The response does not mention the right to interpretation so it remains unclear whether Art. 6 of the Proposed FD is met. There is no emergency scheme for linguistic assistance. Relevant documents are translated and submitted to the suspect in writing. A national register of legal interpreters and translators is administered by the Ministry of Justice. The latter does raise some doubt concerning the independence of the interpreters and translators. Only these qualified interpreters and translators can act in criminal proceedings. Consequently, the quality of the interpreters and translators is carefully monitored and seems to be in accordance with Art. 8 of the Proposed FD.

It is no common practice to audio or video record the interviews, but it is possible. Partial compliance with the prescribed quality control of Art. 9 of the Proposed FD can be found in the fact that if the verbatim language of the testimony is significant, the recording clerk or the translator mentions in the record the corresponding part of the testimony in that language too. There is no separate system of verification other than the above mentioned register.

Denmark

Population (× 1000)	5454
Area (km² × 1000)	43.1
GDP (€, billion)	188.1
Criminal cases dealt by the public prosecutor (per 100,000 inhabitants)	16531
Incoming criminal cases in courts (per 100,000 inhabitants)	2495

Right to interpretation and translation
The provisions regarding free translation and interpretation in the Proposed FD are partly complied with. Linguistic assistance is available for persons who do not speak Danish and for persons with language difficulties or hearing impairments. There is no emergency scheme, but the National Commissioner of Police

administers a list of 1850 authorised interpreters, representing 140 languages and dialects. With this list, the quality of the interpreters and translators is monitored. The interviews are not audio or video recorded. Complaints about the interpretation or translation can be filed to the local police authority. However, this cannot be considered a genuine system to verify the quality and accuracy of the linguistic assistance.

Relevant documents will be translated, but there are no formal time limits within which these documents have to be submitted to the defendant.

Germany

Population (× 1000)	82422
Area (km² × 1000)	357
GDP (€, billion)	2504
Criminal cases dealt by the public prosecutor (per 100,000 inhabitants)	6047
Incoming criminal cases in courts (per 100,000 inhabitants)	1104

Right to interpretation and translation
The suspect will be assisted by an interpreter and a translator if he does not understand the language of the court or if he has speech or hearing impairments. Not the entire proceedings are translated, only the relevant parts and the statements of the defendant. As long as this guarantees a fair trial, it complies with the Proposed FD. Interviews are always audio recorded (sometimes also video recorded). The response does not mention a system for verification. There are no special qualifications required.

Relevant documents are translated and submitted to the suspect within the same time limits as the original documents would have been made available. In conclusion: except for provisions concerning the quality of the translators and interpreters, the provisions of the Proposed FD are complied with.

Estonia

Population (× 1000)	1324
Area (km² × 1000)	45.2
GDP (€, billion)	22.3
Criminal cases dealt by the public prosecutor (per 100,000 inhabitants)	2522
Incoming criminal cases in courts (per 100,000 inhabitants)	638

Right to interpretation and translation
A person with language difficulties or speech or hearing impairments will be assisted by an appropriate interpreter or translator. There is no scheme for

emergency linguistic assistance available. Neither the quality nor the accuracy of the interpretation and translation are guaranteed since there are no specific qualifications required nor is there a system of verification available. The interviews are not audio or video recorded, which makes it difficult to assess the accuracy of the interpretation in case of a dispute. The response to the questionnaire does not mention the translation of relevant procedural documents in great detail. A translation of the summary of the charges is submitted to the suspect.

In short, apart from the fact that an appropriate interpreter or a translator is assigned to assist the suspect, there is very little compliance with the proposed provisions in Art. 6–9 of the FD.

Finland

Population (× 1000)	5231
Area (km^2 × 1000)	338.1
GDP (€, billion)	161.2
Criminal cases dealt by the public prosecutor (per 100,000 inhabitants)	1680
Incoming criminal cases in courts (per 100,000 inhabitants)	1285

Right to interpretation and translation
In Finland, the right to free interpretation is in accordance with the provisions of the Proposed FD, except for safeguards for the interpretation quality. Free linguistic assistance is offered to the suspect who has language difficulties or suffers from speech or hearing impairments. A scheme for emergency linguistic assistance is available covering all needed languages, which means that assistance is guaranteed throughout the entire proceedings. It is difficult to assess the quality of the interpreters and translators, since there are no special qualifications required. The interviews are always audio recorded and sometimes video recorded. A transcript of the audio tape will be offered to the suspect for verification and he is asked to sign it.

Also documents can be translated on State's expenses in accordance with Art. 7 of the Proposed FD.

France

Population (× 1000)	60876
Area (km^2 × 1000)	547
GDP (€, billion)	1816
Criminal cases dealt by the public prosecutor (per 100,000 inhabitants)	8049
Incoming criminal cases in courts (per 100,000 inhabitants)	1549

Right to interpretation and translation
The provisions of the Proposed FD on interpretation and translation are largely met. Suspects who do not understand the language of the court or who have speech or hearing impairments will be assisted by an appropriate interpreter. He will also interpret relevant documents. Documents are translated on the defendant's request. There is no scheme for emergency linguistic assistance. Nevertheless, linguistic assistance is granted throughout the proceedings. When the interpreter is not present, the procedural act will be declared void. In general, the interviews are not audio or video recorded and the suspect has to verify the accuracy of the interpretation himself. This does not comply with Art. 9 of the Proposed FD.

Greece

Population (× 1000)	10688
Area (km^2 × 1000)	131.9
GDP (€, billion)	236.8
Criminal cases dealt by the public prosecutor (per 100,000 inhabitants)	1344
Incoming criminal cases in courts (per 100,000 inhabitants)	1859

Right to interpretation and translation
The response is not very clear on this subject and it seems that the level of provision in the Proposed FD is only partly complied with. The investigative authority will assess whether the suspect has sufficient knowledge of the Greek language and relevant documents will be translated if necessary. The response does not refer to the verification of the accuracy of the translation and the required qualifications of interpreters and translators. There is no explicit provision of assistance by an interpreter during trial. Deaf and mute suspects will receive specific attention.

Hungary

Population (× 1000)	9981
Area (km^2 × 1000)	93
GDP (€, billion)	162.6
Criminal cases dealt by the public prosecutor (per 100,000 inhabitants)	1366
Incoming criminal cases in courts (per 100,000 inhabitants)	1371

Right to interpretation and translation
The provisions prescribed in Art. 6–9 of the Proposed FD are largely met, except the provisions regarding the quality of the interpretation and translation and the audio or video recording. An interpreter will be appointed free of charge, if the

suspect does not know the language of the court or if he suffers from speech or hearing impairments. A public authority translates all written documents and provides interpretation. The prosecutor or investigating authority will provide the suspect with translated decisions and other official documents. There is a list of qualified interpreters available, but if an official interpreter cannot be reached, anyone capable of interpretation can be appointed. The latter does not guarantee the quality of the interpretation. The interviews can be audio or video recorded, but the suspect has to initiate and pay for it himself. It is not clear from the response if there are provisions for indigent suspects in this respect.

Ireland

Population (× 1000)	4062
Area (km² × 1000)	70.3
GDP (€, billion)	164.6
Criminal cases dealt by the public prosecutor (per 100,000 inhabitants)	?
Incoming criminal cases in courts (per 100,000 inhabitants)	8919

Right to interpretation and translation
In general it is difficult to assess whether Irish legislation on this matter complies with the Proposed FD, because the answer is not very clear on most issues.

If a suspect cannot follow the proceedings due to linguistic problems, deafness or muteness, an interpreter will be appointed to him. During the investigation, an interpreter will only be provided when the police think it is necessary for the investigation, or because they need to explain something to the suspect. Hence, provision of an interpreter is not dependent on the suspect's needs, for instance for legal advice.

The interpreter is paid by the State. The response is unclear regarding the existence of a scheme on emergency linguistic assistance and whether the interviews are audio or video recorded. In general, interviews are audio or video recorded, which seems to imply that also the interviews with the assistance of an interpreter are electronically recorded. The response is not clear on the subject of verification. No specific qualifications are required of the interpreters.

Relevant documents are translated and submitted to the suspect within a sufficient time limit for him to prepare his defence. Exact time limits could not be given.

Italy

Population (× 1000)	58134
Area (km² × 1000)	301.2
GDP (€, billion)	1698
Criminal cases dealt by the public prosecutor (per 100,000 inhabitants)	5454
Incoming criminal cases in courts (per 100,000 inhabitants)	2452

Right to interpretation and translation

Except for the recording of the interviews and the verification of the accuracy the provisions of the Proposed FD are complied with. Free interpretation is provided in all stages of the proceedings, when the suspect does not understand the language used during the proceedings. There is no scheme on emergency linguistic assistance. There is no professional register of court and legal interpreters available, but each court has a list of appropriate interpreters, who have attained their university qualifications. Interviews are not audio or video recorded and no formal scheme for verifying the accuracy of the interpretation exists.

Relevant documents are translated and submitted to the suspect.

Latvia

Population (× 1000)	2275
Area (km² × 1000)	64.6
GDP (€, billion)	30.3
Criminal cases dealt by the public prosecutor (per 100,000 inhabitants)	669
Incoming criminal cases in courts (per 100,000 inhabitants)	525

Right to interpretation and translation

A person who does not know the language used in the proceedings or suffers from speech or hearing impairments, will be assisted by an appropriate interpreter. It is not clear whether this assistance is offered on State's expenses and whether the right to free interpretation as proposed in the FD is met There is no scheme on emergency linguistic assistance, but in practice it will be provided within 24 hours. The interpreters and translators have to be knowledgeable on the judicial meaning of the contents and will initially be tested for three months. It is not common practice to audio or video record the interviews, but if so, the entire proceedings have to be recorded. The response is not clear on whether there exists a system of verification, other than the own liability of the interpreter and translator.

Procedural documents will be translated.

Lithuania

Population (× 1000)	3586
Area (km² × 1000)	65.2
GDP (€, billion)	49.2
Criminal cases dealt by the public prosecutor (per 100,000 inhabitants)	507
Incoming criminal cases in courts (per 100,000 inhabitants)	514

Right to interpretation and translation
On this matter, the Lithuanian law complies with the proposed provisions in the FD, since suspects who do not know the language of the proceedings or who are suffering from hearing or speech impairments have to be assisted by an interpreter. Interviews can be audio or video recorded and afterwards a language specialist can be asked to check the accuracy of the interpretation. If no recordings are made, no other system of verification exists. It is striking however, that there are no specific requirements for interpreters or translators working at a police station. They can even be employed by the police.

All relevant documents have to be translated and submitted to the suspect.

Luxemburg

Population (× 1000)	474
Area (km² × 1000)	2.6
GDP (€, billion)	30.7
Criminal cases dealt by the public prosecutor (per 100,000 inhabitants)	10630
Incoming criminal cases in courts (per 100,000 inhabitants)	?

Right to interpretation and translation
An interpreter will be assigned when the suspect does not understand the language used in the proceedings. Interpreters are appointed by the Ministry of Justice and qualifications are demanded. If the suspect is deaf or mute, an interpreter will only be assigned if the suspect does not know how to read and write. There is no scheme on emergency linguistic assistance, which seems to imply that linguistic assistance cannot be guaranteed throughout the entire proceedings. The response does not mention anything about the translation of relevant documents. Apart from the right to interpretation and qualifications of the interpreters, the provisions of the Proposed FD do not seem to be complied with.

Malta

Population (× 1000)	400
Area (km² × 1000)	0.3
GDP (€, billion)	7.9
Criminal cases dealt by the public prosecutor (per 100,000 inhabitants)	?
Incoming criminal cases in courts (per 100,000 inhabitants)	?

Right to interpretation and translation
It is difficult to assess to what extent the provisions of the Proposed FD are implemented. An interpreter is appointed to persons who do not know the language of the proceedings or suffer from hearing or speech impairments. There is a scheme to provide emergency linguistic assistance, but the response does not elaborate on this matter. Interviews are audio and / or video recorded, but again, this is not elaborated.

The response does not mention anything about translation of relevant documents.

Netherlands

Population (× 1000)	16491
Area (km² × 1000)	41.5
GDP (€, billion)	499.8
Criminal cases dealt by the public prosecutor (per 100,000 inhabitants)	1682
Incoming criminal cases in courts (per 100,000 inhabitants)	?

Right to interpretation and translation
As is also stipulated in Art. 6 Proposed FD, the suspect has the right to have an interpreter appointed – free of charge – if he does not understand the language of the proceedings. When it concerns deaf or mute persons the proceedings will be in writing, which does not comply with Art. 6 §3 of the Proposed FD. There is no emergency scheme on linguistic assistance, but a suspect has to be questioned with the assistance of an interpreter if he does not know the language of the proceedings. If an interpreter cannot be summoned within 6 hours, interpretation will be provided by telephone. This seems to comply with Art. 6 of the Proposed FD. The interviews are not audio or video recorded and there is no system of verification, which is below the standards of Art. 9 Proposed FD.

Only the summons will be translated. Other documents have to be translated by a defence counsel or an interpreter. This seems to comply with Art. 7 Proposed FD, provided that the fairness of the proceedings is safeguarded. It is not clear however, whether the assistance of this interpreter is paid by the State and whether the translations of the documents are also submitted to the suspect in writing.

Poland

Population (× 1000)	38537
Area (km² × 1000)	312.7
GDP (€, billion)	514
Criminal cases dealt by the public prosecutor (per 100,000 inhabitants)	4758
Incoming criminal cases in courts (per 100,000 inhabitants)	1436

Right to interpretation and translation
In general, Polish law complies with the proposed provisions as stipulated in Art. 6 – 9 Proposed FD. An appropriate interpreter is appointed if the suspect does not know the language of the proceedings or if he suffers from speech or hearing impairments. The interpreter translates relevant documents orally, but the suspect will also receive written translations. There is no scheme on emergency linguistic assistance, but the suspect cannot be questioned in absence of an interpreter. A list of sworn interpreters is drawn up to ensure that the appointed interpreters are sufficiently qualified as stipulated in Art. 8 Proposed FD. It is not common practice to audio or video record the interviews as is required by Art. 9 Proposed FD, but it is possible. Verification will be done by the Chief Justice of the Court. It is unclear what happens when an interpretation is considered to be inaccurate.

The suspect will receive translations of all documents relating to the preliminary proceeding in due time before the hearing, which complies with Art. 7 Proposed FD. It is not clear whether linguistic assistance is offered on State's expenses so it remains unclear whether the provision of free interpretation and translation is complied with.

Portugal

Population (× 1000)	10606
Area (km² × 1000)	92.4
GDP (€, billion)	204.4
Criminal cases dealt by the public prosecutor (per 100,000 inhabitants)	4739
Incoming criminal cases in courts (per 100,000 inhabitants)	1105

Right to interpretation and translation
As provided in Art. 6 Proposed FD, an appropriate interpreter is provided, free of charge, to suspects who do not know the language of the proceedings or who

suffer from hearing or speech impairments. Interpreters are also asked to translate relevant documents. It is not clear whether this translation is submitted to the suspect in writing. There are no guarantees mentioned to ensure that interpreters are sufficiently qualified, as is stipulated in Art. 8 Proposed FD, since no specific qualifications are required for interpreters. It is possible to audio or video record the interviews, but it is not common practice. There is no system of verification. This does not correspond with Art. 9 Proposed FD.

It is not clear whether written translations of relevant documents are submitted to the suspect, which makes it impossible to assess the level of compliance with Art. 7 Proposed FD.

Romania

Population (× 1000)	22304
Area (km² × 1000)	237.5
GDP (€, billion)	183.6
Criminal cases dealt by the public prosecutor (per 100,000 inhabitants)	3051
Incoming criminal cases in courts (per 100,000 inhabitants)	1922

No further information on the right to interpretation and translation

Slovakia

Population (× 1000)	5439
Area (km² × 1000)	48.8
GDP (€, billion)	87.3
Criminal cases dealt by the public prosecutor (per 100,000 inhabitants)	2581
Incoming criminal cases in courts (per 100,000 inhabitants)	499

Right to interpretation and translation
The response is not clear on the provisions regulating appointment of interpreters, which is regulated in Art. 6 – 9 of the Proposed FD. There is a scheme of emergency linguistic assistance, but the interpreters participating in this scheme are police officers. It is questionable whether these interpreters can be considered independent. Court interpreters are no members of the police force. The response does not mention the recording of the interviews nor verification of the accuracy of the interpretation as mentioned in Art. 9 Proposed FD.

Nothing is mentioned about the translation of relevant documents.

Slovenia

Population (× 1000)	2010
Area (km² × 1000)	20.3
GDP (€, billion)	43.4
Criminal cases dealt by the public prosecutor (per 100,000 inhabitants)	4603
Incoming criminal cases in courts (per 100,000 inhabitants)	727

No further information on the right to interpretation and translation

Spain

Population (× 1000)	40398
Area (km² × 1000)	504.8
GDP (€, billion)	1029
Criminal cases dealt by the public prosecutor (per 100,000 inhabitants)	9214
Incoming criminal cases in courts (per 100,000 inhabitants)	12074

Right to interpretation and translation
As provided in Art. 6 Proposed FD, an appropriate interpreter will be appointed if the suspect does not know the language of the proceedings or if he suffers from hearing or speech impairments. There is a scheme for emergency linguistic assistance, but it only covers English, French, German and Arabic. Contrary to the proposed provisions of Art. 9 Proposed FD, interviews are not audio or video recorded and there is no system to verify the accuracy of the interpretation.

In accordance with Art. 7 Proposed FD, all relevant procedural documents are translated and submitted to the suspect. It is not clear whether linguistic assistance is offered free of charge as is required by Art. 6 and 7 Proposed FD.

Sweden

Population (× 1000)	9017
Area (km² × 1000)	450
GDP (€, billion)	268
Criminal cases dealt by the public prosecutor (per 100,000 inhabitants)	2055
Incoming criminal cases in courts (per 100,000 inhabitants)	759

Right to interpretation and translation
In line with Art. 6 Proposed FD, an appropriate interpreter will be appointed when the suspect does not know the language of the proceedings or if he suffers

from speech or hearing impairments. Interpreters have to be completely independent. There are schemes of emergency linguistic assistance available at police stations. No special qualifications are required of the interpreters, which makes it difficult for the State to ensure sufficiently qualified interpreters as prescribed in Art. 8 Proposed FD. Contrary to Art. 9 Proposed FD, interviews are not audio or video recorded and there is no system to verify the accuracy of the interpretation.

The court is obliged to translate procedural documents if the court has reason to believe that the suspect does not understand the language of the proceedings. This complies with Art. 7 Proposed FD.

United Kingdom

Population (× 1000)	60609
Area (km² × 1000)	244.8
GDP (€, billion)	1830
Criminal cases dealt by the public prosecutor (per 100,000 inhabitants)*	2960
Incoming criminal cases in courts (per 100,000 inhabitants)*	3813

* England and Wales only

Right to interpretation and translation
In accordance with Art. 6 Proposed FD, an appropriate interpreter will be appointed free of charge when the suspect does not know the language of the proceedings or if he suffers from speech or hearing impairments. There is no scheme for emergency linguistic assistance. Since certain qualifications are required for interpreters to be included on recognised lists, the State is able to ensure sufficiently qualified interpretation as required by Art. 8 Proposed FD. It is not common practice to audio record these interviews, but it is possible. Normally the interpreter records everything in writing and the suspect is asked to verify the accuracy of the written record. If he agrees with the contents he can sign the record, if not, he can indicate in what respect the interpretation is inaccurate. The question is how it is possible for the suspect to verify the accuracy of the interpretation. The foregoing does not seem to comply in full with the provisions of Art. 9 Proposed FD.

Prosecution documents are translated on the defendant's request which seems to be in compliance with the provisions of Art. 7 Proposed FD.

With thanks to

Prof. Dr. Taru Spronken, Professor of Criminal Law, Faculty of Law, Department of Criminal Law and Criminology and to **Marelle Attinger**, Research assistant Faculty of Law, Department of Criminal Law and Criminology, University of Maastricht.

Evert-Jan van der Vlis for providing the Cepej data.

APPENDIX III
PUBLIC SERVICE INTERPRETING & TRANSLATION: COMPONENTS OF THE PROFESSION

INTERDEPENDENT, TRANSPARENT, ACCOUNTABLE AND CONSISTENT

Qualified Trainers

Qualified Examiners/assessors

Qualified mentors and supervisors

Selection for
training criteria
- linguistic
- professional
- contextual

Training
- knowledge of the domain
- enhancement of languages
- interpreting and translation
- code and good practice guidelines
- strategies for personal and professional development

Assessment
- linguistic
- professional
- domain

Plus:
Supervised experience

Registration
Criteria:
- qualifications
- experience
- references
- suitability
- agree to observe code
Disciplinary Procedures
CPD
Re-registration systems

Professional practice
- good practice guidelines
- code
- CPD
Employment eg
- contracts
- letters of agreement
- insurance
- support
Deployment
- national registers
- international registers
- suitable agencies
- Quality assurance

On-going communication, at all stages, with and between:
- services (e.g. legal)
- speakers of other languages
- language professional bodies
- other professional disciplines

APPENDIX IV

SUGGESTIONS ON DATA
TO BE COLLECTED

The following minimum data should be collected and collated under three main headings:

1. Current demand in terms of:

    i.   when an interpreter is engaged
    ii.   with what qualifications
    iii.   when a translator is engaged
    iv.   with what qualifications
    v.   in which language/dialect
    vi.   in which context
    vii.   in which geographical location
    viii. length of the interpreting assignment or text
    ix.   payment made/when/how much

and where qualified legal interpreters and translators were needed but none were available because e.g.

    x.   they were doing other assignments
    xi.   of other reasons
    xii.   none exist in the language/dialect required (which)
    xiii. of reasonable geographical distances
    xiv. there were time constraints

2. Broad estimation of predicted demand in terms of potential:

    xv.   new arrivals (immigration and migration)
    xvi.   visitors (e.g. for tourism, trade or education)
    xvii. events (e.g. sporting, conferences)
    xviii. crime
    xix.   availability and access to adequate education of the language of the legal system

3. Supply of qualified legal interpreters and translators in terms of:

    xx.   numbers
    xxi.   which languages
    xxii.   qualifications
    xxiii.   registration
    xxiv.   membership of a professional body
    xxv.   subject to a code of conduct
    xxvi.   location
    xxvii. training courses and qualified trainers
    xxviii. numbers in training, in which languages and locations.

4. Provision of legal interpreters and translators in terms of:

    xxix.   legislation
    xxx.   number of criminal cases employing interpreters or translators
    xxxi.   budget allocated and spent
    xxxii. quality monitoring system

APPENDIX V
PROJECT PARTICIPANTS

Belgium

Erik Hertog is professor of Cultural Studies as well as both Conference and Public Services Interpreting in the Department of Applied Languages of Lessius University College, Antwerp.

Jan Van Gucht is a social and industrial psychologist and a conference interpreter. Currently he is the director of the Central Support Cell for Social Interpreting and Translation and chair of the Flemish Platform of social interpreting services.

Yolanda Vanden Bosch is partner in the law firm Van der Mussele-Vanden Bosch, Antwerp, a member of the Antwerp Bar, Secretary-General of the Association of Flemish Jurists and Associate Professor at Lessius University College.

The Netherlands

Evert-Jan van der Vlis is policy-advisor in the Legal Aid department of the Ministry of Justice in The Hague.

Hans Warendorf is a member of the Amsterdam Bar, a translator and author of articles on legal translation and interpreting and board member of Euromos.

Han von den Hoff is policy-maker at the Raad voor Rechtsbijstand in 's Hertogenbosch.

Jeroen Blomsma is lecturer of Criminal Law at the Maastricht Law Faculty.

The United Kingdom

Ann Corsellis, OBE, is Vice-chairman of Council of the Chartered Institute of Linguists, Vice Chairman of its subsidiary, the National Register of Public Service Interpreters, and a magistrate since 1976.

John Hammond has been Chairman of Council, Institute of Linguists and Chairman of the Board, Institute of Linguists, Educational Trust (2002–2005) and Acting CEO and Legal Counsel, The Chartered Institute of Linguists from October 2005.

Spain

Cynthia Giambruno is professor in the Department of Translation and Interpretation at the University of Alicante, Court Interpreter Trainer at the Agnese Haury Institute for Court Interpreting and Invited Research Scholar, National Center for Interpreter Training, Research and Testing at the University of Arizona.

José Delgado is a practicing translator and interpreter who also designs and teaches translating and interpreter training courses and consults with government agencies, research institutes and businesses on issues related to intercultural communication.

Sonsoles Plaza is a staff translator-interpreter at the Ministry of Justice and president of the Spanish professional association of court interpreters and translators APTIJ.

ECBA

Taru Spronken, representing the European Criminal Bar Association, is professor of Criminal Law and Criminal Procedure, Faculty of Law, Department of Criminal Law and Criminology, at the University of Maastricht.

CCBE

Peter McNamee is a staff member with the Council of Bars and Law Societies of Europe with a special interest in criminal law.